# THE VIKING SPIRIT

## AN INTRODUCTION TO NORSE MYTHOLOGY AND RELIGION

DANIEL MCCOY

ISBN: 1533393036
ISBN-13: 978-1533393036

# CONTENTS

# Epilogue

# PART ONE:
# NORSE RELIGION

DANIEL MCCOY

# Chapter 1:

# Introduction

## THE VIKING WORLD

The longship sways on the windy sea like a seer in a trance. After days of hard rowing through rain and roiling waves, the crew is exhausted. Their rough, gray-brown woolen clothes are heavy with water, and even though the rain has finally given way to a merely cloudy morning, the August air is cool enough that the drenched men shiver as they take turns rowing and amusing themselves with dice games.

They had set sail from the western coast of Scandinavia several days ago, bound for the eastern coast of England, a land about whose riches they had heard many marvelous tales from Vikings under the leadership of neighboring kings and chieftains. None of the men in the king's fleet of five impressive ships have ever yet set foot on that great island. But they are expert navigators, and know the signs to watch in the sky and water to guide them west.

Sverrir removes a soggy barley roll from his sack and takes a bite. The bread, having been threshed on the ground, is full of bits of sand and dirt. Although he's only in his late teens, eating rough bread like this for his entire life has ground his teeth down considerably. He's already lost a few of them. This roll, however, has some of the inner bark of a pine tree baked into it to provide much-needed vitamins to ward off scurvy. Though the meager roll is not enough to fill his belly, he's grateful for the edge being taken off his hunger, as well as the nourishment.

In his childhood, Sverrir had grown up the son of a fairly well-off farmer. Although he had been made to join in the difficult, dangerous, and seemingly neverending farmwork when he was still a young boy, and had lived through two separate occasions of bitter famine that left him shorter than he would otherwise have been, he has often found himself missing the relative certainty and security of those days. He had always wanted to inherit his father's farm, but when his father died from disease when Sverrir was seventeen, he had known that as the fourth and youngest son, he stood little chance of inheriting anything in his father's estate. And he had been right. So, out of hardship as much as ambition, he had gone and joined the king's band of warriors and raiders.

Now, at last, he is on his first raid. Still just eighteen, he is terrified, but eager for the honor that these pursuits will surely bring him back at home. And his leader, King Harald, has so far shown himself to be a noble, generous, and fiercely clever man. Sverrir is proud to serve him.

Just now, Sverrir looks up and sees his king standing at the front of the ship, observing the heavens and giving instructions to the helmsman. This, thinks Sverrir, is how Odin must look when he leads the gods into battle against the giants. Sverrir himself is a man of Thor, and he had sacrificed a goat to his patron god in return for good fortune on this raid on the day before he left home.

A gull cries out as it flies overhead. The crewmembers all cease their tasks for a moment and take notice. It means that they're getting close to land. And, soon enough, through the clearing mist, the first faint outlines of the white and green coast of England come into view.

The clanking and tinkling of metal can be heard from every corner of the ship as the warriors get their weapons in order. The few of them who own some pieces of armor put them on. Sverrir readies his axe. He and Hauk, his best friend from childhood who has also become one of the king's warriors, exchange warm words of encouragement. The king delivers a rousing speech, as do the chieftains for their men in the accompanying vessels.

The ships land and their crews disembark. No one else is in sight, but if their informants have told them correctly, there should be a wealthy trading city just over the dune-like hills that form the perimeter of the sandy beach.

When the king's force rounds the crest of the hills, they see a large town with a magnificent, ornate building with many spires in its center. Still no one is in sight. But as they make their way through the farms at the city's edge and toward the wall that encloses the city proper, they see bread half-kneaded sitting on tables and fires half-smoldering in hearths. The inhabitants of these farms have left very recently – and very quickly.

*well-known Vikings* *and feared*

By the time the force reaches the city gates, many of the warriors have worked themselves up into an ecstatic frenzy and are howling, baying, and roaring like wolves and bears. Everyone is shouting and banging their weapons against their thick wooden shields. The first flurry of arrows rains down upon them from slits in the stone wall above the grand doors. The men raise their shields to deflect them. A few anguished screams are heard, but the band presses forward. In a surprisingly short time, they hack their way through the doors and into the city. But again, they see no one. Even the archers have seemingly fled. The men go around ransacking everything in their path, picking up anything of value they encounter, of which they can find strangely little.

*barbaric culture* *Viking value* *wealth* *live life to the fullest*

At last, they reach the grandiose building at the center of the city. Sverrir whispers to Hauk that the building looks like one of the great temples he's been told exist in this land, where ceremonies so bizarre as to be barely believable take place to honor a god who is said to reign alone and to hate all of the other gods and goddesses. If the legends are true, he says, the people who worship in such a place even eat the flesh and blood of one of their heroes. The ever-skeptical Hauk snorts and dismisses such reports as nothing more than tall tales.

*Christianity*

At first, they hear no sounds coming from within the building. But as they get closer, they can make out the muffled sounds of a man speaking. There is authority and leadership in his tone and cadence, but his voice cracks and scrambles, as if out of mortal fear. The Vikings chop through the doors and smash the high, intricately-colored windows.

As the first warriors pour in, desperate shrieks break out from the crowd of men, women, and children huddled inside. The interior of the building is more lavish by far than any Sverrir has ever seen. This effect is heightened by the fact that the townspeople have evidently brought all of the valuables they could into this place with them, although many of the most expensive items Sverrir can see around him are part of the fixtures of the building itself.

The townspeople perform a strange gesture that involves touching one of their hands to four different parts of their torso and head as the Vikings begin to hew down anyone – man, woman, or child – who stands between them and their plunder. Some seem to murder for no other reason than sport, or perhaps unquenchable, ecstatic rage.

Sverrir approaches a man wearing a long, richly decorated robe, attempting to flee with an axe-sized cross made of gold with the body of a scrawny man carved onto one side. Sverrir grabs him by the shoulder, stares down at him with all the ferocity he can muster, and says, "Give me the gold you're holding and I'll spare your life." Then man hesitates, weeping, but when Sverrir raises his axe, he obliges. Sverrir lets him go, and the man inhales to heave a sigh of both relief and despair before another one of the Viking warriors, a veteran of many raids famed for his reckless daring, rushes up screaming and slashes the man's head halfway off his neck, so that it dangles to one side as the man's body falls to the ground. The young fighter feels his stomach contents lurching up toward his mouth, but he summons all his strength to force them back down. The senseless suffering and gore all around him has turned out to bear little resemblance to the shining vision of battle that had been presented to him in songs and speeches back at home. But, he reminds himself, he is still young and inexperienced; perhaps he's missing something. And after all, are not he and his fellow raiders winning the wealth they set out to win – and,

12

afterwards, a celebrated name in their hometown? Doesn't that make the rest of this really quite grim and sordid expedition worthwhile?

Above the clamor of carnage, a war horn is heard, snapping Sverrir out of his brief reverie. Some of the people rush to the broken windows on the side from which the blast had come. The townspeople turn away with a look of hope on their faces, but the Vikings turn away with a look of great worry. It's a formidable English army, many times larger than the Viking force, arriving with reinforcements for the city.

King Harald shouts an order to return to the boats at once with the spoils. The men run as fast as they can manage with their loot, but shortly before reaching the dunes they are overtaken. A terrible battle erupts. Many die on both sides. The English army is led by the regional king, who ably commands his well-trained ranks. Though the Vikings do eventually make it back to the ships and set sail for home with much of their plunder in tow, they suffer heavy losses. Most distressingly for Sverrir, Hauk falls after having fought valiantly.

After many more days at sea, nursing wounds great and small, eating more stale bread, and dealing with more inclement weather, King Harald's men at last spy the looming mountains and beckoning fjords of their homeland. Upon their arrival in their hometown, the raiding party receives a triumphant welcome. Sverrir is greeted warmly by his brothers and by Thordis, a charming girl of about his age whom he had been courting for a while before embarking on the raid. They've talked about marriage, but Sverrir wants to amass enough wealth by plundering to buy a farm before he settles down with her or anyone else. He's heard that she excels at spinning, weaving, sewing, cooking, milking, making dairy products, and everything else on the seemingly endless list of tasks a capable wife is expected to perform, and to perform well. His feelings for her run deep, but he knows that love alone doesn't keep a farm going.

The following day, the king holds a splendid feast in his hall for his warriors. The long, high, timber building has no windows. Firelight provides the only illumination, and in it, the king, dressed in his finest clothes and armor, much of which contains gold and silver, positively glows, further setting him apart. The band of warriors is seated according to rank and accomplishment around two long, slender tables that run perpendicular to where King Harald sits at the head of the gathering. The queen brings out a large, ornate pitcher of mead and serves the warriors ceremoniously, beginning with the king and going on down the rows. Sverrir, being one of the newest recruits, is seated toward the end of the tables, and is one of the last to be served.

When everyone's horn is filled with drink, rounds of toasts and oaths commence. Then, at last, the women bring out the food. The centerpiece of the meal is a bull that had earlier been sacrificed to give thanks for the (mostly) successful raid. As the men become more and more inebriated, and as their bellies get fuller and fuller from the sumptuous treats placed before them, the mood becomes more and more jovial, and their camaraderie is strengthened.

When the meal is finished, one of King Harald's many poets takes out a small harp and announces that he's written a new piece in honor of his patron. With his fingers plucking a suitable accompaniment, he sings a song whose wordcraft is so intricate and learned that the simple warriors – who, besides, are now quite drunk – can't make sense of parts of it, try as they might. What Sverrir can comprehend is that the king is said to be a descendent of Odin, that he has fought more battles and vanquished more foes than any other human king, and that his generosity is as unparalleled as his warlike prowess. The recent raid is presented as an unmitigated, glorious victory. Deep down, Sverrir finds himself questioning whether or not it had indeed happened as the poet now says it had. Hauk is dead, as are several of the king's other fighters, and besides, the poet hadn't even been there to witness it. What did he know? Nevertheless, Sverrir finds himself swept up in the rousing, artful moment. This reaction seems universal among the warriors, and they all agree afterward that, although some of the poem had gone over their heads, it must have been an exquisite piece.

Next, King Harald dispenses the spoils of the raid. As if in direct fulfillment of the poet's praises, the king's gifts to him are quite ample indeed. All of the men receive shares of the booty that strengthen their warm feelings of fealty to their leader. Sverrir, for his part, receives a few costly golden trinkets – "enough to begin saving for that farm," he thinks.

In the following days, he uses a bit of the gold to pay to have a large memorial stone raised to honor his fallen friend. Although illiterate himself, he pays a local man who is well-versed in the runes to inscribe on the stone, "I, Sverrir, raised this stone for Hauk, who died when kings were fighting."

Such is how one episode in the life of one Viking might have unfolded. The elements in that story were all selected not because they were exceptional, but because they were *unexceptional*. Almost all of them, down to the details, are routinely attested in the archaeological record and contemporary and later literary accounts of the Viking Age.[1]

This was the world in which the Norse myths and religion flourished. It was a world of startling accomplishment. The Vikings raided throughout Europe, conquered large portions of it, established settlements in Iceland and Greenland, discovered North America 500 years before Christopher Columbus, and traded with peoples who lived in such far-flung places as Egypt and the Persian Gulf. But it was also a world of startling squalor and brutality. Short lifespans, famine, malnutrition, rampant illness and infirmity, perilous ways of making a living, incessant toil for paltry benefits, rough treatment of men and women low on the social pecking order, exposure to bitter cold, and any number of other appalling hardships were facts of life for the Scandinavians of the Viking Age. One lived on the razor's edge between life and death, and life was frequently a nasty business.

## DEFINING "NORSE RELIGION"

Before you can have a meaningful discussion of a topic, especially one that centers on terms whose definitions are hotly and endlessly contested, you first have to define the terms you're using so that everyone is on the same page. We'll consider how to define "myth" and "mythology" in Chapter Eleven, but for now, let's go ahead and define "Norse religion." The phrase is comprised of two words, both of which should first be looked at separately before bringing them back together again.

"Norse" here refers to the Old Norse-speaking inhabitants of the lands that are now the countries of Denmark, Norway, Sweden, Iceland, and the Faroe Islands, as well as the colonies they established throughout northern Europe and elsewhere during the Viking Age (roughly from the late eighth century to the late eleventh century CE). The Norse were a northern branch of the Germanic group of peoples, who in turn were a branch of the Indo-European peoples, who immigrated to Europe from the steppes of modern-day Ukraine and Russia over the course of several millennia beginning in about 4000 BCE, absorbing local populations along the way. It's not entirely clear when the Proto-Germanic language (the first Germanic language, which was spoken by all of the Germanic peoples) became distinct from the Proto-Indo-European language, but it seems to have come into its own no later than the first few centuries BCE. By the start of the Viking Age, the Old Norse language had split off from the earlier, common Germanic language. The Viking Age is typically considered to be the latest part of the Iron Age in Scandinavia, and the centuries that follow (from the twelfth century onward) are usually considered to be the first "medieval" centuries in Scandinavia – a somewhat different chronology than the one used when discussing the history of the more southerly parts of Europe.[2]

The closely related term "Viking" is usually used in one of two ways: either it refers specifically to the Norse men who went on raiding voyages during the Viking Age, or it more broadly refers to the whole Norse population during the period. While various scholars and laypeople prefer one usage over the other, both have become established and accepted uses. In this book, I use the second, broader definition of "Viking." Thus, unless it's apparent from the context that

I'm specifically referring to the northern pirates, which I will do only occasionally, "Viking" and "Norse" are used more or less interchangeably here.

"Religion" may be one of the most difficult words in the modern English language to define. Countless definitions have been proposed over the centuries, which vary greatly in substance as well as in usefulness. In this book, we'll use the definition that is probably the most useful and appropriate to date, which also happens to be one of the most famous: that of the esteemed German philosopher of religion Rudolf Otto. In his classic 1917 work *The Idea of the Holy* (*Das Heilige* in the original German), he describes religion as a means of acknowledging and connecting to the "numinous." The numinous is an irreducible category that forms the heart of any and all religions: "There is no religion in which it does not live as the real innermost core, and without it no religion would be worthy of the name."[3] As the greatest theologians and mystics of all religions have pointed out, the numinous is ineffable. Referring to it at all, whether as "the numinous," "God," "nirvana," "Odin," "Freya," or anything else, is an after-the-fact characterization of something that can't be adequately expressed in language, but can only be truly understood if experienced firsthand. (This is surely one of the reasons why the word "religion" is so notoriously difficult to define.)

Nevertheless, Otto offers some characterizations of the numinous that, while they inevitably fall short of the real thing, point to it exceptionally well. The numinous is something "wholly other"[4] than the things that we experience in our day-to-day lives. It seems to come from a different plane of existence. Confronted with it, one experiences oneself as being "but dust and ashes,"[5] utterly insignificant and inconsequential in the face of something immeasurably greater. It has a majestic, daunting, awe-inspiring, even terrifying aspect, which Otto calls the *mysterium tremendum*, as well as a blissful, comforting side, which he calls the *mysterium fascinans*.[6]

"Norse religion," then, was the means the Vikings used to acknowledge and to connect to the numinous. It was a set of symbolic ideas, personages, stories, and ritual actions appropriate to facilitating that pursuit within the context of the Vikings' time and place.

Unlike most of the "world religions" with which people today are familiar, the Norse religion was never systematized or codified. There were no creeds or scriptures that defined what was acceptable and unacceptable to believe or to do. That was left up to social custom and personal preference. There were certainly some common rudimentary patterns of belief and behavior, enough that it's reasonable to speak of "Norse religion" in the singular, but even these common elements were fluid, and the details diverged enormously across time and space. Different communities and different individuals had their own variations of the shared religion. While this somewhat *laissez-faire* approach is appealing to many people's taste for individual freedom, it presents certain frustrations for the scholar, as we'll see momentarily when we consider the sources of our present-day knowledge of Norse religion and mythology.

It should also be noted here that applying the term "religion" to particular aspects of Viking experience, belief, and behavior is somewhat anachronistic. The Old Norse language had no word for "religion," and what we call "religion" was seamlessly integrated into the other aspects of life. The religious hierarchy was the same as the "secular" hierarchy. Kings, chieftains, and other rulers were seen as being divine in some capacity. Their rule was seen as being divinely sanctioned. And it was they who led the public religious as well as "secular" activities of the communities they ruled.[7] The numinous was usually contacted as part of an attempt to gain some practical benefit in war, wealth, health, love, interpersonal disputes, etc. Those activities, in turn, were directed in part according to the people's religious conceptions. So while we today tend to isolate religion as a discrete aspect of life, the Vikings tended to see it as inseparably intertwined with every other part of "the way things are," which is why they didn't have a word for it.

# SOURCES, METHODS, AND THE PRESENT STATE OF OUR KNOWLEDGE

Before we say much more about Norse religion and mythology, let's first briefly pause to consider a crucial question: how do we know what we know (or think we know) about them? The available evidence for Viking Age religion and mythology comes from several different types of sources, but literary sources inevitably contain the backbone of that evidence, so let's look at them first.

The only written sources we possess directly from pre-Christian times in northern Europe are runic inscriptions, which are all brief and, taken together, tell us very little.[8] The rather sparsely-used runes were the only method of writing the Norse had prior to the introduction of the Latin alphabet, which went hand in hand with the introduction of Christianity in the tenth and eleventh centuries. Viking culture was an oral culture, and even though there were surely traditional poems that dealt with mythic and religious topics, none of these have survived – with a few partial and possible exceptions, as we'll see shortly.

However, we do possess court poetry – called "skaldic poetry" after *skald*, the Old Norse word for "poet" – that dates from the ninth century onwards, which was composed and transmitted orally for many generations before finally being written down in the eleventh through fourteenth centuries, usually in the form of quotations in larger prose works. The purpose of the skaldic poems was to please and praise the kings by whom the skalds were employed. They seldom recount myths in their entirety, but they often allude to myths along the way to make a point. The skaldic poems therefore often enable us to see that at least some version of a myth retold by the medieval authors did indeed exist in the Viking Age.[9]

A major collection of anonymous Old Norse poetry called the *Poetic Edda* was compiled and edited in Iceland in the thirteenth century. (*Poetic Edda* is a modern name; the collection was originally nameless, and was given its current title by seventeenth-century scholars struck by the similarity of its contents to those of Snorri Sturluson's *Edda*, which we'll examine momentarily.) The poems in this collection are different from typical skaldic poems in their formal structure and in the fact that they *do* set out to recount whole myths. Therefore, they're called "Eddic poetry" to distinguish them from skaldic poetry. Scholars fiercely and endlessly debate the age of these poems. Arguments range from the ninth to thirteenth centuries, and different poems were of course probably composed at different times (and in different places). Similarly, there's little consensus on whether they started out as oral poems or written ones. What we can be sure of, however, is that the form in which they've come down to us is a product of the thirteenth century, long after the Norse religion had ceased to be a living tradition and had become a topic of antiquarian interest. The editors of the *Poetic Edda* weren't simply compilers; in addition to deciding which poems to include and in which order, they made changes and added a considerable amount of material to the final text of the collection. *Parts* of the collection were *probably* composed during the Viking Age and the period of the transition to Christianity, but other parts of it were *definitely* written by the thirteenth-century editors. These parts include "stage directions" inserted into the bodies of some of the poems, added or subtracted verses, and prose passages that have been placed before and after some of the poems.[10]

Thirteenth-century Iceland has also given us the *Edda* of Snorri Sturluson, often called the *Prose Edda* to distinguish it from the *Poetic Edda*. No one today knows what the word *Edda* means, and speculation has so far proven mostly unfruitful. Snorri (Icelanders were and are referred to by their first names rather than their last names) was a man of great learning and great ambition – a clergyman, historian, politician, and many other things. He wrote his *Edda* in order to provide a handbook on how to write traditional Old Norse poetry.

Since one of the mainstays of that tradition was a system of elaborate, standardized allusions to images, characters, and events from Norse mythology, Snorri endeavored to provide a more or less systematic overview of the old myths as part of his handbook.

Snorri's effort was shaped by two main factors: his sources and his own perspective. Since the oral tradition of retelling the old myths had become a thing of the past by Snorri's day, he had to rely on written sources. These included many of the poems that would later be included in the *Poetic Edda*, skaldic poems, and probably many additional poems that have since been lost. Since we do possess at least some of his sources, we can compare them to Snorri's account to get a sense of his methods. Like any other scholar, Snorri was all too human. He sometimes misinterpreted his sources, glossed over important differences between them in an attempt to present a coherent and systematic narrative, and when his sources left gaps in the story he wanted to tell, he filled them in with his own imagination.[11] Due to his own religious preferences and those of his audience, Snorri presented the Norse religion as the groping attempt of his ancestors to make sense of the world without the all-illuminating revelation that Christ had provided. While it was all manmade folly, Snorri took pains to present his forebears as having anticipated elements of Christianity. He therefore bent and stretched his data to make the Norse myths and beliefs seem closer to those of Christianity than they actually had been, as well as to account for them within a Christian historical framework.[12] While Snorri was a highly capable scholar by the standards of his time, it's important to remember his lack of firsthand experience of the religion and mythology he describes and the fact that he consciously shaped the material to fit the goals of his project.

The next major category of literary sources to consider is the Icelandic sagas. (The word *saga* is simply Old Norse for "story.") The earliest of the sagas date from the end of the twelfth century, while the latest date from the fourteenth century.[13] Their subject matter, however, concerns events that would have happened centuries earlier. They're mostly anonymous, with the most notable exception being the sagas that comprise the *Heimskringla* ("The History of the Kings of Norway"), which were written by Snorri. By modern standards, the sagas occupy a curious place in between history and fiction. But our modern conception of history didn't arise until centuries after the sagas were written. The saga authors saw themselves as presenting traditional lore, creatively adapting it to make it especially palatable to their audiences, not as presenting impartial, factual accounts of past events backed up by extensive research. In other words, while we think of the authority of a work of history as resting on the scope and quality of its research, the medieval Icelanders saw venerable tradition as the firmest basis for a work's legitimate claims to authority.

Around the same time that Snorri was writing his *Prose Edda* in Iceland, a Danish bishop's clerical assistant by the name of Saxo Grammaticus ("Saxo the Learned") was writing another greatly important work, the *Gesta Danorum* ("History of the Danes"). Unlike Snorri and the saga authors, who wrote in their native Old Norse, Saxo wrote in Latin. Since the accepted wisdom of his day traced the Danish people and their rulers back to mythical origins, Saxo included many of these myths in his account. However, he desacralized them by portraying them as events that had happened at particular times and places in this world, rather than in the hazy, almost timeless otherworld in which the myths had originally been seen as taking place. He also turned many divine figures into human ones. Saxo tells us that his sources were Icelanders and runic inscriptions. But his sources have never been found, so it's impossible to really know what to make of this claim. This is an important question, since he presents remarkably different versions of stories known from Snorri and elsewhere.[14]

Other notable literary sources are accounts by foreign authors, such as the German Adam of Bremen, who includes a famous description of a temple at Uppsala in Sweden in his *History of the Archbishops of Hamburg-Bremen*, and Ahmad Ibn Fadlan, an Arabic writer who has bequeathed to us a lavish account of a Viking burial in Eastern Europe.

The most important non-literary sources to consider are archaeological ones, such as graves and picture-stones. Archaeology is an appealing source because of how pure and untrammeled it's often thought to be. After all, it comes directly from the hands of the Vikings themselves. But beneath its apparent purity, archaeology is actually highly problematic. Of all of the various types of sources, archaeological ones are by far the most difficult to interpret, and yet are the ones in most need of interpretation. Generally speaking, we can only make sense of what archaeology gives us with reference to the later literary sources. While archaeology can thereby corroborate some of the information provided in the later literary sources, there is always a risk of forcing the archaeological evidence to fit a particular, artificial mold, since we're essentially ignorant of what it might mean apart from the particular interpretive filters of the later written works. Rather than standing closer to the Vikings than the literary sources of later periods, archaeological evidence is, paradoxically, often actually one step *farther* away from the Vikings than the literary sources.[15]

Another fruitful source of information and insight into Norse religion and mythology is cross-cultural comparisons with other peoples with whom the Norse stood in some particularly meaningful relationship. By comparing otherwise perplexing details from written sources and archaeology with better-known practices and beliefs of related peoples, we can often come to understand Norse mythology and religion more fully. The closest cultures with which we can compare elements of Norse culture are those of the other Germanic groups such as the Anglo-Saxons of England and the continental Germanic tribes; other Indo-European groups such as the Indians (of India), Celts, Slavs, Greeks, and Romans; the Sámi, the traditionally nomadic people of northern Scandinavia; and, in some special cases, other circumpolar Eurasian groups from farther afield, such as the indigenous peoples of Siberia.

Additional sources of note include law codes, place-names, linguistic evidence, and folklore from later periods. When a law code prohibits something, we can be reasonably certain that it was practiced.

Written law codes from the Christian era in northern Europe often prohibit activities that sound like vestiges of pre-Christian practice, which can sometimes provide us with additional clues as to what exactly those practices involved. Place-names from the Norse countries occasionally contain the name of a deity and/or a word that signals the presence of some kind of holy site, which furnishes us with additional information on which gods and goddesses were actually worshipped (rather than just being literary characters), how frequently, and where. Studying the words that the Norse used to refer to particular concepts, beings, etc. can give us clues about the meanings of those concepts and the characters of those beings. We'll find numerous examples of this throughout this book. And folklore from the medieval and early modern periods occasionally preserves elements of beliefs and practices from the Viking Age and earlier, although this type of source must be handled especially carefully due to the difficulty of locating elements of ancient religion and mythology amongst the much larger proportion of more recent innovations.

What does the nature of these sources mean for the study of Norse mythology and religion? As we've seen, there are no sources that we can take at face value. All of our sources carry potential problems and pitfalls, and the most significant sources are also often the most hazardous. Furthermore, since Norse mythology and religion were never codified or systematized by those who actually believed in and practiced them, a source that describes the beliefs or practices of one particular locality or person can't necessarily be assumed to speak for the entirety of the pre-Christian Norse population. Only by critically analyzing all of these disparate sources in relation to one another can we arrive at a reliable and substantial picture of what Norse mythology and religion actually looked like. This picture will never be anything close to complete, and it will never be without its difficulties, but the picture we have is vivid and fascinating indeed.

# CHAPTER 2:

# GODS AND GODDESSES

## THE NATURE OF THE NORSE DEITIES

When you hear the word "god," what kind of image pops into your mind? Perhaps you think of what most Christians, Jews, and Muslims call "God" with a capital "G:" a supreme being who created the world singlehandedly, who is all-powerful yet all-loving, and who has a "plan" for everyone (or at least certain favored people) that is supposed to ultimately work out to their benefit. Or perhaps you think of the Greek gods and goddesses, most of whom could be referred to as the god or goddess "of" one particular thing with a tolerable degree of accuracy: Artemis, goddess of the hunt; Aphrodite, goddess of love; Ares, god of war; or Asklepios, god of healing.

The Norse gods and goddesses were none of those things. They weren't "supreme," they weren't particularly benevolent, and they had personalities as rich and multifaceted as those of the most complicated humans, which couldn't be reduced to any simple formula like "god of x" without expressing only a fraction of the deity's character and sphere of influence.

What *were* they, then?

We can start to answer that question by considering the words that Old Norse speakers used to refer to them. The most widely-used word for "god" was *áss*, or *æsir* in the plural ("gods"). Its corresponding feminine form for "goddess" was *ásynja*, or *ásynjur* in the plural ("goddesses"). When referred to as a collective that included both gods and goddesses, the masculine plural *æsir* was used. These words are all derived from one of two Proto-Germanic roots: *\*ansaz*, "pole, beam, rafter," or *ansuz*, "life, vitality."[1] In either case, this etymology (where a word comes from) suggests that the gods were the metaphorical "poles" or "vital forces" that held together and sustained the cosmos and its order. They were very much a part of the cosmos rather than beings who merely manipulated it from the outside. When the cosmos arose, they arose with it as part of the same process. And when the cosmos will fall, as the Norse prophecies of Ragnarok foretell, the gods will fall with it. Etymology, myth, and religion all complement and reinforce each other here, which points to this having been a central Norse theological concept.

The second most widely-used word for "gods" in Old Norse was *regin*, "rulers." This, too, is perfectly consistent with their recorded role in myth and religion. In addition to being part and parcel of the cosmos, the gods were characterized by their extreme level of power within the cosmos. None of them were "supreme," because each had certain powers that the others didn't have, and they were subject to fate just like all other beings. But they were *more* powerful than any other beings, with the sole exception of the Norns, the carvers and weavers of fate. The structure of the cosmos was seen as analogous to the Norse social hierarchy, with the gods and goddesses as the rulers who established and enforced the order of the system and reigned over those less powerful.

The gods were seen in very anthropomorphic (human-like) and interventionist terms. Far from static models of morals or concepts, they had very human strengths and weaknesses, albeit magnified in proportion to their exalted status, and each deity was involved in a great many aspects of life. While the gods and goddesses were fundamentally invisible and inscrutable, manifestations of their presence, or at least of their power, could often be found in the images of them crafted by their worshippers, the weather, the functioning of the social order, the success or failure of crops and herds, the success or failure of a person's or a group's activities and ambitions, and potentially any other realm of life.

The character of the Norse divinities had important ramifications for the relationship between them and their human worshippers. In the words of archaeologist Neil Price,

> the 'worship' required by the Norse pantheon was not adoration, or gratitude, or even unreserved approval, and was thus utterly unlike the Christian relationship to the divine. The religion of the Æsir and Vanir demanded only a recognition that they existed as an integral and immutable part of human nature and society, and of the natural world, and that as such they possessed an inherent rightness - perhaps even a kind of beauty. If one wished to avoid disaster, it was necessary to come to terms with the gods, and the terms would be theirs, not those of their followers. This is an important point ... because a refusal to acknowledge the gods in this way could have dire consequences.[2]

Finally, while most of the Old Norse sources refer to all of the gods as *æsir*, and occasionally also refer to some or all of the gods as *vanir* (a word whose meaning remains unknown[3]), some late literary sources group the gods into two distinct tribes under these two names. (When we use the capitalized words "Aesir" and "Vanir" to refer to particular groups of deities, as in the above quote from Price, we're talking about this tribal division.) The exact nature of this division is ambiguous and has created considerable controversy amongst modern scholars. Some, most notably philologist Rudolf Simek, have argued that the division is an invention of the medieval authors,[4] while those who have accepted it as authentic have offered varying interpretations of what exactly differentiated the two tribes. The sources themselves never give their own interpretations, and the split can't be found amongst any of the other ancient Germanic peoples, so we're left to guess. Many have advocated some variant of the idea that the Vanir were deities of peace and fertility, whereas the Aesir were deities of war and "culture." Such a schema is unconvincing, however, because the Aesir often played a role in fertility, and the Vanir often played a role in war and the life of the mind. The division is found in too many different sources for it to have been entirely invented by medieval scholars. But it's such a vague and awkward tendency in the sources that it seems to have been a late development in the Viking Age, one that was present in only a half-formed way before the process was aborted with the acceptance of Christianity. Thus, while I point out instances where the Aesir-Vanir distinction might impact our understanding of a particular point, I don't place undue weight on it – because the Vikings evidently didn't, either.

## ODIN

The gods humanity has worshipped over the millennia include many enigmatic, complex, and seemingly contradictory characters among their ranks. But perhaps none have possessed these characteristics more so than the Norse god Odin. He was the chief of the gods, yet he often ventured far from their kingdom, Asgard, on long, solitary wanderings throughout the cosmos on purely self-interested quests, and he had little regard for communal values and standards such as justice, fairness, or respect for law and custom. He was the divine patron of rulers, but also of outcasts. He was a war god, but also a poetry god. He was worshiped by those in search of prestige, honor, and nobility, yet he was often cursed for being a fickle trickster, and he engaged in certain "feminine" activities that would have brought unspeakable shame and dishonor to any flesh-and-blood Norse man. It's no wonder that the Norse had over two hundred names for him.[5] What kind of literary figure – let alone a god whose historical worship spanned much of a continent and several centuries – could possibly have possessed all of these qualities at once, with their apparently glaring contradictions?

Odin's Old Norse name, Óðinn, is comprised of two parts. The first is the noun óðr, a word that could be translated into modern English as "inspiration," "ecstasy," or "fury." Óðr was a frenzied, exalted state that was so overpowering and consuming that it was felt to be intrinsically divine, whether it manifested itself as the rage of the berserker in battle, creative inspiration, the sudden realization of an important insight, the uninhibited power of a king or chieftain, or the trance of a seer or sorcerer. The second element of Odin's name, -inn, is simply the definite article ("the"). Odin's name can therefore best be translated as "The Inspired One," "The Ecstatic One," or "The Furious One." The medieval German historian Adam of Bremen confirms this when he writes, "Odin, that is, Fury."[6] This divine intoxication is the unifying elixir that runs through the many otherwise very different aspects of life in which Odin had a hand, and it is the key to understanding the personality and character of this god who was said to live on wine alone.[7]

The Norse were an extremely warlike people, so it should come as no surprise that they worshipped several war gods. Each presided over particular, although often overlapping, aspects of war. Odin's involvement in war had little to do with its goals or reasons, but was mainly concerned with the raw ecstasy that battle could provoke. The warriors who were especially closely tied to Odin were the berserkers (berserkir, "bear-shirts") and úlfheðnar ("wolf-skins"), who were said to have the ability to take on the spirit – or, in some cases, even the physical form – of bears and wolves. They charged and howled onto the battlefield with no armor and almost less concern for their own well-being, hacking and pummeling away with utter abandon while lost to themselves in their trance.[8] It's hard to imagine a more frightening thing to have encountered on the Iron Age battlefield.

Odin's attitude was similar to that of the hero of German philosopher Friedrich Nietzsche's *Thus Spoke Zarathustra*: "You say it is the good cause that hallows even war? I say unto you: it is the good war that hallows any cause."[9] Odin boasts in the Eddic poem *The Song of Gray-Beard*, "I incited the princes never to make peace."[10] Two of his names, *Hnikarr* and *Hnikudr*, mean "the one who incites to battle."[11] So great was his lust for the frenzy of war that he even inspired kinsmen to fight each other when he could.

*The Song of King Eirik*, one of the grandest surviving examples of skaldic poetry, relates how the heroes in Valhalla, the magnificent land of the dead over which Odin presided, welcomed King Eirik Blood-Axe upon his death. This was after he had risen to power by murdering much of his family, and had been such a brutal figure that he was eventually exiled from Norway. In fact, upon his arrival, Odin states that it was precisely *because of* this very brutality ("for in many lands has he borne a reddened sword"[12]) that his spirit was whisked away to the god's shining hall.

As we'll see in a later chapter, the Norse held quite idealized notions about manly, martial valor. While Odin was one of the foremost battle gods, his role in this regard was – in keeping with his general character – transgressive. When Odin obtained or granted victory, he often did so by breaking the rules of honorable combat. He was known as a devious, fickle trickster who was apt to grant favor and then withdraw it with the flick of a wrist – usually one that held a sword. He was even willing to break oaths he had sworn,[13] which was one of the most disreputable deeds someone could do. Many thought him to be unjust or even, according to one skaldic poem, "malicious."[14] While a war god, Odin was anything but the ideal toward which an honorable Norse warrior aspired. He was more of a reflection of the grim, sordid reality of Viking Age warfare – its unpredictability, its unfairness, its excruciating pain and hardship – but also the sublime ecstasy that could be found at particular moments therein.

Odin's favored warriors were always the elite ones, and this same preference of his extended to all other realms of life; those who claimed Odin as their patron were, like Odin himself, always elite and exceptional in some way or another. Since he was the ruler of the gods, he was a natural choice for the patron of human kings and chieftains. Many royal families even claimed him as an ancestor, often the founder of their line.[15] But Odin was the antithesis of a "law and order" type of ruler like the god Tyr. Instead, he was a "terrible sovereign" who governed by raw power, often of a magical nature.

Intriguingly, he was often the patron of outlaws as well, such as the saga heroes Egil Skallagrimsson and Grettir Asmundarson, both strong-willed warrior-poets. In the Viking world, outlaws were people who had been formally banished from their communities for performing some especially heinous action, often murder. The protection of the law had been stripped from them (hence the title "outlaw," that is, someone who is outside of the law), so anyone who met them could kill them without any legal repercussions. Outlaws were among the most hated and feared people in Norse society. The sources speak of a time when Odin himself was temporarily outlawed by his fellow gods, which we'll encounter in Part Two of this book. Someone with Odin's self-serving disposition and contempt for social mores was bound to do something that would get him outlawed sooner or later, and it's not too difficult to see how Odin and other outlaws – the exceptionally criminal – could be kindred spirits on some level. While a revered king in some contexts, Odin was a despised exile in others, and largely because of the same character traits.

Visual depictions of Odin varied considerably, in keeping with the fiery dynamism of his personality and roles. Sometimes he was pictured as a war leader in full armor, such as on pre-Viking Age jewelry and the famous Sutton Hoo helmet,[16] while at other times he was depicted as a gaunt wanderer with a dark cloak, broad-brimmed hat, and a staff that was surely no ordinary walking stick. But he was invariably visualized with one signature trait: a single eye. He had plucked out his other eye in exchange for rare and precious knowledge. On another occasion, dramatically retold in the Eddic poem *The Song of the High One* (*Hávamál*), he "sacrificed himself to himself" by hanging from the great tree at the center of the cosmos for nine days and nights, foregoing all food and water and peering relentlessly downward into the dark waters of the Well of Fate below, until at last he obtained the object of his ordeal. This was the first glimpse of the runes, the jagged Norse alphabet, whose letters were held to symbolize the foremost cosmic forces. (The word "runes," Old Norse *rúnar*, means "mysteries" as well as "letters.") To know the runes and their secrets was to be able to wield those cosmic forces. Odin's prize, therefore, was far more than merely an alphabet.

We'll explore these stories in greater depth in Part Two. For now, it's enough to note that Odin was willing to undergo any trial in order to gain more knowledge of the innermost workings of the universe. In the Norse worldview, big-picture, esoteric knowledge of this sort was seen as being inherently linked to magic. Indeed, the practice of magic was "simply" putting such lofty understanding to use. To gain this kind of knowledge, therefore, meant to gain colossal power, and power is what Odin was ultimately after.

In the course of his magical and shamanic endeavors, Odin sacrificed something else of almost inestimable worth to any Norse man: his masculine honor. For a man to practice magic meant to bring upon himself unspeakable shame, for reasons that will become clearer later. Odin wasn't one to refuse any activity that would bolster his power, however, and so he accepted even the extreme stigma that went along with the performance of "effeminate" magic. And, to be sure, alongside this "effeminate" aspect of his personality stood a highly masculine side, which manifested itself in Odin's pursuits of war and women.

To aid him in his magical tasks, Odin had numerous attendant spirits. Foremost among them were the Valkyries, the female "Choosers of the Slain;" the ravens Huginn and Muninn, "Mind" and "Memory" respectively; the wolves Geri and Freki, whose names both mean "Greedy;" and the eight-legged horse Sleipnir, "Sliding," whom he rode on his numerous travels to far-flung and dangerous places in the world of spirit.[17]

Odin was said to speak only in poems,[18] and he was the foremost patron god of poets as well as elite warriors, rulers, outlaws, and sorcerers. He owned the potent mead Odroerir (*Óðrœrir*, "Stirrer of

Óðr"), which he personally dispensed to all truly great poets in another example of the overflowing bounty of his ecstasy and inspiration.

Odin was also one of the deities most closely associated with death and the dead. He was the lord of Valhalla, the "Hall of the Fallen," the most prestigious place one could hope to go after death. Of all of the gods, he was perhaps the most frequent recipient of human sacrifice – and, unsurprisingly, those sacrificed to him were seldom commoners, but rather kings and warriors. A frequent – and chilling – way of attempting to secure his favor in battle was to throw a spear over one's foes, sacrificing them to the god with the cry, "Odin owns all of you!" (Óðinn á yðr alla). One of his particular magical specialties was necromancy – the art of raising and communicating with the dead – so as to learn what mysterious knowledge they might possess. During earlier times, the Roman writers even identified him with Mercury, the Roman god who ferried the spirits of the newly dead to the underworld, rather than Mars, the god of war.[19]

Snorri Sturluson tells us that Odin was the son of the proto-god Borr and the giantess Bestla, and that he was the father of virtually all of the other gods and goddesses.[20] Whether this is Snorri's invention or represents a commonly-held view in the Viking Age is anyone's guess, since few deities are named as sons or daughters of Odin in earlier sources. Frigg was generally considered to be Odin's wife, although skaldic poetry sometimes speaks of Jord in that role.[21]

## THOR

Although Odin was the leader of the gods, Thor was the most popular of the northern gods during the Viking Age.

As with Odin, the key to understanding the many facets of Thor's character, and the relationship between them, lies in his name. "Thor" (Old Norse Þórr) means "Thunder,"[22] and Thor was the divine force that manifested in physical thunder.

Also like Odin, Thor was a war god, but of a decidedly different sort. For one thing, Thor was far more inclined to rely on brute force, and far more capable of doing so. Unlike the cunning, intellectual Odin, the sources portray Thor as brawny and hot-tempered. His signature weapon was his hammer, Mjollnir (*Mjöllnir*, "Lightning"[23]), with which he delivered countless death-blows. He also owned a "belt of strength" (*megingjarðar*) that doubled his already almost-unmatched physical strength. In keeping with his muscular strength, his particular domain within Asgard was called Thrudheim (*Þrúðheimr*, "World of Might") or Thrudavangar (*Þrúðavangar*, "Fields of Might").[24] True to his connections to thunder and lightning, his hall within that land was called Bilskirnir (*Bilskírnir*, "Striking Lightning with Rays of Light").[25]

Not only were Thor's methods as a war god different from those of Odin – his motivations and aims were different as well. Unlike the amoral, self-centered Odin, Thor was a dutiful and fiercely partisan defender of the gods, and of cosmic order more generally, against the giants, the forces of chaos. When thunder blasted across the northern lands, the Vikings imagined it to be the embodiment of Thor riding through the sky in his chariot, drawn by the goats Tanngrisnir (*Tanngrísnir*, "Snarl-Tooth") and Tanngnost (*Tanngnóstr*, "Gnash-Tooth").[26] When he spotted an enemy giant, he struck him or her down with his hammer, which was embodied by the lightning flash. The crash and rumble was the sound of the thunder god pulverizing his foes.

Thor's arch-nemesis was Jormungand (*Jörmungandr*, "Mighty Beast"), the great serpent who lurked in the waters at the edge of the known world. So enormous was he that his scaly body actually encircled the land completely. Once, Thor went fishing for the venomous snake, and caught him on his line. As the thunder god was reeling him in, his fishing companion became so terrified that he cut the line at the last moment, and the beast sank back down into the deep. But, the legends say, Thor and Jormungand will face each other again at Ragnarok, the battle at the end of the universe.

As the indefatigable protector of the gods, their holy fortress, and proper cosmic order, Thor was the patron and model of the loyal, honorable warrior, especially those from the non-aristocratic classes. This was a further way in which Thor was differentiated from Odin: the classes with which each were associated. As the Eddic poem *The Song of Gray-Beard* puts it, "Odin's are the earls who fall in battle, but Thor's are the thralls."[27] Thor's status as a champion of the common people and his more straightforwardly admirable character were surely sizable factors behind his popularity overtaking that of Odin in the Viking Age. This trend was especially pronounced in Iceland, which was settled during this period by Norwegian farmers who, according to some sources, were motivated by a desire to find respite from a tyrannical, Odin-worshipping king.[28]

Considering Thor's animosity toward the giants, it's perhaps ironic that he was actually three-quarters giant himself. Thor's mother was Jord (*Jörð*, "Earth," also called *Hlöðyn* or *Fjörgyn* in some sources), who was fully giant, and his father was Odin, who was, as we've seen, half giant. Such parentage, however, was relatively common among the gods.

Thor's role as the protector of sacred order included many other realms of life besides just war. Thor and his hammer were frequently invoked to hallow births, marriages, funerals, the forging and use of weapons, the carving of runic inscriptions, feasting, travelling, the establishment of new settlements, the planting of crops, and the swearing of oaths.[29] In other words, the thunder god was called upon to sanctify and bless potentially any person, place, thing, or event that the worshipper wanted to protect from malevolent, profane chaos, which always had to be actively kept at bay lest it overwhelm all that the Norse cherished in life. While these activities were quite peaceful in and of themselves, they nevertheless carried an undertone of the cosmic struggle in which Thor excelled.

While many of the myths feature Thor in his capacity as a raging warrior smiting giants, they also include scenes that contain traces of this more peaceful side. The most significant of these is probably an episode from the tale of Thor's journey to Utgard. In order to reciprocate the hospitality of a family who had given him a place to sleep for the night, Thor slaughtered his two goats and served them for dinner, instructing the family to lay the cleaned bones back on the hides. The next morning, Thor hallowed the hides and bones with his hammer, and Tanngrisnir and Tanngnost came back to life. (Talk about having your cake and eating it, too!)

Thor had a further hand in the day-to-day affairs and well-being of the common people. As the thunder god, he was responsible for bringing rainstorms that rejuvenated the land and enabled crops to grow. The great majority of Norse commoners were farmers in some capacity. Their livelihoods, therefore, were especially directly tied to how well a season's agriculture fared. Adam of Bremen, for example, writes, "Thor, they say, presides over the air, which governs the thunder and lightning, the winds and rains, fair weather and crops."[30] The signature characteristic of his seldom-mentioned wife, Sif, seems to have been her luscious golden hair, which likely symbolized the fields of grain. The image of a sky god impregnating an earth goddess was a common one among the Norse and other Indo-European peoples, and the marriage of Thor and Sif should surely be understood in these terms.

## FREYA AND FRIGG

The most exalted goddess in Norse mythology and religion was Freya. Freya was the most widely and passionately venerated of all of the many goddesses who had a role in bringing fertility to the land and the people. While most of these goddesses were more or less local figures, Freya's cult enjoyed a considerable popularity across the entire Viking world. Her name, "Lady" (Old Norse *Freyja*), is a title rather than a true name. Snorri tells us that this was due to her going under countless different names while traveling the world in search of her lost husband. There may be some truth to this statement, in a roundabout way; those many local fertility goddesses were probably identified with Freya on some level, making their names her names as well.[31]

Freya had an exceptionally lusty disposition, even for the Norse deities. You could accurately say that she was their "party girl." According to the Eddic poem *Loki's Taunts* (*Lokasenna*), she had slept with every god and elf in Asgard at some point or another – even her brother, Frey.[32] As beautiful as a bright, lush spring morning, she was also a frequent object of desire by less savory kinds of beings such as the giants. Several of the Norse myths involved a giant kidnapping Freya or at least threatening to do so.

She was a great lover of fine material possessions, especially jewelry. Her connection to gold was particularly strong. The precious metal was said to be her tears, which fell over all the earth during the long stretches of time when her husband, the seldom-mentioned Od, was away on his travels.[33] This far-faring Od (Óðr, the same "ecstasy, inspiration, furor" we encountered in our discussion of Odin) was surely none other than Odin himself.

The father of Freya was the god Njord, and her mother was Njord's sister, who, unfortunately, is never named in our sources.[34] As we've seen, a few sources classify this family, including Freya's brother Frey, as the "Vanir," a separate tribe of deities. According to some of them, Freya originally came to live in Asgard when the Aesir (the other divine tribe) and Vanir swapped some members in a hostage exchange at the conclusion of a war that was once waged between them. In all of the other surviving stories involving Freya, however, she's treated as a "normal" member of the inhabitants of Asgard (the Aesir).

Of all of the Norse deities, only Odin rivaled Freya when it came to magical abilities. Freya was the divine model of a Viking Age sorceress. One Old Norse poem describes her traveling from house to house, giving prophecies, chanting, and performing all kinds of rituals for her hosts.[35] In fact, Snorri says that she was the one who taught Odin much of what he knew.[36]

We've noted how Odin and Thor both had particular attendant spirits, and Freya did, too. Freya rode in a chariot driven by unnamed cats, and she also had a boar or a pig called Hildisvini (*Hildisvíni*, "Battle Swine").[37] One of Freya's countless names was *Sýr*, "Sow," which further demonstrates her connection to that particular animal.[38]

Also like Odin, Freya seems to have received some of the dead into her personal domain, Folkvang (*Fólkvangr*, "Field of the People" or perhaps "Field of Armies"), in which stood the hall Sessrumnir (*Sessrúmnir*, "Space with Many Seats" or "Space with Roomy Seats").[39] However, different sources give different accounts of *which* of the dead might hope to have a place there. The Eddic poem *The Song of the Hooded One* (*Grímnismál*) describes her as hosting half of those who fall in battle,[40] while in *Egil's Saga*, a woman who wants to commit suicide declares that she'll never eat again until she dines with Freya.[41] Is this saga referencing a notion that women went to Freya after death, or suicides, or something else? Or is it simply poetic license? In all likelihood, different Viking Age people and communities held different notions about who went to Freya and under what circumstances.

Frigg ("Beloved"[42]), Odin's wife, was a nominally distinct duplication of Freya. Apart from being listed as having a different domain in Asgard - Fensalir, "Marsh Halls"[43] - Frigg's attributes were identical to those of Freya. We've already seen that Freya and Frigg shared the same husband, Odin. He was simply called by a slightly different name in connection with Freya. Like Freya, Frigg was noted for her promiscuity, having slept with Odin's brothers Vili and Ve while her husband was in exile,[44] and on another occasion with a slave.[45] Also like Freya, Frigg had a love for fine jewelry and precious metals.[46] Frigg was a sorceress as well: she could foretell the future,[47] and the two both possessed sets of falcon plumes that could be used to shapeshift into that bird, which Loki made use of in some of the myths.

Nevertheless, the distinction between Freya and Frigg, superficial though it may be, is one that can be found again and again in the sources. It appears, then, that this can't be due to some misunderstanding on the part of authors and poets working after the Viking Age. The separation of this one goddess into two probably began late in the Viking Age, and was never completed because it was interrupted by the acceptance of Christianity. The next question, of course, is: *why* was Freya-Frigg being split into two goddesses? We simply don't know.

## FREY

As with Freya, the name of her brother, Frey, was a title rather than a proper name. It meant "Lord" (Old Norse *Freyr*). Frey, too, was the son of Njord and Njord's unnamed sister,[48] and was counted among the Vanir by Snorri. His more "proper" name seems to have been Yngvi, under which name he was credited with being the founder of the royal dynasty of the Ynglings of Sweden.[49] However, he was referred to as "Frey" much more commonly than "Yngvi." And, unfortunately, no one knows what "Yngvi" meant. Another common name for him was *Fróði*, "Fruitful."[50]

Frey was worshipped primarily as a god who brought fertility and vitality to the land and to people. Those who depended on farming and herding for their livelihood were inclined to regard him as the most important of all the deities.[51] Adam of Bremen reports that the most outstanding feature of the image of Frey at a magnificent temple in Uppsala, Sweden was his enormous, erect phallus, a symbol of his power and fertility.[52]

He was a frequent recipient of sacrifice, especially at weddings[53] – presumably to encourage the fertility and happiness of the couple – and at harvest time. The sacrifice commonly took the form of a boar,[54] an animal with which Frey was closely associated. Like Freya, he was often accompanied by a boar, in his case one named Gullinborsti ("Golden Bristles").[55]

For agriculture to be carried out successfully, an absence of war and conflict was necessary. Understandably, then, Frey was celebrated as a bringer of peace, which went hand in hand with his being a bringer of plenty. However, true to the exceptionally warlike culture of the Norse, Frey, like his divine colleagues, was said to be a formidable and eager warrior as well.[56]

Central to the cult of Frey was the chariot. Chariots that contained a statue of the god were carted from village to village, blessing the land through which they passed and its inhabitants. Frey himself was said to be an expert chariot driver, and his personal chariot was drawn by two of his favorite animal, the boar.[57] Another one of the god's favored modes of transportation was the ship, which indicates that he, like his father Njord, was credited with richly stocking the seas with fish and other useful resources. Frey's ship, Skidbladnir (*Skíðblaðnir*, apparently "Assembled from Thin Pieces of Wood"[58]), was the finest of all ships. It had been built by the dwarves, the greatest craftsmen in the cosmos. Though it was so big that it could carry all of the gods and their weapons at once, it could be folded up and stuffed into a small bag. It always had a favorable wind.[59]

In the Eddic poem *The Song of the Hooded One*, Frey's residence is said to be Alfheim (*Álfheimr*, "Home of the Elves").[60] This might suggest that Frey was sometimes seen as the lord of the elves, but there's nothing else in the sources that directly corroborates this intriguing possibility.

Frey's wife was the giantess Gerd (*Gerðr*), whom he won by force in a reminder that the bestower of "peace and plenty," as a popular formula went, wasn't always so peaceful.

## LOKI

Many people who know nothing else about Norse mythology have at least heard of Loki, the wily trickster god. Loki was a scheming coward who cared only for shallow pleasures and self-preservation. He was by turns playful, malicious, and helpful, but always irreverent and nihilistic. Snorri describes him as handsome, but temperamental and dangerously guileful.[61]

Loki alternately helped both the gods and the giants, depending on which course of action was most pleasurable and advantageous to him at the time. Several of the tales feature him harming the gods in some way, often by stealing something or someone from among them. But it was (almost) always he who then rectified the situation – typically by some bizarre, convoluted means – and often ultimately brought some great benefit to the gods in the process. He was frequently presented as a companion of Thor and/or Odin, but their friendships, though perhaps close, were quite stormy. The equally temperamental Thor, in particular, sometimes found himself in the position of singing Loki's praises one minute and then grabbing him by the collar and threatening his life the next.

Loki's father was the giant Farbauti (Old Norse *Fárbauti*, "Cruel Striker"[62]), and his mother was an otherwise unknown being named Laufey (the meaning of which is also unknown) or Nal (*Nál*, "Needle"[63]). His wife was the goddess Sigyn ("Friend of Victory"[64]), with whom he had a son named Narfi or Nari (perhaps "Corpse"[65]). With the giantess Angrboda (*Angrboða*, "Distress-Bringer"[66]) he also fathered Jormungand, the world serpent who was Thor's particular enemy; Hel, the goddess or giantess who presided over the underworld; and Fenrir, the wolf who bit off the arm of the god Tyr and who will swallow Odin at Ragnarok, the downfall of the cosmos – hardly nice kids, to say the least.

Those were the only children we know of whom Loki fathered. Loki did have other children, but he wasn't their father. He was their *mother.* He gave birth to Sleipnir, Odin's eight-legged horse, after being impregnated by the giant stallion Svadilfari, which we'll read about in the story of how Asgard's wall was built. On another occasion, he was said to have eaten the heart of a woman renowned for many deeds of great malice. He thereby became pregnant once again, and this time he gave birth to all of the female monsters in the world.[67] In a Norse context, these acts weren't merely shockingly "unnatural," although they certainly were that. They also pegged Loki as being *the* most shameful kind of being possible. We've already seen how Odin brought dishonor upon himself by practicing "effeminate" forms of magic. But the idea of a man giving birth was the highest level of dishonor recognized by the Norse, and to taunt a man with having done such a thing was the most extreme insult one could sling at him.[68] We'll examine the Norse honor culture in some detail in a later chapter, but for now it's enough to simply note how, for the Vikings, Loki's giving birth sealed his reputation as being the most transgressive, disreputable being possible.

Had Loki not mothered horses and monsters, he still would have been a supremely reviled personage. In Snorri's version of the tale of Balder's death, Loki was the one who was ultimately responsible for the death of that beloved god. This was his most nefarious act of all, and one for which the gods never forgave him. For this murder, as well as his countless other crimes, great and small, the gods finally dragged Loki into a cave and bound him with a chain made from the entrails of his son, Nari, who was slain before his eyes. A poisonous snake was placed above Loki to drip venom onto his forehead, each drop causing excruciating pain. But Loki's wife, Sigyn, proved her loyalty and steadfastness by sitting by his side and holding a bowl above his head to catch the serpent's poison. Every so often, however, the bowl would inevitably become full, and she would have to momentarily leave the cave to empty its contents. While she was away, and there was nothing between Loki's forehead and the snake's mouth, some droplets would hit his face, which made him writhe in such violent agony that earthquakes were attributed to his tortured convulsions.

But come Ragnarok, Loki will break free of his fetters and captain the ship that brings the giants to Asgard to destroy it, thereby proving once and for all that whatever he may have done to help the gods from time to time, he was ultimately on the side of no one but ruin and annihilation.

Therefore, it shouldn't be surprising that there are no traces whatsoever in the historical record of Loki ever having been worshipped.[69]

While there has been much debate concerning the meaning and etymology of Loki's name, the most convincing case by far is the one recently put forward by philologist Eldar Heide. Scandinavian sayings and folklore from the medieval and early modern periods speak of Loki as a knot on a thread. This can hardly be coincidental, since his mother was called *Nál*, "Needle," and Loki coming after Nal would be akin to the thread following the needle in sewing. Spiders, too, were called *loki* – the webs in which they caught their prey were seen as analogous to the fish nets (made from a series of loops and knots) Loki created in the Norse myths, including the one in which Thor attempted to catch him before his imprisonment. Furthermore, in later Icelandic usage, *loki* was a common noun that meant "knot" or "tangle."[70] The most parsimonious explanation, then, is to accept the later Icelandic definition as the meaning of Loki's name.

The trickster's name meaning "Knot" or "Tangle" would have had two layers of significance. First, it would have pointed to his making and casting metaphorical "nets" in the form of his schemes, in which the gods and other beings were caught like fish. Secondly, we may suspect, it would have meant that Loki was thought of as the "knot" or "tangle" in the otherwise straight thread of the gods, the fatal flaw in the cosmos that would one day lead to its downfall. Such an interpretation fits the ultimately tragic tone of Norse mythology. Even the gods had a traitor in their midst; even their world was not pristine and unshakeable, but compromised and vulnerable.

# BALDER

Balder was said to be the fairest of all of the Norse deities, both in appearance and in character, to the point that he actually radiated light. He was so eloquent and gracious that when he pronounced a judgment on any matter, no one could find a way to criticize it.[71] His hall in Asgard was called Breidablik (Old Norse *Breiðablik*, "Broad Splendor"[72]), where little to no malice could be found.[73] Among the Norse, the ox-eye daisy was called "Balder's Eyelash" on account of its long, slender, and pure white petals.[74]

The main surviving myth in which Balder featured is the doleful tale of his murder by Loki and the blind god Hod (*Höðr*, "Warrior"[75]), most famously told by Snorri Sturluson. Elements of this tale can be found in earlier Old Norse poetry, as well as in archaeological evidence such as pieces of jewelry that predate the Viking Age,[76] so we can be certain that Snorri didn't simply invent this tale out of whole cloth. However, he seems to have gone out of his way to portray Balder as a passive, innocent sufferer – likely in the interest of creating a sense that his ancestors had anticipated the story of Christ's crucifixion.

There's no evidence that Balder was seen in such a manner during the Viking Age. In fact, there's ample evidence that he was seen as an accomplished and formidable warrior – which is, of course, exactly what we'd expect for any Norse god. Skaldic poetry often mentions him in passing in very martial terms,[77] and the one other "complete" version of the story of his death we possess, that of Saxo Grammaticus, portrays him as a zealous fighter. Furthermore, while scholars have offered numerous different explanations for his name, the most straightforward is that it came from the common adjective *baldr*, "bold," which suggests an eagerness for battle.[78]

Balder was the son of Odin and Frigg, and his wife – or at least, in Saxo's version, romantic interest – was the otherwise unknown goddess Nanna. (The meaning of Nanna's name is unknown.[79])The evidence for a cult of Balder is sparse and ambiguous, but it suggests that if he was worshipped, it was largely as a bringer of fertility – a side of him that the literary sources don't particularly speak of, but which is certainly plausible based on the picture of him that they paint.[80]

## HEIMDALL

Heimdall (Old Norse *Heimdallr*, whose meaning/etymology is unknown[81]) was the dutiful sentry who kept watch over Asgard to warn of any approaching giants or other beings who might wish the gods ill. Or perhaps it would be more accurate to say that he "kept his ears open over Asgard;" just as Odin's sight was especially acute, Heimdall's hearing was second to no one else's. It was said that he could hear grass growing on the ground and wool growing on sheep.[82]

There seems to have been a lost myth about Heimdall sacrificing one of his ears in order to gain exceptionally fine hearing, just as Odin sacrificed one of his eyes for his own exceptional perceptual ability. The Eddic poem *The Prophecy of the Seeress* (*Völuspá*) states that Heimdall's *hljóð*, "listening ability and attention," lay in the same well in which Odin had sacrificed his eye, suggesting an obvious parallel.[83]

However he acquired his extraordinary power, he put it to use by tirelessly defending the gods and their heavenly fortress. He required less sleep than a bird, and sat atop the rainbow bridge Bifrost, the entryway to Asgard, in his hall Himinbjorg (*Himinbjörg*, "Sky Cliffs"). In his hand he held Gjallarhorn ("Resounding Horn"), which he will blow when the giants finally storm Asgard at Ragnarok. Snorri calls him the "white god" due to the purity of his honor.[84]

In the Eddic poem *Rigsthula*, Heimdall is said to have fathered the ancestors of the three main social classes in Norse society: aristocrats, freemen, and slaves. The first verse of *The Prophecy of the Seeress* alludes to this or a similar notion of him being the progenitor of humankind, so Heimdall seems to have been credited with fathering humankind in some capacity in ancient times.

The ram seems to have been Heimdall's attendant animal in the same way that ravens and wolves were for Odin, goats were for Thor, and boars were for Freya and Frey. He is associated with the animal in Old Norse literature, but nothing is ever said that indicates what form this connection took.[85] Heimdall was a son of Odin, and, in a feat possible for gods but not humans, he had no less than nine mothers. Who exactly these nine beings were has been the topic of considerable speculation, but no one really knows.[86]

## MINOR AND/OR OBSCURE DEITIES

We've already encountered Njord (Old Norse *Njörðr*, whose meaning and etymology are unknown) as the father of Freya and Frey, as well as, in the estimation of the sources that divide the deities into two tribes, one of the main gods in the Vanir tribe. Like Freya and Frey, Njord was worshipped largely as a fertility god, and he was particularly closely connected to the sea. His kingdom was called Noatun (*Nóatún*), which meant "Place of Ships." He was the patron of fishermen, sailors, and others who made their living from the ocean. Such was the lavishness of the abundance he bestowed that the exceptionally wealthy were called "as rich as Njord." Njord was briefly and unhappily married to the giantess Skadi, as we'll see in Part Two. Place-name evidence indicates that he was once one of the most important deities, but by the end of the Viking Age his role seems to have been all but subsumed by that of his son Frey.[87]

Like Njord, Tyr was once one of the most prominent gods, but by the end of the Viking Age his role had diminished to a downright startling degree. His name was a general Old Norse word for "god" (*týr*), which hints at what cross-cultural comparisons confirm: at some point – probably in the distant Proto-Germanic past – Tyr was *the* highest god, a continuation of the highest god of the Proto-Indo-Europeans, *Dyeus*.[88] By the Viking Age, however, he occupied a narrower and greatly reduced role as a war god known for his bravery and boldness and as a god who guaranteed oaths. The main story in which Tyr featured was the tale of how the giant wolf Fenrir was bound. The wolf declared that he wouldn't let himself be tied in the suspiciously innocent-looking chain in which the gods wanted to tie him – as a game, they said – unless one of them stuck their hand in his mouth as a pledge of good faith. Only Tyr was willing to do so, and when the wolf found himself unable to break free of the magical fetter, Tyr acquired the signature feature of his appearance: a missing hand. According to some sources, he was the son of Odin, but others claim he was the son of the giant Hymir. Place-names attest to his worship throughout Scandinavia.[89]

In the late literary sources, there's a god of poetry named Bragi. He seems to have originally been the ninth-century Norwegian poet Bragi Boddason. So exceptional was his verse that subsequent generations imagined him to be the main court poet in Valhalla, singing the praises of heroes upon their arrival, and skaldic poets often featured him in this role in their works. Medieval authors such as Snorri promoted him to the status of a god in their own works, but he doesn't seem to have been seen in this light in the Viking Age, nor is there any evidence that he was ever worshipped.[90]

Idun (*Iðunn*, "Rejuvenating One"[91]) was a goddess who owned a fruit that conferred longevity of life upon those who ate it. This was the source of the gods' near-immortality. In modern books on Norse mythology, these fruits are almost invariably considered to be apples, but this probably wasn't the case in pre-Christian times. The Old Norse word for "apple," *epli*, was often used to denote any fruit or nut, and "apples" in the modern English sense didn't arrive in Scandinavia until late in the Middle Ages.[92] Loki once accused her of sleeping with her brother's murderer,[93] but any myth in which this may have occurred is now lost. Although the medieval literary sources list her as the wife of Bragi, skaldic poetry confirms that she was an authentic pre-Christian figure (and therefore surely wasn't considered to be Bragi's wife in the Viking Age).[94]

Skadi (*Skaði*, perhaps "Harm" or "Shadow"[95]) was a giantess who was also counted among the goddesses. She lived high in snowy mountains, and seems to have been primarily a patroness of winter hunting and travel. She was widely worshipped in the Viking Age.[96] It was she who placed the viper above Loki's head when he was imprisoned, perhaps as revenge for his killing her father, the giant Thjazi. Intriguingly, her name may be related to the name "Scandinavia," but whether she lent her name to the land mass or vice versa is unknown.[97]

Gefjun ("Giver"[98]) was a goddess who seems to have been particularly associated with plowing and other aspects of agriculture. She was remembered in the literary sources mainly for having been the first to plow the island of Zealand, which she then dragged away from Sweden, where it had formerly been located, and giving it to Denmark. Some sources describe her as a goddess who was worshipped by virgins,[99] while others describe her as being promiscuous, for example trading sexual favors for a piece of jewelry.[100] It's difficult to reconcile or otherwise explain these apparent contradictory notions; perhaps some communities understood her as being a much more sexual entity than others did, but we really just don't know.

Especially since there was never a closed Norse "pantheon," the Norse worshipped numerous other gods and goddesses as well – far too many to ever cover in their totality. Most, for that matter, have been lost forever, their names and deeds unrecorded and therefore unremembered. But this overview of the most widespread and famous deities of the Viking Age should at least indicate something of the extraordinary richness of the Norse conception of the divine.

# CHAPTER 3:

# OTHER NUMINOUS

# BEINGS

The Viking universe teemed with a grand variety of spiritual beings who, while generally not considered gods or goddesses "proper," were nevertheless revered and/or feared. Let's take a look at the most important kinds of them.

## GIANTS

We've seen how the Norse thought of their deities as being, among other things, the powers that held together the proper order of the cosmos and enabled it to flourish. The giants were the exact opposite: they continually sought to undermine that order, to drag the cosmos back to primordial chaos, and to reinstall the uninterrupted reign of its frigid darkness. We can easily imagine how this particular antagonism would have possessed an acute importance for a preindustrial people who lived in a climate and landscape like those of Scandinavia. The homes of the giants were imagined to be like the wildest, remotest, and most desolate features of that landscape: snowy mountain peaks, the depths of the ocean, vast and impenetrable forests, etc. The word *troll* ("fiend, monster") was originally used to refer to giants, but in the folklore of later periods it came to denote a separate kind of being, one grounded in debased memories of the giants.[1]

But the giants were far from unequivocally "evil." While their opposing aims for the cosmos made them natural enemies of the gods, the relationship between the two wasn't always *just* opposition. As we've seen, the giants and the gods frequently intermarried and had children together; most of the deities were descended from at least one giant, and often more, at some point along the line. In the myths, the giants and gods sometimes got together for parties. And the giants provided useful raw materials for the gods' cosmological designs, especially when Odin and his brothers slew the giant Ymir and created the material world from his corpse. In the same way that human civilization depends on resources gleaned from the wilderness, the gods' cosmos depended on the giants and their world. Paradoxically, these forces of entropy and decay made the cosmos possible and guaranteed its survival – as long as the gods could keep them in check. The Vikings themselves seem to have done likewise, offering the giants sacrifices in the hopes of keeping them satisfied and at bay,[2] and otherwise invoking Thor and other divinities to ward them away.

"Giant" is a potentially misleading Anglicization of the name of these beings. In modern English, of course, a "giant" is first and foremost something of enormous size. Calling a godlike being a "giant" can't help but remind one of Michael Palin's famous prayer in *Monty Python and the Meaning of Life*: "O God, you are so very big, and let me tell you, we're all really impressed down here." Seen in this light, the word is a rather frivolous designation for beings who were genuinely dreaded in the Viking Age.

Speakers of Old Norse mainly called them *jötnar* (singular *jötunn*) or *þursar* (singular *þurs*). Jötunn comes from the Proto-Germanic *\*etunaz* and means "devourer."[3] Þurs is derived from the Proto-Germanic *\*þurisaz* and means something like "powerful and injurious one."[4]

How, then, did these "devourers" come to be called "giants?" When the Norman (French) William the Conquerer seized control of England in 1066 CE, the English language became filled with French words. Among these loanwords was the Old French *geant*, the ancestor of the modern English word "giant," which replaced the Old English *eóten*. *Geant* referred to the Giants of Greek mythology, who were a group of spiritual beings who, like the *jötnar* of Germanic mythology, were the enemies of the gods. The Greek ancestor of *geant*, in turn, was once used to translate a Hebrew word that denoted beings of enormous size in the Bible, and over time this connotation of "giant" became the word's dominant meaning.[5]

Nevertheless, since all modern publications on Norse mythology and religion translate *jötnar* as "giants," it would probably be unduly confusing to switch to calling them something more historically appropriate, such as "devourers," for the remainder of the book. Therefore, we'll continue to refer to them as "giants," which is perfectly fine as long as we acknowledge the potentially misleading nature of that word in this context.

## VALKYRIES

The battle has been ferocious. Both sides have suffered heavy losses, and all across the battlefield are strewn countless corpses of fathers, sons, brothers, husbands, and friends. The muddy plain is a haphazard patchwork of brown and red. But those with second sight can see another side to this agonizing scene: beautiful maidens with expressions of calm nobility swoop down from the skies, perhaps on wings, perhaps on horseback. They go amongst the dead, kneeling compassionately beside many of the fallen warriors, picking up their spirit-bodies, and bearing them off to the joys of feasting and fighting with Odin in his shining hall. The clouds close behind them.

Such, at least, is the modern popular image of the Valkyries. And it's essentially historically accurate, although rather limited and one-sided. The name "Valkyrie" (Old Norse *valkyrja*, plural *valkyrjur*) meant "chooser of the slain," which referred at least in part to their choosing which of the dead were to go to Valhalla. After the honored dead arrived in Valhalla, the Valkyries graciously and ceremoniously served them food and drink at their meals. Skaldic poetry sometimes portrays them as courtly and benign, such as these lines from the *The Song of King Hakon*:

> noble women, sitting on their steeds;
> they sat helmeted, in deep thought,
> holding their shields before them.[6]

Modern male fantasies of them as being exceptionally sexy also have some basis in historical reality – even though, of course, the modern men doing the fantasizing are probably unaware of it. The Valkyries were frequently the lovers or wives of human heroes. These relationships were explicitly sexual in nature, and the Valkyries also provided their human companions with assistance in battle, whether directly or through more subtle means, such as esoteric knowledge.

However, while the Valkyries certainly had a pronounced benevolent side, they had an equally prominent sinister side. The name "choosers of the slain" referred not only to choosing who among the already dead were going to get into Valhalla, but also to deciding who was going to die in the first place. The noble "shield-maidens" were also bloodthirsty, terrifying spirits of slaughter. As a counterpoint to the image of them in *The Song of King Hakon*, we can cite the following incantation to the Valkyrie Ruta from *The Song of Bjarki*:

> Arise, too, Ruta, and show your snow-pale head,
> come forth from hiding and issue into battle.
> The outdoor carnage beckons you; fighting now
> shakes the doors; harsh strife batters the gates.[7]

In another particularly haunting image, this time from *The Saga of the Volsungs*, to look at a Valkyrie is said to be like "staring into a flame."[8] But perhaps the most chilling depiction of the Valkyries in all of Old Norse literature comes from the poem *The Song of the Spear* (*Darraðarljóð*). Here, twelve Valkyries are seen prior to the Battle of

Clontarf, sitting at a loom and weaving the tragic fate of the warriors. They use intestines for their thread, severed heads for weights, and swords and arrows for beaters, all the while chanting their intentions with ominous delight.[9]

The highly evocative names of the Valkyries drew from this polarity in their character. Among them were Svanhvita, "Swan-White;" Valthogn, "Hostess of the Slain;" Sigrun, "Victory Rune;" Hild and Gunn, "Battle;" Hrist, "Spear-Shaker;" Geiravor, "Spear Goddess;" Geirahod, "Spear of Battle;" Herfjotur, "War-Fetter;" Herja, "Devastator;" and Svava, "Sleep-Maker/Killer."[10] None of these names were particularly "individual," but rather suggested traits common to the Valkyries as a whole.

Of all of the divine figures in Norse religion and mythology, the Valkyries provide one of the most striking and vivid fusions of Otto's concepts of the *mysterium fascinans* and the *mysterium tremendum*, which we examined in Chapter One.

## ELVES

The elves (Old Norse *álfar*, singular *álfr*) were semi-divine beings who were especially closely tied to the more "proper" deities. In fact, there was a seamless continuity between the two. We've already seen how the god Frey was called the lord of Alfheim, the homeland of the elves. The gods themselves were occasionally referred to as "elves,"[11] although this was a poetic way of signaling the closeness of the two kinds of beings rather than any kind of doctrinal claim (Norse religion had very few of the latter). While the gods and the elves certainly weren't truly synonymous with one another, the elves' proximity to the gods gave them an exalted status among the various types of beings who inhabited the Viking universe. This is likely why they were thought to be, in Snorri's words, "more beautiful than the sun."[12]

Despite playing little role in the recorded myths, they seem to have played a much greater role in religious practice, having frequent interactions with humans. These could be beneficial or injurious for humans, depending on the elves' disposition toward them. For example, in one early saga, a man who was gravely wounded in a duel killed an ox on the dueling field and left its meat, with blood running from it, on a hillock where the elves were known to live. Grateful for the feast of meat and blood, the elves granted him his wish to recover from his wounds.[13]

On rare occasions, humans and elves were said to interbreed and produce half-human, half-elfin children, who often had the appearance of humans but possessed extraordinary intuitive and magical powers.[14]

Just as the line between elves and gods was blurry, so was the line that separated the elves from dwarves, land spirits, and the human dead (and all of those groups relative to one another, too). For example, in a scene from *The Saga of Olaf the Holy*, one of King Olaf's ancestors is repeatedly referred to as an elf as the king and his interlocutor stand beside the forebear's burial mound.[15]

Snorri divides the elves into two groups: "light elves" (*ljósálfar*) and "dark elves" (*døkkálfar*). No other sources record such a distinction, and the "light" and "dark" aspects of the elves seem to have been seen as being seamlessly intertwined. This distinction therefore seems to have been an invention of Snorri's, and doesn't reflect Viking Age views.[16]

## DWARVES

The dwarves (Old Norse *dvergar*, singular *dvergr*) were the master miners, blacksmiths, and craftspeople of the Vikings' mythical world. Among the many matchless treasures they forged were Frey's ship Skidbladnir, which always had a fair wind and could be folded up and carried in a small bag; Freya's necklace Brisingamen, the most beautiful of all pieces of jewelry; Odin's spear Gungnir, which always hit its target; his arm ring Draupnir, from which another eight rings dropped every ninth night; Thor's hammer Mjollnir, the famous crusher of giants; and the resplendent golden hair of Thor's wife, Sif.

They lived underground, often in caves beneath mountains – the places where the metals and gems with which they worked could be found. They made a point to stay in their subterranean halls, or, if they had to come up into the world above, they did so at night. Being aboveground during the day had a dire consequence for them: the touch of sunlight turned them to stone.[17]

The dwarves were exceptionally well-versed in cosmological and magical lore. Iron Age blacksmiths were often thought to possess great magical powers – the ability to transform metal so dramatically was thought to depend on such abilities – and the Norse seem to have perceived the dwarves in this light.[18] They were also noted for their physical strength. Snorri reports that four dwarves – Nordri ("North"), Sudri ("South"), Austri ("East"), and Vestri ("West") held up the sky at its four corners, which, as the dwarves' names imply, were placed at the four cardinal points.[19]

While the elves played a large role in religious practice but little in (recorded) myth, the dwarves played a large role in myth but little in (recorded) religious practice. In fact, despite the myths' portrayal of them as well-disposed toward humans and gods, there's no evidence that they were ever worshipped. Their appearance is never described in the Old Norse sources; the modern idea that they were especially small in size comes from medieval folklore, and there's nothing to suggest that this idea existed during the Viking Age.[20]

## LAND SPIRITS

Although the sources likewise provide no description of the appearance of another group of demigod-like beings, the land spirits (Old Norse *landvættir*, singular *landvættr*), their disposition is described very vividly.

As their name implies, the land spirits were thought to dwell in particular features of the land. They were fiercely protective of these areas. In order to avoid the wrath of the sensitive, finicky, and easily frightened land spirits, these places had a number of taboos attached to them. For example, it was essential to act reverently and solemnly when passing through or by such places; something as seemingly insignificant as making a loud noise could bring grave misfortune upon the perpetrator.[21] The first law code in Iceland (930 CE) instructed those entering the country by ship to remove the carved dragon-heads from the fronts of their boats when they sighted land, lest they frighten the land spirits.[22]

But there was nothing the land spirits hated more than bloodshed. It was said that during the settlement of Iceland, a man was murdered by his thralls, and no one dared to go near the site for a long time after that out of fear of the outraged land spirits, despite its being a prime place to settle.[23]

The land spirits also passionately defended their dwelling-places against foreign invaders. The sagas tell that the king of Denmark once sent a sorcerer to spy on the Icelanders. The man took the form of a whale and made his way to Iceland, swimming along its southern edge and then up its western coast. As he went, he saw that he, too, was being spied upon; the hills and mountains were teeming with land spirits. Each time he tried to make his way inland through one of the countless fjords and bays that indent the island's coastline, the land spirits would come down to the water to bar his way, taking the form of snakes, toads, bulls, and great birds. But when he saw one blocking his course in the form of a cliff-giant, the whale-bodied sorcerer's nerves finally failed him, and he retreated to Denmark.[24]

The land spirits didn't just punish those who trespassed against them. They also rewarded those who gave them their due. These gifts could be an abundance of crops and herds, luck in hunting and fishing, or useful insights in dreams.[25] The land spirits knew much about the future, and sometimes shared this knowledge with those whom they favored. A land spirit was sometimes called an *ármaðr* ("bringer of prosperity") or a *spámaðr* ("seer"), designations which, in this case, often effectively meant the same thing.[26]

An excellent illustration of many of these abilities and gifts comes from the story of a farmer named Bjorn in the Icelandic *Book of Settlements*. Bjorn dreamt that a land spirit came to him and offered him his assistance. Before very long, a billy goat wandered into Bjorn's farm and joined his herd of goats. The goats had so many kids that year that Bjorn could hardly count them all before he sold them to other farmers on the island. He became a rich man in such a short time that the people started to call him "Goat-Bjorn." Those with second sight saw a great throng of land spirits trailing him wherever he went.[27]

The worship of the land spirits continued long after the conversion to Christianity. In fact, in some places, they're still venerated to this day.

# CHAPTER 4: COSMOLOGY

The Vikings thought that the world they lived in on a day-to-day basis was just a tiny sliver of a vast and richly varied universe, most of which was invisible to the average eye. We've already seen some degree of this richness in the previous two chapters' discussions of the beings who inhabited the invisible part of the cosmos. In this chapter, we'll add to that picture by exploring those beings' native realms, as well as the Norse conception of how events in those realms and in our own unfolded in time.

## THE VIKING OTHERWORLD

The part of Norse reality in which the divine beings lived, and in which the myths took place – the "otherworld," as we'll call it – was in some ways very remote from the world of everyday existence, but in other ways it was very close to it.

For one thing, the deities and other divine beings frequently intervened in everyday existence from their spiritual home – Odin deciding the outcome of a battle, the blows of Thor's hammer manifesting in the thunder, land spirits rewarding a favored person with increased herds, etc. Yet the power, decisiveness, and mysteriousness of these interventions indicated their origin in a different plane of reality.

This contact between the two aspects of existence could be achieved from the opposite direction, too – that is, humans could travel to the otherworld and participate in what was going on there (even if their influence in that hallowed land was negligible). Some of the means of accessing the otherworld mentioned in Old Norse literature include traveling over a rainbow, over the ocean, into darkness, into caves, into particular bodies of water, over mountains, into grave mounds, through waterfalls, and into deep forests and bogs.[1] These should surely be interpreted as journeys into extreme places and situations in order to continue the journey in a vision, or possibly – especially in the case of physically impossible feats, like climbing up a rainbow – as journeys undertaken while already in a heightened, visionary state, such as those that seers, sorcerers, and shamans trained themselves to reach. In any case, these methods for reaching the otherworld show that the otherworld wasn't thought of as being located in any particular physical direction relative to the world of everyday existence – up, down, to the north, to the south, etc. The direction one should travel in to reach it was simply "away."[2] The distance was great, but not unbridgeable.

Another instance of this paradox of closeness and remoteness was the way the otherworld was imagined to be once the traveler made it there. The unfamiliar can only be described by comparing it to the familiar, and, accordingly, the world of spirit could only be described obliquely and symbolically with reference to the things of this world. Quite naturally, the Vikings described it in terms of their own social world and natural landscape. They portrayed their otherworld as being a lot like this world, but rarefied and "writ large" – everything was greatly intensified. The rich among the divinities were extraordinarily rich, the virtuous were extraordinarily virtuous, the wise were extraordinarily wise, and the malevolent were extraordinarily malevolent. The grass was greener, the mountain peaks more barren, and the ale stronger and finer.[3] The otherworld was utterly similar to this world and yet utterly dissimilar to it – it, too, had mead, but its mead was unlike any you've ever had before.

Fittingly, the organization of the otherworld matched the way the Vikings themselves constructed and arranged their farmsteads. A proper Viking farmstead featured a tree or pillar at its central point. The pillar was often a "high-seat pillar," which stood at the center of a house and provided its foremost architectural support. High-seat pillars were thought to possess an inherent, mysterious power; some of the earliest settlers to Iceland brought their pillar with them on their boats, and when they got close to land, they threw it overboard, and then settled wherever it came ashore.[4] Centrally-located trees, on whose roots ale was often poured at festivals, were thought to possess the same significance and power.[5]

Around the pillar, or close by the tree, was the house – a place of shelter, comfort, safety, and familiarity. It was, of course, enclosed by walls and a roof. Around the house were fields for crops and livestock, which were themselves enclosed by fences – landscapes actively maintained by the residents of the farm for their benefit, but more exposed to the elements than the interior of the house. Beyond the fences was the wilderness, an uncultivated place of danger and the unknown, where the elements reigned supreme, but which also provided useful materials for the farm, such as timber and game.[6] Fences weren't just there for the "pragmatic" purpose of keeping livestock in; they were also there for the "magical" purpose of keeping injurious denizens of the wilderness, from wolves to giants, *out*.[7] Fences marked a boundary between two different states of being, which the Norse called "innangard" (Old Norse *innangarðr*, "inside the enclosure") and "utangard" (*útangarðr*, "outside the enclosure").

Intriguingly, the Vikings thought of their society as possessing the same structure as their farmsteads. Medieval Icelanders referred to their society as "our law" (*vár lög*), a phrase which shows that they thought of "law" and "society" as two ways of expressing the same thing. Law was a *psychological* enclosure that separated the social from the antisocial, the innangard from the utangard. This is why the punishment for especially heinous crimes was outlawry, whereby a person lost all of his or her legal rights and could be killed on sight without any legal repercussions against the killer. Through the crime, the outlaw had demonstrated that he or she was an utangard being rather than an innangard one, and since the criminal was beyond society's control, he or she was accordingly stripped of society's protection. The very words related to outlawry demonstrate this transition from being a civilized person to a wild one: outlawry was called "going into the forest" (skóggangr), and the outlaw was called a "person of the forest" (skógarmaðr). Fittingly, outlaws often chose to flee as far from human habitations as possible, and for obvious reasons.[8] The king or chieftain probably would have been seen as the equivalent of the central pillar or tree, the axis that held the order of the rest of society together. However, this is never stated explicitly, so it must remain a conjecture.

The Norse otherworld was organized in the same way. At its center was a mighty tree, most commonly called Yggdrasil (Yggdrasill), "the horse of the Terrible One" – that is, Odin – a reference to Odin commonly using its sprawling branches and roots to travel through the otherworld.[9] However, its name, like its species, varied from source to source, another reminder of the diversity and malleability of Norse religion. Several creatures were said to live on or in the tree. In its crown nested an unnamed eagle, while at its base coiled a dreadful serpent named Nidhogg (Níðhöggr, "Slanderer"), who gnawed away at the tree's roots in an apparent attempt to fell it. A squirrel named Ratatosk (Ratatoskr, "Drill-Tooth"[10]) scurried up and down the trunk, ferrying insults between the eagle and the snake. Deer nibbled the tree's shoots.[11]

Different pieces of Old Norse literature mention different wells or springs that lay among the roots of Yggdrasil. The most commonly mentioned are the Well of Fate (Urðarbrunnr), Mimir's Well (Mímisbrunnr), and Hvergelmir (whose meaning and etymology are unknown). Some scholars have (rather arbitrarily) tried to reduce them all to a single, original well,[12] while others have accepted each description at face value, regardless of the apparent confusion on this point in and amongst the texts themselves. There does seem to have been an authentic tradition of wells being located beneath Yggdrasil, but it's impossible to know how many there were and what functions, if any, they served. For that matter, as with countless other elements of

Norse religion, different people and groups of people probably had different views on the topic during the Viking Age itself.

The homeland of the gods, Asgard (Ásgarðr, "Enclosure of the Gods"), was located right around Yggdrasil's trunk, in the same way that the main house of a Viking farmstead wrapped itself around a central pillar or was located right next to a central tree. We can safely assume this due to the "gard" ("enclosure") element in Asgard's name, as well as the fact that the gods were considered to be the forces that held the cosmos together, like the central pillar of a Viking house. Their homeland, then, would have been the central enclosure of the otherworld – the quintessentially innangard part of the cosmos. A rainbow, Bifrost (Bifröst, "Fleetingly Glimpsed Rainbow"[13]), was the entryway into Asgard. Thus, Asgard was likely visualized as a magnificent fortress high in the heavens, perhaps in the upper central branches of Yggdrasil.

Jotunheim (Jötunheimr), the homeland of the giants, was by contrast the quintessentially utangard part of the otherworld. In fact, it was sometimes called "Utgard" (Útgarðr), which means the same thing as "utangard." Appropriately for the dwelling-place of the primordial spirits of chaos, Jotunheim was visualized as being like the parts of the northern European landscape that the Norse dreaded the most. Today, an especially desolate, icy, and remote part of Norway's central mountain range is called Jotunheimen (a modern Norwegian version of "Jotunheim"), which is probably the most appropriate of all possible names for such a place in Scandinavia. Since Jotunheim was the otherworld counterpart to the wilderness outside the perimeter of a Viking farm, it was probably the part of the cosmos most distant from Yggdrasil's stout trunk. At the far end of Jotunheim was an endless ocean, in which Jormungand, that enormous serpent whom Thor particularly hated, encircled the land.

The visible, tangible world in which we humans live our daily lives was called "Midgard" (Miðgarðr, "Middle Enclosure") – which, incidentally, is where J.R.R. Tolkien got the name for "Middle Earth."

As the "gard" element in its name implies, Midgard was thought of as a basically innangard place. However, as the "mid" element in its name implies, Midgard wasn't *as* innangard as Asgard. Instead, it occupied a middle position between Asgard and Jotunheim on the innangard-utangard spectrum, and was always the object of a grand tug-of-war between the gods and the giants. Somewhat contradictorily, Jormungand was thought to dwell in the oceans around Midgard as well as the oceans around Jotunheim in the otherworld – hence one of his titles, "Midgard Serpent" (Miðgarðsörmr).

In addition to Asgard and Jotunheim, there were a number of other places that the sources seem to indicate were similarly distinct realms within the otherworld. No definitive list of them is ever given – and it's highly unlikely that any definitive list ever existed, due, once again, to the unsystematic and non-dogmatic character of Norse religion. However, there might be some merit to the modern idea of "nine worlds" in Norse cosmology, even though the concept is usually overstated today. The number nine was held to possess some deep, intrinsic, and likely magical significance in Norse religion, even though no one really knows why. Philologist Rudolf Simek ably summarizes some of the number's occurrences throughout Norse religion and myth:

> ...[N]ine is the mythical number of the Germanic tribes. Documentation for the significance of the number nine is found in both myth and cult. In Odin's self-sacrifice he hung for nine nights on the windy tree (Hávamál), there are nine worlds to Niflhel (Vafþrúðnismál 43), Heimdallr was born to nine mothers (Hyndluljóð 35), Freyr had to wait for nine nights for his marriage to Gerd (Skírnismál 41), and eight nights (= nine days?) was the time of betrothal given also in the Þrymskviða. Literary embellishments in the Eddas similarly use the number nine: Skaði and Njörðr lived alternately for nine days in Nóatún and in Þrymheimr; every ninth night eight equally heavy rings drip from the ring Draupnir; Menglöð has nine maidens to serve her (Fjölsvinnsmál 35ff.), and Ægir had as

many daughters. Thor can take nine steps at the Ragnarök after his battle with the Midgard serpent before he falls down dead. Sacrificial feasts lasting nine days are mentioned for both Uppsala and Lejre and at these supposedly nine victims were sacrificed each day.[14]

Thus, it's far from unreasonable that the number nine might have featured prominently in Norse cosmology as well. And, indeed, Old Norse literature gives some hints that this might have been the case. One poem, *The Prophecy of the Seeress*, includes a passing reference to "nine worlds" (*níu heimar*) within the branches and roots of Yggdrasil,[15] while another, *The Song of Vafthrudnir* (*Vafþrúðnismál*), mentions nine sub-worlds within the underworld.[16] The Vikings didn't "believe in" "nine worlds" in the same way that some literalist Christians today believe that the earth was created in seven days. Rather, the Vikings believed in a number of distinct modalities of a general otherworld, and since nine was a significant number to them, some or all of those realms were sometimes said to comprise a group of nine.

Due to a number of parallels in the cosmologies of other northern Eurasian cultures,[17] as well as that line from *The Prophecy of the Seeress*, it's very likely that the realms were arranged in and around the branches and roots of Yggdrasil. Beyond that and the farmstead-like, innangard-utangard pattern we've already examined, however, it's impossible to say with any significant degree of certainty how the various realms were organized. No diagrams of them from the Viking Age or medieval periods have come down to us, and it's highly unlikely that the Vikings themselves made such diagrams – or, for that matter, felt the need to make them. (For obvious reasons, the pictures common on the internet of Kabbalah-like or chakra-like schemes are nothing more than New Age fantasies.) Furthermore, as we've seen, the various kinds of spiritual beings that populated the Norse universe – gods, giants, elves, dwarves, land spirits, dead ancestors, etc. – overlapped with each other to a considerable degree, and it's therefore probable that the boundaries between their homelands were blurry as well. In the excellent formulation of historian H.R. Ellis Davidson, "the impression the poems give is not of a planned and rational world, but rather a series of vivid images which build up a vague but powerful world-picture."[18]

The desire to create a "planned and rational world" out of the cosmological lore scattered throughout Old Norse literature is a thoroughly modern one. The Vikings didn't share our lust for rational order. But if we were to indulge that lust momentarily, we might end up with a list of "nine worlds" that looks something like this:

1. Asgard, the gods' celestial fortress;
2. Jotunheim, the chaotic, wild regions of the giants;
3. Alfheim, the homeland of the elves, which is never described in the sources;
4. Nidavellir (*Niðavellir*, "Low Fields"), the cavernous home of the dwarves;
5. Vanaheim (*Vanaheimr*), the homeland of the Vanir, which is never described in the sources;
6. Hel, the underworld where the dead dwelt, which we'll explore in detail in a later chapter;
7. Muspelheim (*Múspellsheimr*, something like "World of Destruction by Fire"[19]), the land of elemental fire;
8. Niflheim (*Niflheimr*, "World of Darkness"), the land of elemental ice;
9. Midgard, the material world and the only one of the nine that wasn't a part of the otherworld.

I emphasize that this list is a modern creation – my own, in fact – *based* on the sources, not one that the sources themselves report. But maybe, just maybe, somewhere, sometime, some Viking taught his son that these nine realms were the basic parts of the cosmos – and he no doubt would have added a great deal of colorful, illuminating information that has been utterly lost in the gaping expanse of the intervening centuries.

# TIME

That, in a nutshell, is how the Vikings thought of the spatial layout of their otherworld, and of their cosmos more broadly. But how did they think of time within that cosmos?

Many people in modern times have asserted that the Vikings had an essentially cyclical view of time, with periodic destructions of the cosmos that were followed by its rebirth. (I used to hold this position in the past, too, for that matter.) However, the only "evidence" for such a view in the sources is a misinterpretation of two particular Old Norse poems that we'll look at closely in a moment. The view that the Norse had a fundamentally linear conception of time, on the contrary, has a wealth of evidence to support it.

For one thing, as we've seen, the gods and other divine beings routinely intervened in linear time to shape the course of historical events. Odin directed the outcomes of battles; the land spirits rewarded those who respected them and punished those who wronged them; Thor crushed a giant every time thunder struck; the giants brought disease, famine, and all kinds of other ills if the people didn't sacrifice to them to keep them at bay; Freya, Frey, Njord, Thor, Sif, and others were responsible for the fertility of the land and for bountiful harvests; and so on. These weren't simply activities the divine beings dabbled in here and there. They were part and parcel of their very essence as the forces who actively upheld the well-being and order of the cosmos – or, in the case of the giants, the forces who actively sought to undermine that well-being and order. The inhabitants of the otherworld lived in linear time, and the cosmos they shaped unfolded in linear time.

Furthermore, this cosmos was seen as having a definite beginning and end. It was created at a particular moment in the past, and it will be destroyed at a particular moment in the future – Ragnarok. We'll explore the myths of creation and Ragnarok in Part Two, but for now it's simply enough to note that the procession of time in the myths was framed by these two decisive, one-off events.

Complicating this picture, however, there are three pieces of Old Norse literature that speak of a rebirth of the cosmos after Ragnarok. What are we to do with them?

Two of these sources are Eddic poems: *The Prophecy of the Seeress* and *The Song of Vafthrudnir*. The third is Snorri Sturluson's *Prose Edda*. Snorri's account of the downfall and rebirth of the cosmos includes no details that aren't also present in those two poems, both of which he quotes extensively throughout the *Prose Edda* and in this particular passage. The most reasonable conclusion is that Snorri used those two poems, and only those two poems, as his sources for his account of a regeneration after Ragnarok. So there are actually only two pieces of Old Norse literature that were (as far as we can tell) composed independently of one another that include a rebirth narrative.

Like many of the poems that comprise the *Poetic Edda*, *The Prophecy of the Seeress* and *The Song of Vafthrudnir* were composed during the latter part of the Viking Age or the early Middle Ages, during the period when the ancient Norse religion was transitioning to medieval Christianity.[20] I say "transitioning" because this was by no means a swift, decisive replacement. It was a process that took centuries. And while it was underway, there was plenty of time for especially thoughtful individuals to interpret and comment on that process and its significance.

*The Prophecy of the Seeress* does just that. Despite many people's insistence on seeing it as a conservative Viking's stirring tribute to the old ways, or even some kind of Norse catechism, it's actually the work of a Christian, or at least Christian-leaning, poet attempting to demonstrate that the traditional religion of his people had prophesied the arrival and triumph of a new, superior religion.

To make its case, it draws on traditional imagery and ideas, but casts them in a radically innovative light. Christian influence permeates the poem. Traditionally, the Norse saw the universe as being basically amoral and working toward no "higher purpose" of any sort. (We've already seen some degree of this in the characters of the gods and goddesses, and the rest of the picture will be filled in by later chapters.) But for the author of *The Prophecy of the Seeress*, this was not so. Instead, the cosmos, and the progression of events within it, was full of moral purpose, just as in medieval Christianity.

The poem imagines that immediately after the gods created the cosmos, there were no giants in it, and a Golden Age of prosperity, peace, happiness, justice, and play prevailed. Then a fall, parallel to that of Adam and Eve, occurred as "three giant maidens" entered the cosmos from the chaos of Jotunheim and brought an end to the earlier bliss and righteousness.[21] Several stanzas later, we find the one and only portrayal of moral punishment in the afterlife in all of Old Norse literature: murderers, adulterers, and other wicked people are torturously dismembered by the monsters Nidhogg and Fenrir in a place called the "Shore of Corpses."[22] The moral worth of the universe (including gods and humans) decays steadily throughout the poem. In a move highly reminiscent of the apocalyptic vision of the book of *Revelation* in the New Testament, Ragnarok is depicted as a necessary purification to rid the world of evil. The world that comes after Ragnarok is a new Golden Age, cleansed of any giants that might otherwise taint it. Stanza 65 is particularly telling:

Then from above
Comes the mighty ruler
To divinely judge
And to rule over all.[23]

Who could this be but Christ?[24] *The Prophecy of the Seeress* is ultimately heralding the coming dominion of the all-powerful, all-virtuous new god from the south, whose victory it sees as inevitable and praiseworthy.

The poet of *The Song of Vafthrudnir* was more neutral, and also less ingenious. His work doesn't seem to have any particular axe to grind.

It's simply a compilation of a large amount of disconnected scraps of mythical lore, which are recounted through a clever framing story about a contest between Odin and a giant named Vafthrudnir. Yet there's every reason to believe that the lore he collected in his poem was already heavily influenced by Christianity – indeed, it would have been difficult for it not to have been. His account of a rebirth of the cosmos after Ragnarok came from the same socio-historical context in which *The Prophecy of the Seeress* was written.

In the tenth and eleventh centuries, when the Norse religion was being replaced by Christianity all across the Norse lands, many Vikings came to believe that they were living through Ragnarok. After all, according to the tales, weren't the gods going to perish in that final battle? Now that the gods were indeed falling, didn't that mean that the prophesied collapse of the gods and their world had come at last? But in that period, a new god and a new world were rising from the ashes of the old gods and the old world. So it seemed to them that while the prophecies of Ragnarok had been correct, they had neglected to mention that Ragnarok wasn't the end of *everything*. Instead, it was followed by another, different world. Could this have been the origin of the idea that a rebirth followed Ragnarok?

All of the evidence suggests that this was indeed the case. Again, there are no other pieces of Old Norse literature that mention a rebirth after Ragnarok. But there are several pieces of Old Norse literature – and, in fact, lots and lots of pieces of literature from all across northern Europe, from poems to folktales to oath formulas – that mention a future cataclysmic end of the cosmos with no subsequent revival.[26] Some of them, such as the skaldic poems *The Song of King Eirik* and *The Song of King Hakon*, are considerably older than *The Prophecy of the Seeress* and *The Song of Vafthrudnir*.[27] Furthermore, the tone of these passages is ominous and tragic. Any hint of the exuberance and hope of the rebirth stanzas of *The Prophecy of the Seeress* and *The Song of Vafthrudnir* is utterly, crushingly lacking. Surely if these passages had simply neglected to mention a widespread belief in a rejuvenation of the cosmos after Ragnarok, there wouldn't be so many of them, and they might have at least alluded to it in their tone or by other subtle means. But nothing of the sort is anywhere to be found.

The striking conclusion is that, at least originally, the Norse saw Ragnarok as a one-off event in the future that would obliterate every trace of the cosmos to which they belonged and which their cherished gods upheld.

The Norse view of time and its end might strike us as exceptionally gloomy, even despairing. And on one level it was indeed gloomy and despairing. But as we'll see in the next chapter, the Vikings found existential comfort not in what was going to happen to them in the future, but in how they met whatever it was that happened to them.

# CHAPTER 5:

# FATE

"What have I dreamed?" wondered Odin as he awoke. "It seemed to me that I was going around and waking the noble warriors who dwell with me here in Valhalla. I told them to cover the benches of the feasting hall with fine furs, and to wash the drinking horns. I told the Valkyries to fetch the mead and prepare to serve it. It seemed we were getting ready for a sumptuous feast, as if to welcome a great hero into our midst."

The walls of Valhalla began to tremble, first just enough to be perceptible, then with mounting intensity. A low, insistent rumbling could be heard approaching from afar.

Odin left his chambers and found Bragi, his court poet, sitting in the main hall. He asked the learned minstrel, "What's causing all this commotion? It sounds like some fierce army approaching."

Bragi replied, "Aye, the timbers of the benches are creaking as if Balder himself were coming back from the depths."

Although Bragi had said these words lightly and innocently, Odin couldn't help but be stung by the reminder of his beloved son's death. Regardless of how much he yearned to see Balder again, he knew that it was impossible. "Stop being foolish, Bragi," admonished Odin, with an unintended curtness that surprised even him. Regaining his composure, Odin went on: "No, you who are so wise and learned must surely know that this is someone else. And I have an idea of who it is."

"Who, then?" asked Bragi with eager curiosity.

"It can surely be no other than King Eirik Blood-axe," replied Odin, who had himself arranged the death of the fearsome king.

By now, the warriors who lived in the hall had all woken and assembled around their ruler and his poet, anxious to know what was going on. Odin turned to Sigmund and Sinfjotli, two of his best men. Pointing to the door, he told them, "Go and welcome King Eirik, if it is indeed him."

Before obeying his commander's orders, Sigmund summoned up the courage to ask him a question he had been struggling with for some time: why did the god strike down the best and noblest warriors and bring them to his hall? Rather than posing his question directly, which might have seemed impertinent, he couched it in more concrete language. "My lord, if I may, why is it that you desired to bring Eirik to your hall rather than any of the many other kings in the world?"

"Because," Odin answered casually and quickly, "he has reddened his sword in too many countries to count."

Sigmund's curiosity overcame his prudence, and he blurted out in response, "But why did you snatch out of his hands the victory that was due to him, when by your own admission he was so valiant?"

Sigmund realized only after he had spoken that he had just questioned his master's judgment. He braced himself for whatever would happen next. But instead of being wrathful, or even cross, Odin's expression became one of dejection. He sighed deeply and stared down at the floor for a long moment. Despite the tumult going on outside, the total silence of the astonished warriors within the hall was palpable. Finally, his eyes still on the floor, he answered gravely: "Because no one knows when Ragnarok will arrive, and the wolf will finally make his way here to kill me."

So goes *The Song of King Eirik*.[1] How could Odin have known that a dreadful beast (Fenrir) would one day slay him, which spurred him to amass an army of the most elite human warriors in the futile hope of averting his death? It was partly due to how far-seeing Odin was. But in order for him to have had knowledge of what was going to happen in the future, that future had to have been foreordained.

# THE NORSE CONCEPTION OF FATE

The idea of fate permeated the religion of the Vikings at every turn. Everything in the universe, even the gods, was subject to it.

There were at least six terms for "fate" in Old Norse: *ørlög, sköp, mjötuðr, auðna, forlög,* and *urðr*. Of these, *auðna, mjötuðr,* and *urðr* meant "fate" in a very direct sense with few subtleties. *Forlög* and *ørlög* both meant "first law," the original and most powerful set of guidelines that governed behavior. And *sköp,* from the same root as the modern English word "shape," referred to a coherent structure that produced a reliable outcome.[2] Fate occupied roughly the same position in the Norse worldview that the laws of science do in the modern world; it provided an unseen guiding principle that determined how events in the world would unfold, and could explain them after they occurred. Questioning the reality and omnipotence of fate would have been laughable and almost unthinkable. The Eddic poem *The Song of Fafnir* warns its readers that it's as ridiculous and foolhardy to struggle against fate as it is to row a boat against a strong wind.[3]

Fate had nothing whatsoever to do with notions like morality or justice – the Vikings' standards of morality and justice or anybody else's. Karma, for example, is a concept that was completely alien to the Viking Age view. This was a quintessentially "blind fate," utterly apathetic to the well-being of those caught up within it.

To be sure, what we today would call "cause and effect" was taken into account – judicial proceedings, to cite but one example, operated on the basis of assuming personal responsibility for one's own actions. But notions of cause and effect and of personal responsibility were seen as necessary superficialities, and were contextualized by the deeper explanatory framework of fate. For example, those same judicial proceedings were often seen as the instruments of fate, and the laws they upheld were seen as having been built on the "first law." After all, in such a perspective, how could they not be?

## THE NORNS

Several Old Norse sources mention a group of female entities who personally shaped the fate of all beings: the Norns (Old Norse *nornir*, singular *norn*). They lived at the base of Yggdrasil, the mighty tree at the center of the cosmos, in a great hall by the Well of Fate (*Urðarbrunnr*). They took mud and water from the well and poured them over the tree's roots, preventing them from drying out or rotting.[4] Runes, the magical alphabet of the Norse, were inscribed on their fingernails.[5]

Different images were used for the Norns' fate-crafting activity. Sometimes they were said to weave a person's life like an intricate web, ending it by cutting the last thread.[6] At other times, they were said to cut a person's fate into a piece of wood. This has usually been interpreted to have meant that they wrote out the course of a lifetime in runes, and it very well could have meant that. However, in Norway, time was traditionally reckoned by cutting notches into a wooden plank above a window, and it's equally plausible that this practice is what such passages were referencing.[7]

The sources don't share any consensus on how many Norns there were. Some say there was a large but unknown number of them,[8] while others hold that there were exactly three.[9] In the latter case, their names are usually given as Urd (*Urðr*, "Fate"), Verdandi (*Verðandi*, "Becoming"), and Skuld ("Debt") – fitting names for such beings.[10]

There's no evidence that the Norns were ever worshipped. Perhaps we shouldn't be surprised by this. After all, what could the Vikings have hoped to gain by worshipping entities who were utterly implacable?

## RESPONSES TO FATE

The concept of fate provided the Norse with a means of addressing timeless existential anxieties. Naturally, different people took different approaches to this task, and the same person might have taken different approaches at different times.

All people have always wanted to be able to predict the future – consider how seriously we take meteorologists in our own society, for example. But whereas we see the future as an open field of possibilities, and we typically issue and receive weather forecasts with a grain of salt, the Norse had to come to terms with a future whose core structure was rigidly fixed. Fundamentally, things could only happen one foreordained way. Thus, they often sought out the help of seers and seeresses, those with privileged access to the future shape of things, either out of a desire to take that shape into account when making plans, or out of simple fear. Kings and other military leaders would consult with seers and seeresses on the eve of battle, and communities might invite a seer or seeress before the spring planting began, to cite but two examples. Humans weren't the only ones who called upon professional soothsayers – the deities did, too.

At other times, fate was helplessly cursed. "Evil is the decree of the Norns," moans one saga.[11]

But the attitude toward fate that Viking society held up as the ideal one was a heroic stoicism. In the words of archaeologist Neil Price, "The outcome of our actions, our fate, is already decided and therefore does not matter. What is important is the manner of our conduct as we go to meet it."[12] You couldn't change what was going to happen to you, but you could at least face it with honor and dignity. The best death was to go down fighting, preferably with a smile on your lips. Life is precarious by its very nature, but this was especially true in the Viking Age, which made this fatalism, and stoicism in the face of it, especially poignant.

The model of this ideal was Odin's amassing an army in Valhalla in preparation for Ragnarok. He knew that Fenrir, "the wolf," was going to murder him one way or another. Perhaps on some level he hoped that by gathering all of the best warriors to fight alongside him, he could somehow prevent the inevitable. But deep down he knew that his struggle was hopeless – yet he determined to struggle just the same, and to die in the most radiant blaze of glory he could muster.

Another example of this same attitude, this time on a less cosmic and more humble scale, comes from the life of the warrior-poet Egil Skallagrimsson. According to his saga, toward the end of his life, one of his sons died, after others had died before him. Such was the depth of Egil's grief that he planned to kill himself, but his surviving daughter convinced him to instead use his poetic talent to compose a memorial poem for his lost children. Egil's poem is called *The Wreck of Sons* (*Sonatorrek*). In it, Egil bemoans his lot in life and curses Odin, his patron god, for having made him suffer so much. But Egil finds that this suffering has also carried a gift within it, for his anguish inspires him to compose better poetry than ever before. He lets loose an eloquent cry of both despair and joy, or at least contented acceptance. The final three stanzas read:

> I offer nothing
> With an eager heart
> To the greatest of gods,
> The willful Odin.
> But I must concede
> That the friend of the wise
> Has paid me well
> For all my wounds.
>
> The battle-tested
> Foe of the wolf
> Has given me
> A towering art,
> And wits to discern
> In those around me
> Who wishes well,
> Who wishes ill.

Times are dire,
Yet glad is my heart,
Full of courage,
Without complaint.
I wait for the goddess
Of dirt and of death
Who stands on the headland
To bear me away.[13]

# CHAPTER 6:

# MORALITY

You don't need me to tell you that the relationship between religion and morality is a question that people argue over constantly and heatedly. Today, some people believe that morality is inherently God-given, and that without a belief in (a particular kind of) God, all morality would vanish. Others seek a basis for a moral system in Darwinian evolution, or in the desires and fears that are common to all of humanity. Regardless of what justification someone might use to defend a system of morality, virtually everyone equates the word "morality" with a code of conduct based on altruism and universal compassion (even if the details may differ between various systems).

The Vikings would have thought of all of that as a stinking pile of dragon excrement.

The only connection between religion and morality in the Norse world was that they were both part of the same cultural system. Morality didn't derive from religion, and religion didn't derive from morality.

Gods and goddesses didn't decree moral codes. There was no Viking "Ten Commandments" or anything like that. Naturally, deities looked favorably upon ritual piety and unfavorably upon ritual impiety and negligence. But that kind of religious piety was and is categorically different from morality, because performing rituals properly and reverently has nothing to do with how one conducts oneself in daily life.

Nor did the gods and goddesses exemplify moral behavior. There's a common misconception that myths, the stories of the lives and deeds of the deities, were supposed to teach proper morals. *Maybe* that was true for some other peoples, but it definitely wasn't true for the Norse. The myths assumed that their readers held particular moral conceptions in mind, which were sometimes implicitly referenced in some of the details of the stories, but the stories didn't go out of their way to *teach* morals. Their intent(s) lay elsewhere, and they often featured the deities doing things that would have been unspeakably shameful to the Vikings, such as breaking oaths and committing incest, without any subsequent "lesson" for their human listeners. The behavior of the gods and goddesses was more of a reflection of the often sordid realities of the Viking Age than it was a reflection of the Vikings' moral ideals.

Morality, therefore, belonged to the human social sphere rather than the religious sphere.

Furthermore, whether or not the Vikings even *had* a standard of morality is debatable, and depends on how you choose to define the word "morality." If morality is defined broadly and loosely as simply a standard of conduct that one is expected to follow in one's day-to-day life – the definition we'll be using here in this chapter – then the Vikings did have their own morality. Such a definition is wide enough to include what the German philosopher Friedrich Nietzsche famously called the "morality of mores" – that is, a system of morality that consists of nothing more than social norms.[1] That was the only kind of morality the Vikings had.

As you can probably guess from the preceding chapter, the Vikings weren't big on the idea of "free will," which we today tend to see as the basis for moral action. The idea of a fixed fate greatly constrained the range of moral choices, such that will was only ever "free" in a partial and provisional sense, and those choices that were left were essentially just matters of meeting that fate in a particular way.

Norse morality differed so much from our modern notions of the concept that it was almost unrecognizable. The final, and probably most important, factor that made it this way was its content. The actions the Vikings labeled "good" or "bad" were a far cry from what would be considered "good" or "bad" according to most modern systems of morality. In some cases, the two kinds of systems are even diametrically opposed. Some things that most people today would deem to be exemplary moral behavior would have been, for the Vikings, either neutral or actively *immoral*, and vice versa. We'll spend the rest of this chapter exploring this particular point.

## HONOR AND SELF-INTEREST

The Vikings saw themselves as living in a basically hostile universe. They were helpless against the cruelly capricious dictates of fate. The climate was icy, and the landscape was perilous and unyielding. Enemies were always close at hand, whether from outside of one's trusted social group or from within it. Nothing in life was a given; one had to toil and fight for whatever one had. It should come as no surprise, therefore, that the Norse placed a high value on the capable, accomplished warrior and the traits that such a person embodied.

Things like peacefulness, kindness, and compassion were not held up as inherently positive ideals. People were frequently peaceful, kind, or compassionate, but just as often, and perhaps more often, they were violent, gruff, or vengeful. And those latter behaviors were often valued just as highly as, or even more highly than, those more pleasant ones. For example, in a remarkable and chilling reversal of the common practice of comparing one's enemies to "beasts" and "animals" as a way of justifying one's slaughtering them, the Vikings routinely cast *themselves* as "beasts" – and in particular predators like bears or wolves – and their enemies as their prey. By invoking such imagery, the Vikings justified their own brutality not on the basis of their innocence of having committed some transgression, but rather on the basis of their simply being the superior power and fulfilling the natural order of things.[2]

But just as there was no "Golden Rule" ("do unto others as you would have them do unto you"), and no altruistic rationale that determined what was valued, savagery for the sake of savagery wasn't valued, either. Instead, the basis of Norse morality was self-interest as defined by and expressed through a certain code of honor. The concept of honor enabled the Vikings to channel their inherent selfishness into pursuits that also served the interests of the communities to which they belonged.

For the Norse, as in most other historical cultures that have placed a high value on personal honor, the chief good was one's own "name" or reputation. Particular kinds of actions increased one's stature in the eyes of others, and other kinds of actions diminished it. The most honorable behaviors and character traits, as evidenced especially in the sagas, were manliness, generosity, hospitality, valor, courage, eloquence, and loyalty.[3] Most of these were actions that benefitted others in one's community (but, crucially, not those outside of it). Some of these actions could even be seen as altruistic in a different context. The poet Egil Skallagrimsson, for example, once said, "I am quick to sing a [generous] man's praise, but stumble for words about misers."[4]

But in this context, even generosity and hospitality weren't truly altruistic actions. They may have helped others along the way, but that wasn't their ultimate intent. In the words of anthropologist Richard Bauman, "Not only did honor have to be enacted and observed, it had to be publicly acknowledged, by being talked about and evaluated. ... The quest for honor was thus centrally a quest for reputation, resting on the need to be well talked about."[5] A chieftain gave his warriors prized gifts and threw lavish feasts for them because he wanted them – and poets like Egil – to praise him for his generosity. A family who let a traveler spend the night in their house did so because they wanted others to see them as being hospitable. And so forth. Of course, it could be argued that even altruistic morality is actually motivated by this same selfish impulse, but either way, the Vikings harbored no illusions about their ultimate self-interest.

## SEXUAL AND GENDER-BASED MORALITY

Now we come to an aspect of Norse honor and morality that many people find to be upsetting, or at least ugly. But it was a central element of Viking Age values, and was referenced throughout Norse mythology and religion, so it's something that anyone interested in this topic has to grapple with sooner or later. Consider the following episode from *Gisli's Saga*:

A farmer named Thorbjorn had a gorgeous, strong-willed daughter named Thordis. When she reached the age of marriage, a suitor by the name of Skeggi the Dueller – a rough brawler, as his nickname implied – came to Thorbjorn's farmstead and asked for Thordis's hand in marriage. Thorbjorn refused, and offered a half-hearted excuse. But everyone knew the real reason why Thorbjorn had turned down Skeggi's request: Thordis was already seeing another man by the name of Kolbjorn, a well-to-do local farmer.

So the Dueller, angry and humiliated after being rebuffed, stormed off to Kolbjorn's house and challenged him to a duel for the hand of Thordis. Kolbjorn was terrified, but agreed, noting that no one would think him worthy of Thordis if he declined.

On the night before the duel was to take place, however, Gisli, Thordis's brother, went to Kolbjorn and asked him if he was prepared. He found Kolbjorn panic-stricken and questioning whether he would actually go through with the duel. During their conversation, Kolbjorn asked the stronger, bolder Gisli to fight in his place. Gisli harshly ridiculed Kolbjorn, calling him the most despicable lowlife in the world, and saying – correctly – that Kolbjorn would bear a heavy shame for the rest of his life. But, in the end, he agreed to take Kolbjorn's place.

The next day, Skeggi and his men arrived at the appointed location and waited for Kolbjorn. A long time passed, and neither Kolbjorn nor Gisli showed up. So Skeggi said to his carpenter, Ref, "Carve two life-sized, wooden statues of Kolbjorn and Gisli. Set them

82

up with one standing behind the other, penetrating him. And may this monument of scorn (*nið*) remain here forever to mock them!"

At that very moment, Gisli appeared from the woods. "Give your farmhands something better to do," he sneered at Skeggi. Waving his axe in the air, he growled, "Here is a real man, one who will fight you!"

The duel raged. Both men fought fiercely and skillfully. But eventually, in one tremendous sweep of his axe, Gisli sliced through Skeggi's shield and into his leg, severing it at the knee. Despite his unbelievable pain, Skeggi had the presence of mind to know that he had seconds to save his life. So he immediately offered to pay Gisli a great sum of money to end the duel then and there and not kill him. Gisli accepted. From that day forward, Gisli's victory increased his reputation considerably, while Skeggi had to walk with a wooden leg - presumably this was the use to which he ended up putting Ref, his carpenter.[6]

The single most important word in Norse notions of honor and morality was *drengskapr*,[7] which meant "manliness," "high-mindedness," and "courage."[8] For the Vikings, therefore, "manliness" meant much more than simply having one kind of genitalia rather than another. It connoted all sorts of virtues - the ones discussed above in the examination of the code of honor - that were thought to make the difference between being a merely biological man (a *maðr*) and a "real man" (a *drengr*).

The opposite of *drengskapr* was *ergi*. *Ergi* meant first and foremost "unmanliness," but, like *drengskapr*, it contained a host of other connotations. The primary insinuation was that such a man had adopted the receptive role in homosexual intercourse. In the words of philologist Eldar Heide, "for a man to be penetrated by another man was the ultimate unmanliness, because that symbolically turned him into a woman. Injury in the buttocks had the same effect."[9] Someone who would do something so extremely unbecoming of a *drengr* was thought to necessarily also lack the other qualities of a *drengr*. In particular, he was a coward[10] - hence Skeggi's estimation of Gisli and

Kolbjorn as homosexuals for having failed to show up for a duel. Someone who was willing to adopt a passive role sexually must have also been willing to adopt a passive role in life more generally, or so the thinking went.[11] The practice of sorcery, or at least certain kinds of sorcery, was also thought to be quintessentially *argr* (the adjectival form of *ergi*) for reasons that will become clearer in Chapter Ten.

*Ergi* was the subject of formalized insults (*níð*), which are mentioned in Norse law codes. They included comparing a man to a female animal ("mare," "bitch," etc.), saying he had given birth, saying he had played the part of a woman every ninth night, and saying he had performed sorcery. A *níð* was typically given verbally or in wood, whether through writing in runes or through sculpture, as with Skeggi. *Níð* was a crime as heinous as rape and murder, and was punishable by full outlawry – in many cases, effectively a death sentence.[12] It's surely no coincidence that Gisli appeared from the woods to kill Skeggi immediately after the latter had accused him of *ergi*. Gisli was defending his *drengskapr*, his honor, with the same fervor and violence that would have been stirred up had Skeggi killed or raped one of Gisli's family members. *Ergi* was so shameful that legal officials would sometimes try to persuade the involved parties to settle matters on their own so that the case wouldn't have to be brought before the legal assembly for everyone to hear.[13]

Among the deities, Odin could be seen as *argr* due to his being a practitioner of sorcery. He was taunted for being such, and was once exiled – outlawed – for this and other shameful behaviors. Loki, however, was virtually the model of *ergi*. This can be seen most clearly in his having mothered a foal in the story of how Asgard's wall was built. Not only did he adopt a receptive homosexual role to do so, but he actually turned himself into a mare (a formal *níð*) and gave birth (another formal *níð*) along the way.

What about Viking women?

Unfortunately, the sources provide far less information on Viking conceptions of honor and morality as they pertained to women. But they do drop at least a few clues. For one thing, women were occasionally said to be *argr*, and judging by the context of such passages, this seems to have been an accusation of nymphomania.[14] Additionally, while acts that determined a person's or a family's honor were almost always carried out by men, women also played a more or less socially defined but behind-the-scenes role in such matters by goading men into action, whether for conflict or for peace, when the men failed to take what in their eyes were the appropriate actions. The sagas are replete with examples of such goading.[15]

Needless to say, the Vikings didn't exactly share our modern ideals of gender equality and sexual freedom. Gender roles and expectations were quite sharply defined, and "manliness" was a much higher ideal than "womanliness." While women did enjoy certain rights that would later become unavailable to them with the acceptance of Christianity, and while the Eddas and sagas contain numerous examples of strong and independent women, Viking society as a whole granted men considerably more power and prestige than women.

# Chapter 7:

# The Self and Its

# Parts

Today, most of us think of the self as having two or three parts: a body, a mind, and perhaps – depending on your own religious convictions – a soul. The Vikings, too, thought of the self as having different components, but they believed in more and different components than we do.

The Viking self was an integral being; all of the parts added up to a more or less cohesive whole, as they do in our view of the self as well. But the parts could also function independently of one another, and could dissociate themselves from the others and go their separate ways under certain circumstances.[1]

We've already seen on numerous occasions how Norse religion was never made into a neat and tidy system while it was a living tradition, and how informal and fluid it was. The Norse view of the self was another prime example of this resistance or apathy toward foisting a smooth order upon the roughness and boisterousness of lived experience. The sources never offer a list or a "map" of the different parts that comprised the self. Different sources mention different and contradictory parts, and characterize them in different and contradictory ways. This tendency is too pervasive to be due to mere misunderstandings of what was originally a totally orderly and coherent system. No worldview is, has ever been, or will ever be totally orderly and coherent. Those that are more coherent than others are generally those whose creators have gone out of their way to impose a rational organization upon them. But in the case of ancient, tribal religions that no one ever attempted to make into a doctrinally tidy system while they were still believed in and practiced, expecting the same level of tidiness one finds in the worldviews of individual philosophers, for example, is just plain ridiculous.

That being said, the sources do indicate that some parts of the self were more widely believed in, and the concepts more fully developed, than others. In this chapter, we'll explore four particularly widely remarked-upon parts of the Viking self and their *dominant* characterizations.

One of these four parts was physical, and the other three were spiritual. However, intriguingly, in the Norse religion, for something to be spiritual didn't necessarily mean that it was truly immaterial or incorporeal. Instead, spirit was an especially fine kind of material substance, much like air – and, as in many ancient cultures, spirit was synonymous with breath. Like Latin (*animus/anima* and *spiritus*) and Hebrew (*ruach*), Old Norse had one word for both breath and spirit: *önd*. Spiritual parts of a person could leave through her or his respiratory passages after death, and, while the person was still alive, spirits could enter him or her through the same respiratory passages. For example, when a spiritual part of a person detached itself from him or her and traveled to another person, the recipient of the spirit would often yawn or develop an itchy nose.[2]

## THE *HAMR*

The first of these four parts of the self, and the only one made of solid matter, was the *hamr*. *Hamr* literally meant "skin" or "hide,"[3] but was essentially the same as what we today would call the "body."[4] It was the visible part of the self that housed the invisible parts.

However, whereas we tend to view the body as fixed and mostly unalterable, the Norse saw the *hamr* as something that could be changed radically by some people. *Hamr* was the central word in the vocabulary of shapeshifting, because the *hamr* was the "shape" that was "shifted" in that magical process. A shapeshifter was called a *hamhleypa* ("*hamr*-leaper"),[5] and the verbal phrase for "to shift one's shape" was *skipta hömum* (*hömum* was the dative form of *hamr*).[6]

## THE *HUGR*

One of the three invisible, spiritual parts of the self was the *hugr*. The *hugr* was someone's personality or mind, the intangible part that corresponds most closely to what we mean when we speak of someone's "inner self."[7] It encompassed thought, desire, intuition (the Old Norse word for "foreboding" was *hugboð*[8]), and a person's "presence" – the feeling others get when they're around the person.[9]

People described as having an especially strong *hugr* could make things happen somewhere far away without being physically present.[10] At times, the *hugr* could even leave its original "owner" and enter into someone else. One could make a person sick by thinking about them in an envious way; the *hugr* of the thinker traveled to and entered into the one who was thought about and instigated physical reactions. This could be done in a more or less involuntary and unconscious way, or as part of a deliberate attack. If it was an attack, it could have simply harmed the person directly, or it could have proceeded by more subtle and indirect means, making the victim sleepy, depressed, or generally weakened, so that the attacker could overpower the victim, whether physically or by getting the victim to do something that he or she wouldn't otherwise do.[11]

## THE *FYLGJA*

The second of the spiritual parts of the self was the *fylgja* (plural *fylgjur*). The verb *fylgja* meant "to accompany," "to help," "to side with," "to belong to," "to follow," "to lead," "to guide," or "to pursue" depending on the context.[12] The *fylgja* spirit did all of those many things, and the best translation of the noun *fylgja* is probably "attendant spirit," in both senses of the word "attendant" – one who accompanies and one who helps.

*Fylgjur* were always visible to those with second sight (the ability to see invisible, spiritual phenomena on a regular basis), and they were visible to those without second sight during dreams and at the moment of the death of the "owner."[13] Just before someone died, he or she sometimes caught a glimpse of her or his dead *fylgja*. In this and other ways, the well-being of the *fylgja* and that of the "owner" were intimately bound up with one another.[14] This shouldn't surprise us, since, after all, the *fylgja* was *part* of the owner on some level, even though it could separate itself from the rest of the self at times, just as could all of the other parts of the self.

The *fylgja* often worked to protect the person of which it was a part. In one of the sagas, for example, a sorceress planned to kill a man at an upcoming party. The man's *fylgja* warned him about the danger in dreams for three nights in a row, and then finally gave him an illness that prevented him from being able to go to the party, thereby saving his life.[15]

The only constant in the visual form these attendant spirits assumed was that they were always female.[16] Sometimes they appeared in the form of a human woman, but more commonly they appeared in the form of an animal. The particular animal form taken by the *fylgja* often signaled something about the person's character. Someone with a bear for a *fylgja* was likely high-born,[17] while someone with a wolf *fylgja* was bound to be especially aggressive, and someone with a fox *fylgja* was cunning and shrewd.[18] Sometimes, however, the form in which the *fylgja* appeared could be situational. For example, an attacking army might be accompanied by a host of wolf *fylgjur*.[19]

To avoid a possible confusion, the *fylgja* having an animal form was different from a person shifting his or her shape (*hamr*) into that of an animal. The *fylgja* accompanied its "owner" in a spiritual capacity while he or she was in his or her usual form, while shapeshifting involved transforming one's physical, sensory presence.

## THE *HAMINGJA*

The final part of the Viking self we'll examine here is the *hamingja*, "luck" or "fortune" (plural *hamingjur*). In the words of Old Norse scholar Bettina Sommer, "luck was a quality inherent in the man and his lineage, a part of his personality similar to his strength, intelligence, or skill with weapons, at once both the cause and the expression of the success, wealth, and power of a family."[20] The surest test of the strength of a person's *hamingja* was his or her fortune in battle.[21]

Like the *fylgja*, the *hamingja* was always female, even for men. The appearance of the *hamingja* is seldom described in the sources, but *Viga-Glum's Saga* provides a striking image of one: an enormous woman whose shoulders were so wide that they touched two separate mountains.[22]

The *hamingja* was typically passed down through family lines. Naming a newborn child after a relative would ensure, or at least increase the likelihood, that the relative's *hamingja* would be passed down to the child. Sometimes it seems like the dying or dead person could decide to whom his or her *hamingja* went, and at other times it seems like the *hamingja* decided herself.[23] A living person could also lend his or her *hamingja* to others to accompany them on particular endeavors in which extra luck would be of great use, such as a battle or a long and perilous journey.[24]

The lines between the *hamingjur*, *fylgjur*, and Valkyries were especially blurry. All were female helping spirits, and all at least sometimes moved from one person to one of that person's children or grandchildren when the original "owner" or partner died.[25]

There was, of course, a substantial conceptual tension between luck and fate, just as there was between fate and moral choice. But, true to form, the Norse didn't seem to have been particularly bothered by such philosophical niceties. In the harsh world of the Viking Age, with its constant strife and unforgiving Nordic weather and landscapes, any means of explaining one's fortune and/or gaining more control over it was highly prized.

# CHAPTER 8:

# DEATH AND THE

# AFTERLIFE

The intrepid Vikings have spent a successful year in the south and east, trading with the locals in the many different lands through which they've passed. Now, at the Volga River, thousands of miles from their home by sea, one of their leaders has died. They place him in a temporary grave with a wooden covering while they hold his elaborate, ten-day funeral. His great fortune they divide into thirds: one third for his family, one third for exquisite garments for his body, and one third for the liquor that the mourners will drink night and day for the next week and a half. This is no party; a few of them will die, with cups in hand, while ceremoniously carrying out their leader's funeral arrangements.

The members of the dead man's family who have accompanied him on this trip assemble his slave girls and ask them which one will agree to die with him. After a long silence, one of them, a beautiful, blonde twenty-year-old, musters the courage to say, "I will." She has spent these last years being sold by and to various different owners, all of which have forced her to cater to their every desire, and have raped her at their pleasure. Although she doesn't say it out loud, this, finally, is her way out. And it carries an additional benefit: despite the horrors that await her shortly before she is killed, until then she will be treated like a queen. Two of her fellow slaves are appointed to accompany her and to do whatever she orders them to do (and, we may surmise, to prevent her from changing her mind and trying to run away).

While the slave girl indulges her every whim with merry abandon, the people busy themselves with crafting the dead man's clothes and preparing his ship for its final use. The cups in their hands and by their sides are never empty. They feel increasingly ill, and the thought of sobriety seems like a happy dream they had long ago. Yet, for the sake of their master, they drink on.

At last, the day arrives in which the bodies of the high-ranking man and his slave are to be burned. His boat is drawn out of the river and dragged up to the top of a great wooden platform. A group of men place a bed in the center of the boat, with pillows and a mattress of fine Byzantine silk, and erect an A-shaped pavilion above it.

They remove the wooden covering from the noble's temporary grave and exhume his body. It has turned an eerie coal-black, but otherwise it is the same as before. He doesn't even smell. With him in his grave had been liquor, fruit, and a drum; these, too, are removed. The corpse is dressed with the clothes the people have spent the last several days crafting: a brocade caftan with buttons of gold and a brocade cap with sable fur. He is borne up to his boat and placed on the bed in the pavilion. Next to him are placed basil, onions, fruit, meat, bread, and, of course, more liquor.

The people bring a dog before the ship, and two men hold its trembling body in place while a third man cleaves it in half with one massive chop of his axe. The two halves of the unfortunate animal, gushing blood, are thrown on board. Next, the dead man's weapons – axes, daggers, a spear, a sword, and a shield, all of uncommonly fine workmanship – are placed beside his corpse. Two horses are forced to run, and run, and run, until they are almost at the point of collapsing from exhaustion. They are then rushed by sword-bearing men who furiously hack their still-living bodies to pieces. Two cows are made to suffer the same agony. The chunks of muscle, bone, skin, and organs of these four animals are collected and thrown onto the boat. A rooster and a hen are killed as well, this time by beheading, and likewise thrown onto the ship.

Now it's the slave girl's turn. Her days of indulgence have come to an end, and one final, short period of torment awaits her before her death.

First, she's passed around by the other noblemen, each of whom has sex with her in turn. "Tell your master that I only did this out of love for him," each says to her. Then, she's led to a wooden doorframe built in the open air. The men lift her up over the top, with her feet on their palms. She says the words the ritual requires: "There I see my father and mother." They let her down, then hoist her up again, and she says, "There I see all my dead relatives sitting." They set her on the ground briefly before lifting her over the frame a third time, and she says, "There I see my master sitting in paradise, and paradise is green and beautiful. There are men with him, young and old, and I see him motioning to me to come to him. Take me to him." Though the words are only a formality to her, as she says them, she finds, unsettlingly, that she almost *can* see what she tells the others she's seeing. They lead her to the boat where her master's corpse lies.

A thick-bodied sorceress, whom the people call the "Chooser of the Slain" ("Valkyrie"), takes the girl's bracelets off her arms. The girl removes her two anklets and gives them to the two fellow slave girls who have served her these past several days. They are, in fact, the daughters of the witch. The men lift her onto the boat. They hand her a cup of liquor, and she drinks it and sings a song, wherein she bids her fellow slave girls farewell. She continues singing as the men give her another cup. Eventually, the Chooser of the Dead cuts her off and orders her to down the cup and enter the pavilion where her master's body lies.

The girl does as she's told, but hesitates at the last moment, leaning her head out of the pavilion. The witch grabs her head and pushes her in. The men standing around the boat take up wooden clubs and bang them against their shields so that when the girl cries out in terror and agony, her screams will be drowned out, and the other slave girls won't be discouraged from following their masters to death at some later date.

Six more men have sex with the girl inside the pavilion with the ten-day-old corpse. After they're finished, they lay her next to her master on the bed. Two hold onto her feet, and two others hold onto her hands. The sorceress wraps a cord around the girl's neck and gives the two ends to the remaining two men. Then, the Chooser of the Dead takes out a dagger and begins to stab the girl between her ribs over and over and over, while the two men pull on the cord around her neck. At last, her suffering comes to an end, and she finds the respite for which she has been yearning. The men and the sorceress exit the ship.

The closest male relative of the deceased nobleman strips naked, picks up a torch, and walks backwards toward the ship, holding his hand over his anus to prevent that orifice from being penetrated by any uncouth spirits who might be lurking around such a highly-charged proceeding. He lights a fire in the wooden structure that holds the boat. All the people then throw torches of their own onto the wood. The fire slowly reaches the bottom of the boat, then the top of its sides, and finally engulfs the pavilion where the bodies of the dead man and girl lie. The stench of burning flesh fills the air. A fierce wind comes out of nowhere, emboldening the already roaring blaze. A man shouts joyfully that Odin has sent this wind, so that he can have the nobleman in his company sooner.

Within an hour, nothing remains of the ship, nobleman, slave girl, animals, and treasures but a smoldering pile of ashes. Over the ashes, the people build a huge grave mound. At its crest, they place a wooden pillar into which has been carved the name of the dead man and his king. Then, with their long and arduous task finally complete, they pack up their belongings, get into their ships, and resume their journey up the Volga River.

Such is how a Viking nobleman's funeral in the land that is today western Russia was described in the tenth century by an Arab traveler named Ahmad Ibn Fadlan.[1] (This particular retelling is informed by the interpretation of archaeologist Neil Price,[2] and includes my own conjectures about the characters' possible inner thoughts.) Ibn Fadlan's account can't be taken as being representative of *all* Viking funerals, or even all funerals of men of a particular class. For example, many Vikings, including those of noble stature and even kings, were buried rather than cremated. Modern scholars take issue with some of the details, but many of the other details – a much greater number – are corroborated by archaeological and literary evidence. And there is certainly a ritual formality involved at every step of the intricately choreographed, ten-day funeral, which suggests that it's an enactment of a traditional procedure, perhaps even one with a now-lost myth behind it.[3] All in all, we can be reasonably certain that Ibn Fadlan's account is a broadly honest and accurate description of one particular Viking funeral.

Clearly, the nobleman's passing was a big deal for his community, who took great pains to ensure that he was given a proper send-off. But what kind of place was he sent off *to*?

## THE LAND OF THE DEAD

The safest and most widely applicable characterization of what the Vikings thought happened to a person after he or she died is historian H.R. Ellis Davidson's comment that "There is no consistent picture in Norse literary tradition of the fate of the dead,"[4] to which she adds that "to oversimplify the position would be to falsify it."[5] This is yet another instance of the lack of rigid doctrine in Viking religion.

The only point the sources *generally* agree on is that the deceased went to live in the otherworld in some way or another. Archaeological evidence seems to confirm this. The dead, including human sacrifices, were buried or cremated in such a way that suggests they were being prepared for a journey to somewhere far, far away. Sometimes they were burned – changed into air or spirit – along with their ships, servants, and provisions, as we saw in Ibn Fadlan's description of the funeral on the Volga. When the dead were buried, they were often buried with some means of transportation, such as a wagon, a horse, or a boat, as well as food and other things that would be useful to them on a long journey.[6]

Old Norse literature contains vivid portrayals of the journey of the dead to the otherworld. One had to traverse deep and dark valleys, torrential rivers spanned by creaking bridges, caves, high walls, and other such foreboding places. Giants often guarded the way, and had to be appeased before one was allowed to progress further. All of these elements served to depict the distance between the otherworld and this world, as well as the perilousness of the path to the other side.

Sometimes, the sources speak of the land of the dead as a single place for everyone. In such cases, it's often referred to as "Hel," which meant simply "the grave."[7] Despite the name's coincidental resemblance to the Christian "Hell," the two ideas have essentially nothing in common. We've already seen that the Vikings didn't believe in any kind of moral punishment in the afterlife.[8] And although Snorri tends to describe Hel as a vaguely bad place, he is alone in doing so. His version is highly confused on a number of points, and has a strong air of Christian influence.[9]

The other sources, even when they mention Hel, rarely describe it. But when they do, it's cast in neutral or even positive terms. For example, the mention that the land of the dead is "green and beautiful" in Ibn Fadlan's account is mirrored in a passage from Saxo (the medieval Danish historian, as you likely recall). In Saxo's telling of the story of Hadding, the hero travels to the "underworld" and finds "a fair land where green herbs grow when it is winter on earth." His companion even beheads a rooster just outside of that land and flings its carcass over the wall, at which point the bird cries out and comes back to life – a feat which is highly reminiscent of another detail from Ibn Fadlan, namely the beheading of a rooster and a hen whose bodies are then tossed into the dead man's boat shortly before it's set aflame. In both cases, the emphasis is on abundant life in the world of the dead, even when death and absence prevail on earth.[10]

At other times, the dead were said to go to specific and different places. Many of these were simply local variants of Hel, "the grave."

One prominent example is the hill called Helgafell in Iceland, which was said to be the resting place of the early settler Thorolf Mostrarskegg and his family. Even those who died a great distance away from the hill went into it after death. According to *Eyrbyggja Saga*, Thorolf's son was Thorstein, a fisherman. One night, at the age of twenty-five, Thorstein and his crew were fishing, and drowned out at sea. Before word of Thorstein's death reached Thorolf and his family, a shepherd happened to be walking near Helgafell. In the darkness, he saw one side of the mountain open up. Firelight glowed from within. He could hear the sounds of feasting and celebration, and heard someone exclaim that Thorstein was about to be welcomed into the hall of his ancestors, and would sit at the head of the table opposite his father.[11] Here, too, the "underworld" is hardly a place of punishment, but rather one of merriment and reunion. (Recall that the slave girl in Ibn Fadlan's account likewise sees her dead relatives waiting for her in her vision of the afterlife.)

Some of the more specific places to which the dead went seem to have had something to do with the manner in which one died. For example, those who drowned were sometimes said to go to the underwater realm of Ran, a female giant.[12] (Note that this contradicts Thorstein's situation.) One poem credits Freya with receiving half of the "weapon-dead" into her domain of Folkvang.[13] And while there are no explicit references to Thor ever being a recipient of the dead,[14] one line in *The Song of Gray-Beard* might imply that some or all of the people of the lower classes did indeed go to him upon death.[15]

## VALHALLA

But the most prestigious of all of the distinct or semi-distinct afterlife worlds was Odin's Valhalla (Old Norse *Valhöll*, "Hall of the Fallen"). According to *The Song of the Hooded One*, the "gold-bright" hall of Odin had a roof made of shields, which was held aloft by spears that served as rafters. The benches of the feasting tables were breastplates.

Wolves guarded the door, and eagles circled above it.[16] And *The Song of Vafthrudnir* tells us that the men who dwelt there, who were called *einherjar* ("those who fight alone"[17]) battled each other every day, but at the end of the day, their wounds all healed, and they sat down to drink and feast in full health and happiness.[18] They ate the meat of a boar that came back to life every time it was killed and eaten, providing an endless supply of food for the hungry warriors.[19]

To gain entrance to Valhalla was seen as a high privilege, and was an honor for which many Vikings evidently yearned with great ardor. For example, when the saga hero Ragnar Lodbrok is about to be executed at the hands of an Anglo-Saxon king (Aella of Northumbria) by being thrown into a pit of writhing, venomous snakes, he defiantly declares, "I shall not come into [Odin's] hall with words of fear on my lips. ... I am eager to depart. ... Gladly I shall drink ale in the high-seat with the Æsir. ... I die with a laugh."[20]

However, the question of how one earned admittance to Valhalla has been the subject of considerable controversy. As with so many other aspects of Norse religion, the answers provided by the sources are ambiguous and conflicting. The most commonly-repeated distinction is the one given by Snorri in the *Prose Edda*: those who died violently went to Valhalla, while those who died by peaceful means went to Hel. But Snorri himself contradicts this in his version of the story of the death of Balder; Balder died by stabbing, yet nevertheless went to Hel. The most straightforward conclusion is that Snorri is here, as elsewhere, trying to artificially systematize the religion of his forebears, and that this tidy distinction is his own invention.[21]

Nevertheless, Snorri doesn't seem to have been entirely off-base. Other pieces of Old Norse literature suggest something similar. *The Song of the Hooded One*, for example, holds that half of those who died in battle were taken to Valhalla, while the other half were taken to Folkvang, Freya's realm. (It says nothing about what criteria were used to divide the "weapon-dead," however.)[22] As we've already seen, *The Song of King Eirik* has Odin state that his reasons for admitting the king to Valhalla are Eirik's bloodthirstiness and success in battle.[23] Hints of the same view can also be found in Saxo, various sagas, and other skaldic poems.[24]

However, this picture becomes more complicated when we note that – in addition to the contradictions on points of detail between the aforementioned sources – Odin often brought about the deaths of heroes himself, which would seem to spoil the notion of entrance to Valhalla being granted based on something that the warrior himself did. We can also note that Bragi – a poet rather than a warrior – was a prized resident of Odin's hall.

It seems that the necessary credential for entering the "warrior's paradise" of Valhalla upon death was, first and foremost, simply being chosen to enter by Odin and his Valkyries. This decision was largely influenced by things like having been a great warrior during one's life, having died a violent death, having had a high social status, and having piously kept up with the proper ritual observances connected to Odin during one's life. But ultimately it was up to Odin, and he chose whom he chose for the perfectly personal and selfish reason that he wanted to have the mightiest possible host to defend himself against Fenrir, "the wolf," at Ragnarok. For that was the ultimate fate of all of Valhalla's residents: to fall by their master's side in his hopeless struggle during the downfall of the cosmos. Death was only a respite, a change of state, before the utter obliteration of Ragnarok.

Was Valhalla a part of "Hel" – "the grave" and the more general land of the dead – or a separate realm altogether? There's good evidence that it was seen as being a part of Hel. In Saxo, when Hadding travels to the realm of the dead, he finds a battle raging without end in one area, which can't help but remind us of the daily fights of the *einherjar*.[25] In southern Sweden, there are a number of prominent rocks that bear the name *Valhall* (apparently from *valhallr*, "the rock of the fallen"), which seem to have been seen as local resting places for the dead, much like Helgafell in Iceland, or entrances to a more general land of the dead. Given that the names *Valhall* and *Valhöll* are practically identical (especially since, in Old Norse, *a* became *ö* under certain circumstances, and vice versa), it's difficult to cleanly disentangle the two.[26]

Then again, some sources seem to treat Valhalla as being a part of Asgard, which was located in the heavens. The question of Valhalla's relationship to Hel, therefore, must ultimately remain an open one. It seems that the Vikings themselves held conflicting views on this point, as they did on so many others.

## THE CONTINUING PRESENCE OF THE DEAD

Even from the grave, the deceased still influenced and interacted with the society of the living.

Sometimes, famous people, especially kings who had enjoyed a particularly prosperous reign, were thought to bring fertility to the land far beyond the mere nutrients and minerals their corpses provided the soil. Take, for example, the treatment received by King Halfdan the Black:

> His reign had been more fortunate in the seasons and crops than those of all other kings. So much trust was placed in him that, when they learned he was dead and his body carried to Hringaríki to be buried, there came influential men from Raumaríki and Vestfold and Heiðmörk, all begging to have the body and to bury it in their own district; for they thought it would ensure prosperous seasons if they could obtain it. So it was decided that they should divide the body between four places; the head was laid in a howe at Stein in Hringaríki, and each man bore home a part of the body and laid it in howe; these howes are called 'the howes of Hálfdan'.[27]

Likewise, sacrifices were offered to the dead in hopes that they would return the favor by blessing their descendants with success in any and all areas of life.

People sometimes sat or slept on burial mounds in order to receive something from the dead buried there: creative inspiration, insight, or various other kinds of gifts. Intriguingly, archaeologists have noted that surviving burial mounds sometimes have flat platforms built into their tops or at their base, quite possibly to enable people to comfortably sit or lie on them, or to perform other kinds of solitary or communal ceremonies there. Sometimes these areas are encircled by stones in the shape of a ship's hull, suggesting a vessel for a journey to the otherworld.[28] Even the extraordinarily wise and learned Odin sought knowledge from the dead on numerous occasions.[29]

There's some evidence in the sources for rebirth of a person within his or her own family line. The closest we can probably come to an "if-then" statement that would trigger rebirth is the practice of naming a newborn child after a deceased relative, but this certainly doesn't seem to have been the case invariably. There don't seem to be any examples in Old Norse literature of a human being reborn as an animal or vice versa – nor, for that matter, do there seem to be any examples of a human being reborn into another human family.[30] And, as we've seen, one particular part of the self, the *hamingja* ("luck," as you might recall) was frequently passed down along a family line.

However, there was no clear boundary that separated the deceased from other types of spiritual beings. For example, *The Saga of King Olaf the Holy* refers to the king's namesake as "Olaf, the Elf of Geirstad," implying that he was believed to have become an elf – a suggestion that makes the fervently Christian king profoundly uncomfortable.[31]

Sometimes the dead would come back bodily (not as disembodied ghosts) and cause great harm to the living, as in the case of Hrapp and several other characters from *The Saga of the People of Laxardal*[32] and Glam in *Grettir's Saga*.[33] The characters' walking about occurs for no discernible reason, and it ends when their bodies are beheaded, burned, or both. This seems to have been a possibility against which the Vikings took precautions. Some Viking Age graves, for example, feature heavy stones placed over the bodies of the dead, which could have been an attempt to prevent them from escaping and wreaking havoc.

Finally, a kind of pseudo-immortality cherished by the Vikings was a "good name" that would be remembered with fondness and admiration long after its bearer had died. In words that bring to mind Shakespeare's 55th sonnet, *The Song of the High One* proclaims:

> Wealth will pass,
> Men will pass,
> You, too, likewise, will pass.
> One thing alone
> Will never pass:
> The fame of one who has earned it.[34]

# Chapter 9:

# Formal Religious

# Practice

The Vikings put their vibrant religious conceptions into practice in a number of different ways. Over the course of the past several chapters, we've noted some of them: hallowing weddings and oaths with a symbolic Thor's hammer, casting a spear over an enemy host to offer them as a sacrifice to Odin, constructing farmsteads in imitation of the spatial layout of the otherworld, and many others. In this chapter, we'll round out the picture by looking directly at four particularly important, and particularly formal, aspects of Norse religious practice: holy places where public rituals were conducted, the composition of the public rituals themselves, human sacrifice, and private rituals carried out by individual men and women. Discussions of most magical and shamanic rituals, however, will be left for the next chapter.

## HOLY PLACES

Most - and perhaps all - sites where the Norse held formal religious ceremonies were located outside in the open air. Few, if any, were enclosed by buildings or "temples."[1] The main words the Norse used to refer to the places where they felt the presence of the otherworld the most intensely were *vé*, *hörgr*, and *hof*,[2] all of which seem to have been more or less synonymous. If the place was located in a wooded area, the more specific term *lundr*, "grove," was sometimes used.[3]

These sites were often characterized by striking geographical features. One, for example, was located on the island of Frösö ("Frey's Island") in Sweden, in the middle of a large lake with expansive views of the surrounding low mountains. A stately tree, much like Yggdrasil, the tree that stood at the center of the Norse otherworld, marked the center of this ritual site. Archaeological excavations there have revealed the stump of a deliberately-felled birch directly beneath the altar of the church that currently occupies that spot. Amongst its roots, the archaeologists discovered a vast array of animal bones, including five whole bears, six elk heads, two stag heads, five sheep or goat heads, eleven pig heads, two cow heads, and countless miscellaneous bones from those species, as well as from reindeer, squirrels, horses, and dogs. This was clearly a sacrificial site of considerable importance. Radiocarbon dating tells us that the bones were placed there during the tenth century. Two Viking Age burial mounds are located in the churchyard, and may have been part of a larger cemetery now obscured by the presence of the churchyard. Tellingly, the site of the church is called *Hov*, a modernized Swedish rendering of *hof*.[4]

Other burial mounds throughout the Norse lands served as ritual sites,[5] as did bogs and other bodies of water. Many of these bodies of water were held to possess healing powers.[6] Sacrifices and offerings were commonly dropped into them – perhaps as a gift to local spirits, or perhaps as gifts to a more general otherworld to which the water served as a portal.[7]

Helgafell, the hill where the early Icelandic settler Thorolf and his family were held to reside after their deaths, fits this same pattern. It's an elongated rocky outcropping with a magnificent view of the nearby plains, hills, and ocean. Intriguingly, when seen from a certain angle, the hill looks like a Viking Age house with a door.[8] Surely it was this side that the shepherd saw opening up to welcome Thorolf's son Thorstein upon his death (as per the story of Helgafell in Chapter Eight).

Perhaps the most remarkable Viking Age holy site of all, however, was Thingvellir in Iceland, the place where the country's legal assembly was held. (Recall that the Vikings didn't separate their religion from other aspects of life. Thus, it shouldn't be surprising that their legal assemblies had elements of religious ceremonies in them.) Every year at Midsummer, people came from all over the island to take part in the assembly, in which the laws were recited and disputes were settled. The gods were thought to preside over the gathering, which was, after all, modeled on the deities' own council at Yggdrasil. The Icelanders' council began on Thursday – Thor's Day – in honor of the patron god of most of the earliest Icelandic settlers. Sacrifices and feasts punctuated the gathering's legal aspects.[9] And just as Yggdrasil was the center of the otherworld where the gods lived, Thingvellir was the symbolic (although not the strictly geographical) center of Iceland.[10]

In the evocative words of historian H.R. Ellis Davidson, Thingvellir

is formed by a natural volcanic rift in a large sunken valley, where the swift-flowing river (Öxará) runs into a large lake. A line of sinister twisted rocks provides an impressive background and natural sounding board, which would have been effective when a section of the laws was recited every year at the 'Law Rock' by the Speaker or Lawman who presided over the Assembly. ... It is no sheltered site, but lies open to strong winds and blizzards and even sandstorms at all times in the year. The sense of wide distances and far views of lakes and mountains give it something of the same numinous quality as is possessed by Helgafell. These two sacred places of the Viking Age have no need of monuments or permanent buildings to render them memorable.[11]

Committing any kind of violence at holy sites was a heinous crime, and was punishable by outlawry.[12] People were generally prohibited from even taking weapons into their precincts. Because of this, people – and, according to the sagas, even animals – fled to these sites for safety when they were pursued by their enemies.[13] In keeping with the cosmological significance of the *garðr* (which we explored in Chapter Four), holy places were often enclosed by a fence, hedge, or rope.[14] The upkeep of holy sites was financed by dues (*hoftollar*) collected from everyone who used them – essentially the same thing as Christian tithing.[15]

At these sites, deities were frequently represented by roughly carved wooden statues. Some of these were very large, and others were small enough to be carried around in a purse.[16] Ibn Fadlan describes wooden figures of gods that the trading Vikings brought with them. This was likely a common practice among travelers, enabling makeshift shrines to be built (or found) potentially anywhere.[17]

Religious ceremonies were also commonly conducted inside the hall of a king or a chieftain. This did make such halls partial temples in some sense, but their religious function was only one of several. True temples – dedicated buildings of worship akin to Christian churches or Islamic mosques, for example – have left no clear evidence in the archaeological record.[18] Foreign writers such as Adam of Bremen have left us descriptions of large, lavish Norse temples, but these accounts are likely influenced by portrayals of similar buildings among other polytheistic peoples in the Old Testament and the works of classical authors.[19] The sparse references to religious buildings in Old Norse literature seem, in context, to refer to small, local shrines.[20] Given all of this, it seems reasonable to conclude that the Vikings never built or used true, large-scale temples, preferring their majestic outdoor sanctuaries instead.

## FESTIVALS AND OTHER PUBLIC CEREMONIES

What kinds of practices went on at these sites?

In addition to legal assemblies such as the one at Thingvellir, major public rituals were part of the celebration of the three big festivals around which the Viking calendar turned. One of these was the Winter Nights, which was held over several days during our month of October, which the Vikings considered to be the beginning of winter and of the new year more generally. The boundary between the realm of the living and the realm of the dead was thin, and all sorts of uncanny things were bound to happen. At this festival, the divine powers were petitioned for the general prosperity of the people. The second critical festival was Yule at midwinter – late December and early January – which, with the arrival of Christianity, was converted into Christmas. Offerings were made to the gods in hopes of being granted bountiful harvests in the coming growing season in return. The third major festival was called "Summer Time" (*sumarmál*), and was held in April, which the Vikings considered to be the beginning of summer. When the deities were contacted during this festival, they were asked for success in the coming season's battles, raids, and trading expeditions. The exact times of these festivals differed between communities.[21]

Public ceremonies to win the gods' favor were also held at times when circumstantial events posed problems for the community's well-being, such as when enemy forces threatened to attack or when a chieftain or king died. The time between the death of a ruler and his replacement was a dangerously unsettled period, when the community was vulnerable to incursions from the forces of chaos – both rival human groups taking advantage of the group's temporary leaderlessness and malevolent spirits taking advantage of the group's temporary lack of one of the primary intercessors between them and the gods.[22]

As part of these ceremonies, an animal was ritually selected. The exact means differed from ceremony to ceremony, but steps of one sort or another were taken to ensure that the animal was divinely chosen.[23] Usually, this would be a horse, a bull, a boar, or a pig. All of these species were readily available to the ancient Scandinavians, and all possessed cosmological significance.[24] The chosen animal was hallowed and then sacrificed to the gods upon an altar. After the sacrifice (*blót* in Old Norse), the meat of the animal was cooked. The animal's blood, which had turned the altar a thick, shiny red, was collected in bowls and sprinkled on the premises and on those in attendance to consecrate them and the event in which they were taking part. In fact, the participants often went out of their way to drink this blood and to literally lick clean the bowls that contained it. This sacrificial blood was called by a special name, *hlaut*, to distinguish it from ordinary blood (*blóð*).[25]

Once the meat had finished cooking, it was served to the participants. For their drink, they had beer, mead, or some other kind of alcoholic beverage, which was hallowed before it was served in either individual vessels or a large communal bowl.[26] Toasts were offered to various gods and ancestors, as well as to the ruler and perhaps other humans who were present. After these solemnities, a merry feast commenced.[27]

Such ceremonies were communions between living people, deities, and deceased ancestors. The bonds between them, which the ritual strengthened, were embodied by the sharing of special, consecrated liquids (alcohol and *hlaut*).[28] Alcohol was the drink of choice at these feasts due to its power to open the mind to suggestion, inspiration, and emotional elevation, which placed the participants in closer contact with the divine world.[29]

In addition to strengthening bonds, the sacrifice was offered to the gods with the expectation that they would reciprocate by bestowing some desired blessing upon their human worshippers – abundant harvests, victory in battle, general prosperity, or some other condition for which the people yearned. In a sense, there was a spiritual economy involved here, where divine favors were purchased with the currency of sacrifice.

Other kinds of events often peppered these festivals, especially the big three annual ones. Oaths – which the gods were typically charged with overseeing – were sworn on the sacrificial animal. All kinds of entertainment and sports, including racing, wrestling, and storytelling, could be enjoyed by the audience. And since the otherworld was especially close during these times, divination was thought to be especially potent. Seers and seeresses went into their trances and told their listeners what fate had in store for them.[30]

Who led these ceremonies? There's no credible evidence for "priests" – full-time religious specialists – in the Viking Age. Instead, public worship was led by the "secular" authorities, especially kings and chieftains, whose offices were religious roles in addition to their more worldly duties.[31] The Icelandic word for "chieftain," goði (female gyðja), comes from the word goð, one of the many words for "god," a sign of the closeness between the bearer of that title and divinity.[32] This is another powerful instance of the inseparability of religion from all other realms of life in the Viking way of looking at things.

## HUMAN SACRIFICE

The Vikings indisputably practiced human sacrifice as part of some public ceremonies. It doesn't seem to have been an especially routine practice, but was reserved for special occasions of many different kinds. Men and women were sacrificed to the gods as a way of appeasing them when the people were threatened with the failure of the harvest or some other grave communal misfortune. One or more of those in the service of high-ranking men and women could have been sacrificed when their masters died, as in the case of the slave girl on the Volga in Ibn Fadlan's account. Criminals were sacrificed as a form of capital punishment. Prisoners of war, too, were often sacrificed, sometimes in very large numbers and along with the spoils of war, to the deities the victorious army credited with enabling their victory, as a way of giving thanks and returning the favor.[33]

Human sacrifice is also listed as a central part of obscure but massive and extravagant rituals that seem to have been held once every nine years, which were attended by the people who inhabited an area much of the size of a modern-day country. According to Adam of Bremen,

It is the custom moreover every nine years for a common festival of all the provinces of Sweden to be held at Uppsala. Kings and commoners one and all send their gifts to Uppsala, and what is more cruel than any punishment, even those who have accepted Christianity have to buy immunity from these ceremonies. The sacrifice is as follows: of every living creature they offer nine head, and with the blood of those it is the custom to placate the gods, but the bodies are hanged in a grove which is near the temple; so holy is that grove to the heathens that each tree in it is presumed to be divine by reason of the victim's death and putrefaction. There also dogs and horses hang along with men. One of the Christians told me that he had seen seventy-two bodies of various kinds hanging there.[34]

While many of the details in Adam's account can be readily disputed (such as the ritual being held at a "temple"), the eleventh-century German historian Thietmar of Merseburg describes a similar ceremony taking place every nine years at Lejre, Denmark. It's unlikely, therefore, that Adam made up the entire rite himself.[35]

Unsurprisingly, those lower down on the ladder of social status were more likely to be sacrificed than those higher up on it. However, in especially dire predicaments, not even kings were immune. *The Saga of the Ynglings*, for example, describes such a situation. A famine had devastated a kingdom. The people's response was to work their way up the ladder of status until, after each sacrifice proved ineffective, they reached the very top:

The first year [of the famine] they sacrificed oxen, and there was no improvement in the harvest. The next autumn they sacrificed men, but the harvest was as before or even worse. And the third autumn many Swedes came to Uppsala when the sacrifice was to take place. The chiefs took counsel then, and decided unanimously that the famine must be due to their king Domaldi, and that they must sacrifice him for a good season and redden the altars with his blood, and this they did.[36]

The sacrifice of the king apparently worked; the saga tells us that the reign of Domaldi's successor was characterized by bountiful harvests.[37]

An especially gruesome form of human sacrifice was the "blood-eagle" (blóðörn). The victim's ribs were cut apart from the back, exposing the lungs, which were then drawn out of the chest and placed over the back like the wings of a bird. This ghastly act seems to have been reserved for occasions where the person leading the sacrifice had some extreme personal vendetta against the victim.[38]

Odin was the main recipient of human sacrifice, but any or all of the deities could demand or receive them at times.[39]

## PERSONAL DEVOTION

But the religious practices of the Vikings didn't just consist of public ceremonies. Individuals often had intense personal spiritualities of their own.

An individual might encounter divine powers through sacrifice or other deliberate methods – much as in the communal ceremonies, just on a smaller scale – or otherworld beings might come "involuntarily" via dreams or omens. The content of such communications could include foreknowledge of the future, directions for the guidance of present or future action, a change in the nature of the relationship between the person and the divine power(s), or other kinds of hidden knowledge.

Norse men and women often had a *fulltrúi*, a patron god or goddess with whom the worshipper was particularly close.[40] For example, Thor was the *fulltrúi* of Thorolf Mostrarskegg, the early Icelandic settler whose family drank and ate beneath Helgafell after their deaths. Thorolf was originally from Norway, but got into a bad dispute with the king. So he asked "his dear friend" Thor whether he should stay in Iceland and reconcile himself with the king or leave for Iceland and start a new life there. The god instructed him to depart for the island, so he did. Many of the other earliest settlers of Iceland were guided there by their patrons: Helgi the Lean landed at Eyjafjord due to Thor's directions; Ingimund lost a cherished amulet of Frey that mysteriously turned up in Iceland, so Ingimund settled in the spot where it was found; and others were guided to particular parts of the island by Odin's ravens.[41]

As was the case with the public mode of religion, maintaining good relations with one's *fulltrúi* brought success, and neglecting one's *fulltrúi* brought failure. For example, in *The Saga of Eirik the Red*, when Thorhall and his community were in urgent need of food, Thorhall composed a beautiful poem of praise to his *fulltrúi*, Thor. Soon, a whale beached itself on the shore. Thorhall proudly proclaimed to the religiously mixed community: "Red Beard proved a better friend now than your Christ. This is what I get for the poem I made about Þórr [Thor] my patron. Rarely has he failed me."[42]

A particularly interesting and telling example of two competing modes of private religiosity comes from *Viga-Glum's Saga*. Two rivals, Thorkell and Glum, are locked in a bitter dispute over cattle and family honor. Both appeal to their patrons for help. Thorkell leads an ox into Frey's sanctuary to sacrifice it to the god, in hopes that Frey will come to his aid in his dispute with Glum. He asks for a sign that Frey accepts the bargain, and the ox promptly lets out a tremendous bellow and falls down dead on the spot.[43] Glum, by contrast, states at a feast that he has three patrons: "the first is my bag of money, the second is my axe, [and] the third the storehouse."[44] In other words, he is basically what we today would call a materialist, and trusts in his wits and possessions rather than any spiritual being. This could be Christian literary symbolism crafted by the saga's author, but it's not at all a stretch to imagine that people of such a persuasion existed during the Viking Age. People like Glum could have been accommodated by the wider societal religious framework, which demanded participation in the public rituals but didn't reward or punish individuals for their private beliefs or practices.

Sometimes, a person's *fulltrúi* was another kind of divine being besides a god or a goddess. Land spirits seem to have been especially common patrons. We've already seen one example of this in the case of Goat-Bjorn, who became rich through the land spirits' aid.[45]

Occasionally, someone might even have a giant as his or her *fulltrúi*. Such seems to have been the case with Earl Hakon Sigurdarson, who is widely reported to have had a giantess named Thorgerd Holgabrud for his patron. *The Saga of the Jomsvikings* recounts how he won a great naval battle with her support – for a hideous price:

Hakon left his companions and rowed to an island alone. He knew that the dreaded Jomsviking fleet was headed toward him, and that he and his men stood little chance of overcoming them in battle. With the seemingly endless vastness of the grim fjords all around him, he turned to the north and prayed to Thorgerd. His entreaties only angered the capriciously temperamental giantess, and she refused every sacrifice he offered to her, even a human victim. At last, Hakon made her an offer she was willing to accept: for the aid of her and her sister Irpa in the coming battle, the life of Hakon's seven-year-old son. Hakon fetched the boy and had a slave kill him. The deal was sealed.

The earl returned to his ship and prepared for the fight with a newfound confidence. His fleet rowed out to meet the Jomsvikings, and a terrible battle ensued. From the north came a storm so thick it blotted out the daylight almost as if the sun had been eclipsed. Lightning flashed and thunder roared all around the fighters. A piercingly cold wind blasted against the Jomsvikings and battered them with driving rain and hail. They hurled rocks, arrows, and spears at Hakon's army, but the wind turned all of their missiles back on them, doubling the onslaught from Hakon.

Those few Jomsvikings gifted with second sight could barely glimpse, through the torrent, two shockingly sinister beings standing amongst Hakon's men, shooting arrows from their fingertips into the Jomsvikings. When they told this to Sigvaldi, the Jomsvikings' leader, his face grew pale. He shouted above the clamor, "In that case, I am going to flee. You and the other men should flee, too. I have vowed to fight against men, but I have not vowed to fight against giantesses."[46]

# Chapter 10:

# Magic and Shamanism

A dire famine had seized Greenland. The Viking settlers had been able to rely on their stores to provide them with a spare, bleak diet over the winter, but it was clear that if the famine swallowed the coming year as it had the previous one, they would all starve to death.

Thorkell, the leading farmer in his settlement, sent for Thorbjorg, the island's premier seeress. Thorbjorg usually spent the winter traveling from farm to farm, receiving room and board in exchange for foretelling what the coming year held. This winter, Thorkell and his neighbors were especially anxious to hear what she had to say.

When Thorbjorg arrived with the man who had been sent to escort her, she was dressed in a dark blue cloak that glistened with the countless precious gemstones that had been sewn into it. A glass bead necklace hung around her neck. Her head was partially covered by a hood made of black lambskin and lined with white catskin. In her hands, she held a staff with a knob on top that was covered by brass and more gemstones. A large leather pouch sat on her wooden belt. In this pouch were all kinds of mystifying charms. Her feet were covered by hairy calfskin shoes with metal knobs at the toe. Her hands were covered by white, furry catskin gloves.

The people received her with meticulously respectful greetings, which she responded to based on her opinion of the person. Thorkell took her by the hand and led her to the high-seat that had been prepared for her, upon which had been placed a cushion newly stuffed with fresh hen feathers. This would be the platform from which she would give her prophecies. She seemed pleased by it, but said little.

Besides, before she would tell the people about their future, her stomach had to be filled – and not with just any food.

The tables were prepared for dinner, and all sat down to eat. Thorbjorg was given a porridge made with goat's milk, and for her main course, a heart from every species of livestock kept at Thorkell's farm. They even gave her special silverware: a brass spoon and an ivory-handled knife with the point broken off. After dinner, Thorkell approached Thorbjorg and asked her when she might be ready to give the people what they wanted. She replied that she would first have to spend a night at the farm. So she was provided with one of the finest beds they had, and all went to sleep.

The following evening, she was provided with all of the tools she requested to aid her in her sorcery. Then she told the people to find women who knew the proper chants (varðlokkur) to accompany her work. But this was the late tenth century. Many of the people had already converted to Christianity, and old customs like the varðlokkur were falling into disuse. As a result, no one could be found who knew the incantations. At last, Gudrid, a young woman, spoke up: "I am not skilled at sorcery, nor can I be counted among the wise women, but my foster-mother in Iceland taught me the songs when I was a child, and I think I still remember them." Thorbjorg smiled at her and said, "Then you know more than I expected." But Gudrid added that she was a Christian woman, and therefore wasn't comfortable with participating in the rituals of her forebears who hadn't revered Christ. Thorbjorg pointed out to her that her people were in great need, and performing the chants would be a great service to them. She then insinuated, in a not-so-subtle manner, that Thorkell should force Gudrid to sing. Thorkell took the hint and pressured the girl until she agreed to sing.

Then Thorbjorg got up onto the high-seat, and the women made a circle around her. Gudrid began to recite the chants. Afterwards, everyone would say that the sounds had flowed from her so beautifully that they had never heard anyone do a better job.

When Gudrid had finished, Thorbjorg thanked her and said that the incantation had proven successful. A great number of spirits, many of whom had earlier hardened their hearts against the people, had come to assist the ritual. And now, she said, with their help, she could see the year ahead: "When this winter ends, so, too, will this famine. When spring arrives, the land will heal, and you shall lack nothing." Then she turned to Gudrid, and said: "As for you, Gudrid, I will reward you for you work by telling you what fate has in store for you, for it is very pleasant indeed. You will marry the most honorable man in all of Greenland, but it will not last long. That is for the better, however, because your path leads over the seas to Iceland. There, you will become the mother of a line of men and women so great that it will be as if a bright ray of sunlight went out of its way to shine on your family. Health to you, and fare you well."

Then each person who was present went before Thorbjorg in turn and asked what the year held for them. Few of her answers didn't come to pass.

Thorbjorg was called away to another farm, and bade goodbye to Thorkell and his people. And when spring came, the famine abated, and the people had full bellies and peaceful minds.[1]

The tale of Thorbjorg's divination in *The Saga of Eirik the Red* is one of the most detailed and telling depictions of Viking magic in Old Norse literature. Lots of the particulars that appear again and again in other, more limited accounts of the practice of magic in the Viking Age are contained in this one passage.

In a Norse context, "magic" can probably be most appropriately defined as the knowledge of how to manipulate spiritual forces, and the skilled application of that knowledge in practice. Magic was distinguished from the rest of religion by the fact that the practitioner of magic didn't just worship spiritual forces and humbly ask them for favors; he or she sought to actively *control* some of them in order to accomplish particular outcomes. It should go without saying that there are no recorded instances of anyone attempting to control the deities themselves through magic – that would have been futile, and might have brought dire consequences for any mere human who attempted something so insulting to the very powers who held the cosmos together. But spiritual entities of a lesser stature, such as the parts of the self discussed in Chapter Seven, were fair game. The practitioner would also work with spirits as powerful as, or more powerful than, the practitioner himself or herself, with whom the sorcerer or sorceress had a working relationship.

Knowledge was central to the magician's craft. The most general Old Norse word for "magic," *fjölkyngi*,[2] meant "great knowledge." It was derived from the verb *kunna*, which meant "to know," but didn't refer to just any kind of knowledge. It signified an understanding of the inner workings of people, things, and the world as a whole, as well as a mastery of ancient lore and traditions.[3]

Such insight and erudition was the necessary basis of the successful practice of magic. Any random person couldn't just say "abracadabra" and expect something "magical" to happen any more than a modern person could just say "car" and "magically" end up with a new car. Building a car is an impressive feat that requires highly specialized knowledge and skill, and so, for the Norse, was the manipulation of spiritual entities.

In the Viking Age way of looking at things, magic wasn't irrational, nor did it violate what we would call the "laws of nature." The potential efficacy of magic was perfectly rational relative to the Vikings' fundamental assumptions about reality, and it worked *with* the "laws of nature" – which, as we've seen, essentially came down to fate – rather than against them.

## SEID

The Old Norse sources use the word "seid" (*seiðr*) in what appear to be two different ways: as one type of magic among others, and as a synonym for "magic" in its totality. This is yet another instance of the fluidity and lack of systematization in Norse religion, a theme we've already noted and discussed several times. While some modern writers have attempted to isolate seid as a particular kind of magic cleanly distinct from other kinds, the very vagueness with which the sources delineate seid seems to argue against this interpretation. Furthermore, there aren't *any* magical practices that aren't referred to as "seid" at some point in Old Norse literature, so the idea that there were other forms of Norse magic that were never thought to be a part of seid rests on rather shaky ground. The safest and *most* widely applicable interpretation, therefore, is that seid was seen as being *effectively* synonymous with magic as a whole.[4]

The common Old Norse noun *seiðr* meant "string, cord, snare, halter." For a long time, scholars were reluctant to accept that *seiðr*, the name of the magical tradition, came from the common noun *seiðr*, because it isn't clear at first glance what the relationship between weaving and ecstatic sorcery would be. But closer and more recent research has made sense of this conundrum, and along the way has revealed much about what seid consisted of in practice.[5]

Consider Thorbjorg's jewel-studded staff, for example. The staff seems to have been a near-universal accessory of seid practitioners ("volur," Old Norse *völur*; singular "volva," *völva*).[6] It was a symbolic distaff – a tool used in the process of spinning fiber. With his or her ritual distaff in hand, the sorcerer or sorceress would send out spiritual parts of himself or herself, or other spirits, to do his or her bidding. They would be tethered to the distaff by an imagined string so that they could be readily called back when they had achieved their purpose.[7]

Another part of the connection between "magic" and "string, cord, snare, halter" was surely the prevalence of imagery of binding and loosening bonds in instances of magic in Old Norse literature. To control someone by magical means was to metaphorically bind them, and the evidence suggests that this was more than just a metaphor for the Norse. The tethers that tied the traveling spirits to their masters' staffs could also "ensnare" victims – or break snares.

For example, one of the most dreaded circumstances in the Viking Age was to find oneself paralyzed in battle by the so-called "war-fetters" (*herfjöturr*) of an enemy magician, as happened to the protagonist of *The*

*Saga of Hord and the People of Holm.* At a crucial moment in battle, a volva placed the war-fetters around Hord. Such was the warrior's strength that he was able to break free and continue to fight. The war-fetters came upon him again, and after great exertion, he again escaped and took up his weapons against his enemies. But then he was ensnared a third time, and he found himself helpless against the ring of enemies closing in on him.[8]

Furthermore, recall the weaving imagery that was sometimes used to depict the Norns' crafting of fate (Chapter Five). The volur, too, are occasionally called "norns" in Old Norse texts. Given this striking convergence of images, it seems reasonable to assume that the spinning activities involved in seid also had something to do with threading additions to the web of fate. It's highly unlikely, however, that human sorcerers and sorceresses were thought to be capable of undoing what the Norns "proper" had already woven – they probably "only" contributed a few extra patterns around the web's edges.

Seid rituals were often performed at the top of a raised platform called a *seiðhjallr*, as Thorbjorg did in *The Saga of Eirik the Red*.[9] The *varðlokkur* ("guardian spirit enticements") chants that Gudrid sang were another common feature, and summoned spirits to aid the volva in his or her work. The songs were said to be exceptionally pleasing to the ear, and this allure was thought to naturally attract the spirits. Due to this pleasantness, the songs could also be used to draw soon-to-be victims of injurious magic to the situation where they would be harmed.[10]

How did the volur enter the trance states in which they performed their work? The sources don't tell us directly, but they do offer some clues. For one thing, there's no evidence for a widespread use of entheogens (mind-altering plants used in a religious context, literally "substances that bring one into the presence of the divine") among the Norse. It probably occurred here and there, but it certainly doesn't seem to have been anything like an extensive practice.[11] (The sole – and obvious – exception to this is alcohol, but that was used in larger, more regular, more communal rituals like the ones we saw in Chapter Nine, and no source records a volva imbibing a significant amount of alcohol before beginning his or her rituals.)

Instead, it's probable that the volur got themselves into the proper frame of mind via the sweet music of the *varðlokkur*, as well as deep breathing exercises – the sources sometimes refer to volur "yawning" at the start of a ritual, which could point to such a practice (and would accord with the Norse identification of breath and spirit). But, once again, we don't really know for sure.

Words, whether spoken, sung, or written, were another central feature of the practice of magic in the Viking Age. For the Norse, words weren't merely symbols that referred to something else in the "real world" after the fact. They weren't spoken idly. Instead, a word was thought to bring into being that which it symbolized. By being spoken or sung aloud, or written on a physical surface, words had a physical presence of their own, and were part of the fabric of physical reality. They transformed an abstract intention or idea into something concrete. Words – and the intentions and ideas behind them – had the power to change physical reality, just like any other physical phenomenon. Therefore, when someone pronounced a blessing or a curse, for example, that blessing or curse was believed to actually take place simply because it had been articulated.[12]

The volur harnessed this incredible power in several ways. One was writing the text of a spell in runes, the Norse alphabet. After the words were recorded, the letters were typically reddened with sacrificial blood (*hlaut*) to render them more potent.[13]

Another was singing the spells aloud, a practice which was called *galdr*. The word *galdr* primarily meant simply "sung or chanted spell," but it carried a secondary connotation of "animal noises," especially those of roosters and other birds with especially piercing calls. An insane person was said to be *galinn* – roughly "the object of *galdr*." Nevertheless, *galdr* was said to be pleasing to the ear, and it may have been intoned in a special meter, preserved in a few pieces of Eddic poetry, called *galdralag*.[14]

Another technique used by sorcerers and sorceresses was *útiseta*, literally "sitting out." While not a ritual in and of itself, it formed a framework that could give rituals a context that would make them particularly effective. *Útiseta* involved sitting outside at night in places of great spiritual power, such as burial mounds, beneath the dangling bodies of the hanged, or beside running water. Unsurprisingly, it seems to have been used especially often in rituals that involved communication with the dead.[15]

## THE USES OF SEID

Magic may seem like something hopelessly exotic and bizarre. But even at its most outlandish, it was (and, in some corners of the world, still is) a way of addressing big and small anxieties that are an inherent part of the human condition. Being as old as humanity itself, they are naturally still with us today, even though our methods of attempting to overcome them may be different.

What are the things that stress you out in your own life, and which you spend a lot of time trying to control? Money, love, lust, friendships, reputation, health, and/or an uncertain future, perhaps? These are the same things the Vikings struggled with, and magic – the skilled manipulation of subtle, unseen forces – was one of the techniques they used to try to make important events turn out the way they wanted them to turn out.

Seid was sometimes a matter of passively perceiving the future, like in Thorbjorg's ritual in Greenland, and at other times a matter of actively altering it. Sometimes it was used within the context of "domestic" or "civilian" life, and at other times as part of war. Archaeologist Neil Price offers an elegant summary of its uses:

There were *seiðr* rituals for divination and clairvoyance; for seeking out the hidden, both in the secrets of the mind and in physical locations; for healing the sick; for bringing good luck; for controlling the weather; for calling game animals and fish. Importantly, it could also be used for the opposite of these things - to curse an individual or an enterprise; to blight the land and make it barren; to induce illness; to tell false futures and thus to set their recipients on a road to disaster; to injure, maim and kill, in domestic disputes and especially in battle.[16]

Divination served first and foremost to discern the workings of impersonal fate, and secondarily to discern the wills of deities that were thought to have a hand in the situation in question. As we've seen, the Vikings lived in a world characterized by a constant tension between fate and free choice. Peering into the future through divination – a Viking Age version of a weather forecast, if you like – enabled people to have a clearer sense of the range of possibilities that were available to them, and which ones were beyond their reach. Then they could develop plans for acting within these limits.[17]

Given the prevalence of war and strife in the Viking Age, it makes sense that one of the main uses of seid to actively produce change was directing the outcome of violent disputes. To quote Price again, seid's battlefield applications included

> instilling fear and confusion, conferring courage and clarity of mind, instilling physical weakness, conferring physical strength, magically hindering the body's movements, breaking or strengthening weapons and armour, providing invulnerability in battle, killing people, resurrecting dead warriors to fight again, providing protection from sorcerers, [and] fighting or killing sorcerers.[18]

In other words, it could influence essentially any and every aspect of Viking Age conflict, and it frequently played a significant role in turning the tide of battle.

## THE SEXUAL DYNAMICS OF SEID

Seid had a pronounced sexual component, even in instances where the ultimate intentions of the workings weren't sexual in nature.[19]

Recall the discussion of sexual and gender-based morality in the Viking Age from Chapter Six. To briefly recap, the most shameful and dishonorable thing a Viking man could be was *argr*, a word that meant "unmanly," "cowardly," and "receptive homosexual." For the Norse, these were three ways of saying the same thing – hence their one word for all three. The noun form of *argr* – the state of being *argr* – was *ergi*.

The Norse considered the practice of seid to be inherently *argr*. In the Eddic poem *Loki's Taunts*, Loki accuses Odin of being a volva – "And that, it seems to me, is wholly *argr*."[20] Likewise, *The Saga of the Ynglings* says that after seid was invented, "it was found to bring so much *ergi* to those who practiced it that honorable men wanted nothing to do with it, and it was taught to the sorceresses instead."[21] While it was more or less okay for a woman to practice magic, the same can't be said for men.

Why would the Vikings have considered it to be so profoundly disgraceful for a man to practice magic? At first glance, this seems bizarre. And the sources never tell us explicitly. However, they give us several clues that, taken together, form a consistent picture.

For one thing, in a culture where the forthright, physical, violent defense of one's honor was so central to the concept of "manliness," gaining an upper hand in a dispute through a method as surreptitious and intellectual as magic was likely seen as being highly cowardly.

For another thing, the association between seid on the one hand and spinning and weaving thread on the other gave seid an air of being "women's work," unfitting for any "true" man.[22]

Also, during the seid ritual itself, the staff seems to have been held between the legs in a sexually suggestive manner, as if the performer was "riding" it.[23] (Could this be the origin of the popular image of witches riding broomsticks?) The sexual connotations of this position were underscored by the fact that the word *gandr*, one of the words used to refer to the magic staff, could also mean "penis."[24]

*Gandr* could also mean "spirit,"[25] and it is here that we find the clue to what seems to have been the single most important reason why seid was considered to be *argr*. As a seid ritual began, the practitioner yawned, which had the intent of breathing in spirits that would help the work.[26] In the Viking way of thinking, he or she was thereby allowing one of his or her orifices to be penetrated by those spirits – and was therefore effectively the receptive partner in a sexual act.[27]

By the same token, a man who was affected by a seid ritual became *argr* as the practitioner's emissary spirits entered his body. An especially vivid example of this can be found in *The Story of Thorleif the Earl's Poet*. An earl was attacked by seid, and his anus became so unbearably itchy (due to the spirits entering it) that he found himself unable to sit still. The only way he could find relief was to have two men pull a coarse, knotted cloth between his buttocks. As if the tale's early medieval audience needed any additional confirmation of just how "unmanly" the earl had become, his beard rotted away as another side effect of the magic.[28]

Nevertheless, despite the supreme stigma associated with seid, men from all social strata were apparently drawn to practice it due to the extraordinary powers it gave them. According to *The Saga of Harald Fair-Hair*, this even included a king's son. When King Harald admonished his poet Vitgeir for practicing seid, Vitgeir retorted that the king would do better to direct his order to his son Rognvald, who was a known sorcerer. This was so humiliating for King Harald that he had another one of his sons – none other than the brutal Eirik Blood-Axe – murder Rognvald by burning him alive in a hall where he and eighty other "seid men" had gathered.[29] Evidently, King Harald's shame at having a sorcerer in the family was deeper than his love for his own son.

## THE SOCIAL STATUS OF PRACTITIONERS OF SEID

As you'd probably expect, the social status of those who practiced the fearsome art of seid depended largely on the gender of the volva in question. Male volur seem to have been more or less universally reviled, although they would still be called upon to perform their services when their clients had need of them. Their clients' contempt was also mitigated by a sense of fear and awe at their powers.

The status of female volur was more complex. Seid-women were still quite marginal characters, but more in the sense of being "set apart" than scorned. They inhabited the hazy borderlands between the worlds of humans, divinities, and other kinds of beings. To emphasize this, even their graves are described as being literally "set apart" from the graves of others at the margins of burial grounds.[30]

They were also seen in a highly ambivalent light. On the one hand, they were often received with honor, with feasts and lavish gifts, including expensive jewelry, as if they were of exceptionally high status. We saw some of this in the story of Thorbjorg from *The Saga of Eirik the Red*. However – and this, too, can be glimpsed in Thorbjorg's tale – they were seen as untrustworthy and therefore bad company to keep, since their hosts' hospitality was often dependent on them prophesying good fortune and not mentioning bad fortune. In other words, the volur were held to a Viking Age version of our own platitude that "If you can't say anything nice, don't say anything at all." Price aptly characterizes this aspect of their social role as largely being one of "ritual reassurance."[31] They were thought to truly possess the ability to see into the future, but they were expected to report back something pleasant regardless of what they actually saw.

When seid was used to actively accomplish some particular purpose rather than to merely perceive the future, its effects could fall anywhere in the spectrum between help and harm. For that matter, these two poles were often two sides of the same coin; to help one person often meant to harm another. This was especially the case for the Vikings, who believed in an "economy of fortune:" there was a fixed amount of luck in the world, and when one person's luck changed for the better, someone else's luck necessarily must have changed for the worse.[32] When seid harmed someone – especially in cases where someone actually died – the volva who had caused the harm was dealt with just like anyone else who had committed such a crime.

Sorcerers and sorceresses were not infrequently killed by official or vigilante justice. The sagas in particular are replete with examples of this. To cite but a few: in *Gisli's Saga*, an elderly volva named Audbjorg kills twelve people, and is stoned to death. Her brother Thorgrim, likewise a performer of injurious sorcery, is later killed, too.[33] In *The Saga of the People of Laxardal*, a man named Hrut is involved in a dispute over the ownership of some horses. The sorcerer Kotkell and his sons are enlisted by Hrut's opponent to harm him. One night, they climb onto the roof of Hrut's house and begin chanting an exceptionally pleasing and soothing song. Hrut, understanding what's going on, orders his family to stay inside and to stay awake. However, everyone is soon lulled to sleep by the music except for Hrut's youngest and favorite son, Kari. Enthralled by the enchanting sounds, Kari steps out of the house. In the words of the saga, "he walked into the seid and fell down dead at once."[34] For this and other crimes, Kotkell, his wife, and his sons are all stoned to death or drowned.[35] In *Eyrbyggja Saga*, the sorceress Katla makes sexual advances toward a man named Gunnlaug. After he repeatedly refuses, Katla's spirit attacks him and leaves him incapacitated for many months with severe injuries. When the people discover what has happened, Katla is executed.[36]

Those who practiced magic weren't rounded up and killed indiscriminately, like in the infamous Witch Trials of the early modern period. In the above examples from the sagas, the executed sorcerers aren't killed *because* they're sorcerers, but rather as part of the more general honor/blood feud culture, where any murder or grave injury was liable to be avenged by another murder or grave injury. The one partial exception to this in the examples we've seen is the case of the king's son Rognvald and his companions. Apparently, a man's becoming a volva was seen as sufficient grounds for him to be killed by his family due to the dishonor he had brought upon them all.

## SHAMANISM

"Shaman" and "shamanism" are notoriously difficult words to define. The most precise and generally applicable definition to date is probably that of anthropologist Åke Hultkrantz: "we may define the shaman as a social functionary who, with the help of guardian spirits, attains ecstasy in order to create a rapport with the supernatural world on behalf of his group members."[37] That's the definition we'll use here.

The term "shaman" comes from the Evenki word *šaman*. (The Evenki are a Siberian indigenous people.) Technically, the concept of "shamanism" in the sense of "what the shaman does" was invented by modern anthropologists and applied to sufficiently "shamanic" activities in cultures from around the world in order to more readily discuss them in relation to one another. But they didn't invent the term or the concept out of whole cloth, since there *are* ritual functionaries in many, many cultures from all over the world whose roles and activities are *more or less*, but of course never *exactly*, the same as those of the Evenki *šaman*. This makes the concept a highly useful one – even necessary in some contexts – but it can become problematic when used to gloss over cultural differences rather than merely highlighting very real commonalities amongst very real differences. In this regard, it's no different from the concepts of "religion," "ritual," and "worship."[38] To throw out those latter concepts in a book of this sort would be to lose the forest for the trees – and so, too, with the concept of "shamanism." A discussion of Norse shamanism is therefore not only appropriate, but necessary in order to illuminate and contextualize particular aspects of Norse religion.

While the elements in Norse religion that could legitimately be considered to be "shamanic" in some way or another are too numerous to discuss in full here, two aspects of Viking religious practice stand out as being especially noteworthy in this regard. Broadly speaking, we can divide the shamanism practiced by the Vikings into a female sphere and a male sphere.

The female sphere, in a word, was seid. The volva performed her or his ritual actions in the ecstatic trance that forms one of the hallmarks of shamanism, as per Hultkrantz's definition. As we've seen, the practitioner summoned and sent out helping spirits during the course of the seid ritual. And while volur performed rituals on their own behalf in many cases, they were more commonly commissioned by others. Seid-workers – and Freya and Odin as their divine models – were classic shamans.

The male sphere of Norse shamanism consisted of the elite warrior groups known as the *berserkir* ("bear-shirts") and *úlfheðnar* ("wolf-skins"). The berserkers (as we'll refer to members of both of those groups for the sake of convenience), were shamans of a very different sort. After undergoing a period of rigorous training and initiation, they developed an ability to fight in an ecstatic trance that rendered them fearless – and, according to some sources, impervious to danger[39] – while nevertheless inspiring a tremendous amount of fear in their opponents by their behavior, which was at once animalistic and otherworldly. Perhaps needless to say, there was no *ergi* associated with being a berserker. Quite the opposite, in fact – the berserker was seen as being something of a model of manliness.

In the year 970, the Greek historian Leo Diaconus witnessed a band of far-traveling berserkers as they fought against the army of the Byzantine emperor, his employer. He says that they fought in a burning frenzy beside which ordinary battle rage paled in comparison. They roared, growled, bayed, and shrieked like animals, and in an especially eerie and uncanny way. They seemed utterly indifferent to their own well-being, as if lost to themselves. Their leader, who embodied all of these traits to an extreme degree, was thought by Leo to have literally gone insane. Leo and the Byzantine forces were veterans of countless battles, so the reactions elicited by the Scandinavian's behavior in Leo and his companions strongly suggests that what they witnessed in that battle was something unique to the Scandinavians, and something which chilled Leo and the Byzantines to their core.[40]

The berserkers seem to have worked with a number of helping spirits of their own, such as the bear-spirits and wolf-spirits indicated by the groups' names and antics. Some had Valkyries as their "spirit-wives," a practice they had in common with other northern Eurasian shamanic traditions.[41] When they fought, they usually fought for the good of their warband, as well as, in many cases, their civilian communities. Thus, the berserkers, too, fit Hultkrantz's definition of a shaman.

Both the female and male spheres of Norse shamanism had Odin, "The Ecstatic One," as the exemplar of their traditions. Their wild, empowering ecstasy was a gift bestowed upon them by that "terrible sovereign" of a god who kept vats of spiritual mead to be dispensed to those whom he found worthy. When the volur and the berserkers went into their intoxicating trances, they were thought to have been given a coveted sip of this mead.

But how did Odin acquire this mysterious liquor in the first place? That myth, and many others, will be the subject of the second part of this book, to which we now turn.

# PART TWO:
# NORSE MYTHOLOGY

DANIEL MCCOY

# CHAPTER 11: WHAT IS NORSE MYTHOLOGY?

The question "What is Norse mythology?" may seem very simple and straightforward at first glance. But it's actually a good bit more complex than one might think.

Let's begin to answer the question "What is Norse mythology?" by breaking the phrase "Norse mythology" into its two parts: "Norse" and "mythology." We've already defined and discussed what the word "Norse" means in Chapter One. What about "mythology" and its root word, "myth?"

## WHAT IS A MYTH?

The word "myth" can be most appropriately and simply defined as a story intended to convey some kind of timeless, sacred truth.

Why use a story, instead of some other means, to convey what are perceived to be timeless, sacred truths? Stories engage more – and arguably deeper – parts of ourselves than bare, conceptual discourse usually does. They're more entertaining, and they can be more emotionally moving. They're not necessarily *irrational* – especially when one understands the basic assumptions of the worldview out of which they spring – but they *are* generally *nonrational*. They don't *necessarily* contradict a particular rational understanding of the world, but they're not concerned with the rational validity or lack thereof in what they purport to describe. They bypass reason altogether, for better or for worse. Rather than stating an idea and then arguing for why that idea is an accurate reflection of reality, stories go straight to the example, depicting the cosmos as seen through the lens of the idea. They show rather than tell. These factors make stories more persuasive than rational argument, for most people and as a general rule, which is why most if not all societies have entrusted their core beliefs to myth more often than to rational argument.

Some people have a tendency to think of myth as an early, "primitive" groping toward our modern conception of history, so in the interest of arriving at a fuller understanding of what myth is and is not, let's go ahead and dispel that notion. While myth and history both take the form of narrating events that supposedly happened in some kind of past, that's where the similarity between them ends. Myth and history have fundamentally different goals, and because of that, they have fundamentally different methods as well.

History tries, by rational means, to determine what's most likely to have factually happened in the past. Myth tries, by nonrational means, to depict the past as it must have been or should have been in order to give rise to the world (the social world as well as the natural world) in which the person narrating the myth lives or wants to live. Rather than trying to depict the past as factually accurately as possible, myth tries to depict the past in whatever light best serves to legitimize the world it wants to legitimize. This isn't to say that myth attempts to actively subvert what we would call a "historical" understanding of the past, but rather that it treats such a historical understanding as irrelevant. To think of myth as merely deficient history is to fundamentally misunderstand myth.

A "mythology" is simply a collection of myths. It doesn't have to be a rationally coherent system – and most mythologies aren't. Norse mythology, for example, definitely wasn't such a system. At least not originally.

## THE TWO NORSE MYTHOLOGIES

Despite the fact that Norse mythology was never systematized or codified during the Viking Age (this common refrain from Part One of this book applies equally to Part Two), numerous attempts have been made since then to create a single, tidy system out of the disparate stories and fragments of stories that have survived the death of the religion to which they originally belonged. This endeavor goes all the way back to the *Poetic Edda* and the *Prose Edda* of the early medieval period, and continues to the present day.

This effort toward rationalization and systematization, rather than clarifying aspects of "original" Norse mythology that would otherwise be enigmatic or contradictory, actually creates an additional and unnecessary barrier to understanding both the letter and the spirit of Viking Age Norse mythology. This is because these new elements that have been introduced to "smooth out" the old myths are just that: new additions. This tendency has, over time, created what is effectively a second Norse mythology that overlaps with the first, but shouldn't be confused with it.

The first or "original" Norse mythology is simply the collection of scattered sacred stories that the Vikings told to each other. Different communities had their own myths and their own versions of the relatively few myths that seem to have been known and told across the entire Norse world. Even within particular communities, stories would have naturally changed over time. Recall also that Viking society was an oral one in which writing was rarely practiced until the introduction of Christianity. For these reasons, by far the majority of "original" Norse mythology is now lost and irrecoverable.

But even though the *majority* of "original" Norse mythology has been lost, the literary sources discussed in Chapter One preserve some magnificent fragments of what was once evidently an incalculable richness. As we saw in that same discussion, few if any of those literary sources can be taken at face value. The tendency toward rationalization and systematization began with them. Their authors were mostly Christians with centuries of distance between them and the living practice of the traditions they purported to describe. And those authors, even the ones writing in the later part of the Viking Age itself, had agendas that were often antithetical to the faithful recording of their ancestors' lore. The voice of the "original" myths is frequently muffled in these sources, but they're all we have to go on.

Nevertheless, by critically analyzing the contents of these sources – the second Norse mythology – in comparison with one another and with the other kinds of sources we examined in Chapter One, we can make some educated guesses about which parts of them preserve something authentic from the first Norse mythology of the Viking Age, and which parts represent creations by the authors themselves. All is not lost.

## INTERPRETING THE NORSE MYTHS

Once we determine which of the tales from the second Norse mythology are most likely to preserve authentic myths from the first, how should we go about trying to interpret them?

When trying to interpret any myth, many people reflexively turn to the theories of people like James George Frazer, Carl Jung, Sigmund Freud, and Joseph Campbell. While each of those thinkers has developed an intriguing personal philosophy that uses various ancient mythologies as points of reference, their works are dubious guides to any one particular mythology. Their goal is not to understand any one mythology as deeply as possible on its own terms, but rather to identify supposed universal patterns within myth as such, which inevitably turns a blind eye toward the factors that make any given mythology unique. These thinkers, while fascinating in their own right, have little to no light to shed on how the Vikings themselves understood their own myths – which is, after all, the kind of interpretation that matters by far the most in a book of this sort.

So, then, how were the Norse myths interpreted during the Viking Age, when they were still part of a living tradition? The sources never tell us explicitly. But when we attentively examine the content of the myths themselves in their historical and cultural context, we can get a pretty good idea of what they were trying to do and how their listeners would have understood them. The myths seem to have served to convey cosmological lore, to depict the personalities and roles of the gods and other larger-than-life beings, and to provide examples of concepts like fate and honor at work. They illustrated sacred ideas and beings in action. For the Vikings, it would seem, the truth of a myth lay not so much in, for example, "Did Thor actually do such-and-such?" but rather in, "Does this story demonstrate something authentic about Thor's character and roles?"

Finally, we shouldn't underestimate the importance of looking at the Norse myths as, at least on one level, simply "good stories." Humanity being what it is, this was surely the only capacity in which many Vikings cared about them. And in addition to providing high entertainment value, a well-composed and well-told story can be meaningful in a way that has little intrinsic connection to ideas. As scholar of religion Elaine Pagels has pointed out in one of her studies of early Christian texts and communities, which contained an incredible and seldom-acknowledged diversity of perspectives and opinions, "What sustained many Christians, even more than belief, were stories – above all, shared stories of Jesus' birth and baptism, and his teachings, his death, and his resurrection."[1] The stories themselves were what tied people together in the communal religion, despite the great diversity of the interpretations people who belonged to that community had of their shared stories. The same was surely true for the Norse in relation to their own sacred stories.

# THE STRUCTURE OF NORSE MYTHOLOGY

There's no indication that Norse mythology was ever given an overarching, rationally coherent structure in the Viking Age. Given all of the other instances we've found of the lack of systematization in Norse religion as a whole, it would be strange if the Vikings' mythology alone was rigidly and precisely codified. In the words of historian H.R. Ellis Davidson,

> Some scholars... have persevered in the hope that a convincing structure could be built up from the scattered clues, accepting all as of equal value; but this is a hopeless quest, based on the erroneous assumption that a set mythology once existed that was logical and tidy in every detail, and remained so over a long period. All that can be claimed is that certain conceptions concerning the Otherworld were generally accepted, and that the most powerful myths were enacted against this vivid but [by modern standards] confused background.[2]

Our modern zeal for rational structure can't reasonably be projected onto societies far removed from ours, especially when they have given us no indication of sharing that value. Thus, while the lack of systematization in Norse mythology might be a deficiency to us, the Vikings seem to have been utterly untroubled by it. Perhaps they even saw it as giving the myths a certain vitality that kept them swept up in the dynamic flows of lived experience, rather than isolated and static fossils.

In keeping with the Vikings' linear view of time (Chapter Four), Norse mythology does seem to have had a clear beginning in the creation of the cosmos, and a clear end in Ragnarok, the destruction of the cosmos. However, everything that was said to take place in between these two points doesn't seem to have been thought to have occurred in any particular chronological order. Instances in which myth A assumes that the events of myth B have already taken place, but myth B assumes that the events of myth A have already taken place, are common. To someone hearing any one of these stories (or something much like it) in the Viking Age, the tale would have been recognized as both a standalone narrative and part of a greater whole, but its precise position in that greater whole simply wasn't of much interest, as far as we can tell.

The chapters that follow retell the entire body of the most significant Norse myths contained in the literary sources described in Chapter One. Each of these stories about the deeds of gods and human heroes begins with a brief introduction that notes the sources for that specific tale and provides evidence-based guesses as to whether or not (or to what degree) that story is an authentic pre-Christian myth, and if so, how widespread it may have been. The retellings make a point to be faithful to the sources from which they come, while fleshing out some scenes in minor ways that don't alter the plots themselves. Where possible and relevant, I've provided English translations of Old Norse proper nouns.

# Chapter 12:

# The Creation of the

# Cosmos

Fragments of a Norse creation myth can be found in three poems in the *Poetic Edda*: *The Prophecy of the Seeress* (*Völuspá*), *The Song of the Hooded One* (*Grímnismál*), and *The Song of Vafthrudnir* (*Vafþrúðnismál*). The medieval Icelandic scholar Snorri Sturluson used all three of these poems as sources for his account of a Norse creation myth in his *Prose Edda*, and quotes each of them.

Snorri's version of the Viking story of creation is the only one we possess that's actually a full story, but we shouldn't let that trick us into assuming that it's therefore necessarily an authentic product of the Viking Age. The elements in Snorri's story that aren't found in those three Eddic poems are found in no other sources, either, so we have little basis for evaluating which ones originated in the Viking Age, and which ones originated in Snorri's own imagination. This is a topic of fierce and probably irresolvable debate among scholars.

Furthermore, as we've seen, the Eddic poems are problematic for their own reasons. This is particularly true of *The Prophecy of the Seeress*, due to the Christian or at least Christian-leaning theological intentions that apparently frame much of the narrative. But even that poem certainly preserves much true Viking lore along the way. To cite but one especially striking example, one of the lines in the third stanza, *jörð fannsk æva né upphiminn* ("neither the heavens nor the earth existed"), is a formula that can be found virtually word-for-word in religious poetry from throughout the Germanic world.[1] The poet who composed *The*

*Prophecy of the Seeress* evidently possessed an expert knowledge of the lore of his or her ancestors, regardless of the way the poet chose to frame that lore.

Despite the difficulties inherent in Snorri's version of the Norse creation myth, it's the only ostensibly "complete" one we have, and regardless of the degree of its authenticity, it's quite a grand story in its own right.

## THE CREATION OF THE COSMOS

Before there was sky, or ground, or sun, or ocean, or grass, or anything we know from our world, there was nothing but Ginnungagap, the "Yawning Abyss." This void of uninterrupted silence and darkness stretched infinitely in all directions.

Then in the south appeared Muspelheim, the "Land of Fire," and in the north, Niflheim, the "Land of Fog." The fires of Muspelheim blew sparks out into the void, while the icy waters of Niflheim overflowed into the void as well. Fire and ice crept toward each other until, at last, they met in the middle. Amid the hissing and sputtering, the drops from the melting ice formed a being named Ymir, "Scream," the first of the giants. When Ymir slept, he sweated, and from the sweat of his hands and feet came more giants. And so their kind was established.

The drops from the ice also gave rise to another being: the first cow, whose name was Audhumbla, "The Hornless One Rich in Milk." She nourished Ymir with milk from her bulging udder, while she, in turn, was nourished by blocks of salt in the ice. After she had licked the ice for a whole day, a man's hair emerged in the evening. By the end of the second day, his entire head had been uncovered. And by the end of the third day, Audhumbla at last licked the man free of the ice. He was handsome and strong. This was Buri, "Father," the first of the gods.

Buri had a son named Bor, "Son." Bor slept with a maiden from the giants, Bestla. Her name meant "Wife," and she was the daughter of Bolthorn, "Thorn of Misfortune." Bestla conceived and bore three sons: Odin, Vili, and Ve. "The Inspired One," "Will," and "Holiness" turned on the progenitor of their mother's line, and slew him. So much blood gushed forth from Ymir's body that all of the giants were drowned. Well, almost all of them, that is – one named Bergelmir, "Mountain-Bellower," escaped with his family, and from them are descended all the giants in the cosmos.

Then the sons of Bor fashioned the world from Ymir's corpse. From his blood they made the seas, rivers, and lakes. His flesh they sculpted to form the ground, with all of its subtle contours, and from his bones they made the great stones that lie beneath the ground and sometimes stick up from it. Smaller rocks were made from his teeth and from the bones that were broken during his murder. Green and woody plants were shaped with his hair. When the land had taken its shape, they set the oceans in a ring around it. His skull they made into the dome of the sky, and appointed four burly dwarves – who had begun their lives as maggots writhing in Ymir's putrid flesh – to hold it up at the four cardinal points: Nordri in the north, Austri in the east, Sudri in the south, and Vestri in the west. Odin, Vili, and Ve next took embers and sparks from Muspelheim, some great and some small, and placed them in intricate formations rotating around the earth. When they are above the earth, their light shines down upon it, and by them time can be reckoned.

The brothers appointed the outermost part of the land, that which abutted the encircling sea, as the dwelling place of Bergelmir and his kin. But in the center they made a place for humans, who at that time had not yet been made. They called this part of the world Midgard, and to protect it from the giants, they made a great wall around it from Ymir's eyebrows.

By that point, out of all of the pieces of Ymir's corpse, only his brain was left unused. The crafty brothers tossed it into the sky and teased it apart into many strands, which became the clouds. Ymir had been quite hard-mooded, as you might expect for a giant, and this is why clouds are so gloomy and somber to this day.

Finally, from the finest parts of the cosmos, the gods constructed a magnificent dwelling-place for themselves, and called it Asgard.

# CHAPTER 13:

# THE CREATION OF THE

# FIRST HUMANS

The tale of how the first human pair was created comes primarily from *The Prophecy of the Seeress* in the *Poetic Edda*. Snorri repeats the account from that poem in his *Prose Edda* with a few changes.

In its broad outlines, the tale is probably an authentic literary artifact from the Viking Age. Humans first emerging from trees or groves is a theme that's found in several instances throughout the ancient Germanic world, and Ask ("Ash Tree") the name of the first man, was a mythical ancestor of at least one Germanic family.[1] Some of the details of the version in *The Prophecy of the Seeress* seem confused and arbitrary, and it can be reasonably assumed that Snorri's version is the more authentic of the two. The following retelling therefore follows the account from the *Prose Edda*.

## THE CREATION OF THE FIRST HUMANS

After Odin and his brothers had formed the cosmos from Ymir's corpse, and appointed a dwelling place for humans at the center of the visible world, the task of creating the first humans to inhabit that land still remained.

One day not long thereafter, Odin, Vili, and Ve were walking along the beach of the newly-raised landmass. They came upon two large and curiously-shaped pieces of driftwood that had washed up onto the shore. Odin, with a look of solemn excitement on his face, stopped the other two. This was the moment he had been waiting for.

The three gods picked up the two pieces of driftwood and carefully carved them until they had taken on the forms of a human man and woman. But these wooden sculptures, though shapely, were still lifeless.

Odin bent down over them and imparted to them the breath of life. The two humans began to awaken a little bit, opening their eyelids into slits and taking their first breaths. Then Vili leaned in and gave them wits and emotions. Their eyes opened wider, and their muscles began to twitch. Next it was Ve's turn. He gave the pair speech, hearing, sight, and the final details of their appearance. Now the former pair of logs became fully awake and aware, and stared at everything around them with a startled wonder. The gods brought them clothes and dressed them. Then, they gave them names: the man they called Ask, and the woman they called Embla.

The three divine brothers escorted them to their home in Midgard at the center of the land, ringed by the newly-erected wall to protect them from the baleful giants. From them have come all of the humans who have ever inhabited the earth.

# CHAPTER 14:

# HEIMDALL FATHERS

# THE SOCIAL CLASSES

This tale comes from *The Song of Rig* (*Rígsþula*), a poem inserted into one (and only one) of the surviving manuscripts of Snorri's *Prose Edda*. Scholars are divided on the questions of its age and how well it represents views that were held during the Viking Age.

While some elements of the poem may be as young as the fourteenth century – approximately three hundred years after the close of the Viking Age – others are surely much older than that. The idea that Heimdall had a hand in fathering humankind, for example, can also be found in *The Prophecy of the Seeress*, which suggests that both poems drew from a common body of lore.[1]

However, since the actions of Rig are ones that could be expected much more readily from Odin than from Heimdall, it's quite possible that Odin was the original protagonist of this particular story.

## HEIMDALL FATHERS THE SOCIAL CLASSES

When the gods wanted to travel amongst humans and accomplish their often-inscrutable goals, they often took up a disguise and a nickname so that no one would know who they really were. So, when Heimdall left Asgard for Midgard, he called himself Rig, "King," to those he met along his way. At this time, humankind was wayward. No one knew what his proper work should be, and no one knew who should command whom, and toward what ends. Heimdall set out to remedy this situation by organizing humankind into a true society, one with classes, ranks, and titles. Each class would have its own appointed task to carry out.

Rig walked along the grassy pathways that connected the few houses that stood in Midgard at that time until he came to a small, shoddily-built hovel. This was the home of a couple whose names were Ai, "Great-Grandfather," and Edda, "Great-Grandmother." Ai and Edda hospitably invited the traveler in to have dinner with them and spend the night. After the three had eaten their meager portions of coarse, husk-filled bread, the couple lay down to sleep. The clever Rig convinced them to let him sleep between them.

After three nights of this sleeping arrangement, Rig went on his way. Edda, meanwhile, found that she was pregnant, and in due time she gave birth to a son named Thraell, "Farmhand." He had an exceptionally ugly face, rough skin, oversized hands and feet, gnarled fingers and toes, and a twisted back. But despite his uncomely appearance, he proved to be quite strong. He was given hard manual labor to perform, and he performed it ably, carrying heavy burdens all day long. Thraell married Thir, "Bondwoman," a maiden with bent legs, sunburnt arms, and a flat nose. Thraell and Thir had many children, who had names like "Hay Stack" and "Cow Shed." The family spent their days caring for their house, digging turf, spreading manure over the soil, and tending goats and pigs. From them is descended the lowest class, the manual laborers.

Rig came next to a house of ample size and built with some degree of care and art. When he knocked on the door, he was greeted by a couple who introduced themselves as Afi, "Grandfather," and Amma, "Grandmother." Afi was a woodcarver by trade, and Amma spent her days spinning and weaving. Both had neatly trimmed hair, and both were dressed in nice, well-fitting clothes. In the corner of the hall was a chest filled with their possessions.

After a hearty dinner of boiled calf meat, vegetables, and wine, it was time for bed. As he had done before, Rig charmed the couple into letting him sleep between them in their bed. After three such nights, Rig departed.

Amma soon found herself with child, and nine months from Rig's visit, she gave birth to a son named Karl, "Freeman." He had a ruddy face and bright, intelligent eyes. As he grew up, he became an expert craftsman and a deft handler of the plow. He married Snor, "String," a pretty girl who dressed in nice clothes. Together, they had many children, including "Smith," "Man of Honor," and "Farmer," and from their line came the middle class of skilled professionals, merchants, and yeomen.

Rig continued on his way, and at last came to a broad hall with wide doors and a regal ring on the door-posts. Inside, he found a couple dressed in fine clothes and much jewelry. The man was polishing a new hunting bow, and the woman was smoothing out a small wrinkle she had found in her flowing blue gown. The man introduced himself to Rig as Fadir, "Father," and the lady introduced herself as Modir, "Mother." They invited Rig to eat and spend the night with them.

Modir laid a finely embroidered linen tablecloth over her large, intricately carved table. All kinds of rare meats and wines were served in silver vessels. After eating their fill, they got up to go to bed, and once again, Rig persuaded the couple to allow him to sleep in between them in their bed. After three nights, he went on his way.

Nine months later, Modir gave birth to a son who was called Jarl, "Earl." Jarl was exceptionally handsome in every way, and his eyes flashed with all the knowledge and cunning of a serpent. As a youth, he demonstrated consummate skill at archery, hunting, war, horsemanship, and all kinds of sports.

One day, while he was honing his skills by the side of a wood, Rig emerged from the trees and called the boy by his name. He revealed that he was his father, and taught him the runes so that he could broaden his training to include their mysterious, esoteric knowledge and powers.

Jarl became a mighty warlord, expanding his domain through countless military conquests. He married Erna, a beautiful maiden from another noble family. Their children bore names like "Noble" and "Young King." From them came the highest class, that of the aristocrats. In time, one of them surpassed even their father Jarl at all his skills, and took the name Rig in honor of the founder of his line.

# CHAPTER 15:

# THE WAR OF THE GODS

The earliest source that tells a version of the story of the first war in the cosmos is *The Prophecy of the Seeress* from the *Poetic Edda*, which contains it in an abbreviated and very vague form. Snorri Sturluson gives two more partial accounts in his *Prose Edda*, and a fuller one in *The Saga of the Ynglings*.

All four of these accounts are mutually contradictory on various basic points. It's difficult to tell whether this is due to misunderstandings or creative liberties on the part of the authors of those sources, or whether they simply recount different versions that were current in the Viking Age. The following retelling is necessarily a synthesis that picks elements from each in order to form a single, coherent narrative. Where possible, I've made a point to include parts of the various versions that are corroborated to some degree by scattered allusions elsewhere in Old Norse literature, and to leave out uncorroborated elements that conflict with the corroborated ones.

## THE WAR OF THE GODS

One day, as the Aesir gods and goddesses went about their business in Asgard, a sorceress traveled up the rainbow bridge to the entrance of their fortress. At the gate, she gave her name as Gullveig, "Lust for Gold" – although she was surely none other than Freya, the beautiful witch-goddess of the Vanir. The gods were wary of her, and all agreed that those who practiced sorcery weren't the best company to keep. Nevertheless, in the end, they were won over by her charms and her promise to bring them success in all realms of life.

Once in Asgard, Gullveig began going into her trances and running spiritual errands on behalf of whichever deities would pay her handsomely. For a while, the Aesir appreciated her talents. But as time went by, her magical interventions in the affairs of the gods created strife amongst them. Each deity became jealous of the unearned privileges that others were gaining, especially when they allowed one god or goddess to win an upper hand in a dispute against another. Eventually, the discord amongst them reached a fever pitch. The Aesir held an emergency assembly to decide what to do about the situation, and in the end they decided that they had to get rid of Gullveig and make her atone for what she had done to them. The only fitting way to do both, they agreed, was to put the sorceress to death.

They seized Gullveig and tied her up. Then they hurled spears at her from all directions – so many that, under ordinary circumstances, her body would have been reduced to one scarcely recognizable, spear-ridden wound. But the gods failed to take into account the sorceress's ability to turn away weapons, and the sharp points blithely bounced off of her. She laughed gleefully and mockingly at her would-be executioners.

The Aesir then resolved to burn her. But as with the spears, the flames failed to so much as singe a toe or a finger. They attempted to burn her no less than three times, adding more fuel to the flames each time, but each time they accomplished nothing but triggering a long train of scornful cackling from their captive.

But the Aesir did accomplish one thing with their attempts to murder Freya: they earned the vengeful ire of her kin, the Vanir, who promptly declared war on the Aesir. The two sides met on the plain of battle, and when Odin cast his spear over the Vanir, symbolically sacrificing them to himself, both sides knew that the fight was on.

A furious struggle ensued. Both the Aesir and the Vanir fought valiantly. Though the Aesir had more and better warriors, the Vanir had Freya's sorcery on their side. With it, she reduced the mighty planks of Asgard's wall to a heap of splinters and dust.

After the fighting had stretched to encompass many battles, both sides found that they were evenly matched. Neither could gain a decisive advantage over the other, and both were growing weary of what had proven to be an unwinnable conflict. So the warring parties sat down together and forged a truce, agreeing to live in harmony with each other and to share as one body the tribute humans paid to them through their sacrifices.

To seal their pact, they exchanged hostages. The Vanir deities Freya, Frey, and Njord went to live with the Aesir, while the Aesir deities Mimir and Hoenir were sent to the Vanir.

The Aesir were quite satisfied with the gifted gods and goddess they had received. Unfortunately, however, the same can't be said of the Vanir. Though Hoenir had been presented to them as a keen, just, and perceptive ruler, they found him to be dismayingly indecisive. The Aesir knew that Mimir was the wise and impartial one, and Hoenir's beautifully fitting pronouncements were simply repetitions of what Mimir whispered into his ear. Hoenir made up for his lack of wits with his strength and courage in battle, but the Vanir never tested him in that field, and remained unaware of his martial abilities. Neither did they realize that Mimir was the source of Hoenir's apparent wisdom. All they knew was that at times, Hoenir would become inexplicably incapable of issuing judgments, and would stammer out an anxious "Let others decide." They never noticed the pattern: when Mimir was present, Hoenir spoke beautifully and righteously, but when he was absent, Hoenir could barely speak at all.

Thinking they had been sorely tricked, the enraged Vanir beheaded Mimir and sent the god's severed head to Asgard. When Odin laid eyes on it, he was overcome with grief, for Mimir had been one of his most trusted counselors.

By that time, however, Odin had learned some of Freya's magic. He embalmed the head of his fallen companion with herbs and chanted spells over it, preserving it and giving it life once again. From that day, Odin consulted Mimir's head whenever he was in grave need of advice.

# CHAPTER 16:
# THE MEAD OF POETRY

The plot of the tale of Odin's acquisition of the Mead of Poetry begins as an alternate version of the truce between the Aesir and the Vanir that we read about in the last chapter. Rather than exchanging hostages, this version goes, they all spat into a container and produced a new, exceptional being from the pool of saliva.

The Eddic poem *The Sayings of the High One* (*Hávamál*) alludes to three different and mutually contradictory versions of the tale of the Mead of Poetry. But we do possess one complete retelling of one particular version of the tale in Snorri Sturluson's *Prose Edda*, which is the version upon which the retelling below is based. Where Snorri's version differs from the accounts in *The Sayings of the High One*, the details of his version are often corroborated by kennings and other passing references from skaldic poetry, so we can be certain that Snorri based his tale on legitimate sources that are now lost.[1]

In addition to these textual sources for the narrative, scenes from this story are also portrayed in pictorial form on the Lärbro St. Hammars III runestone from Gotland, which was erected around 700 CE.[2] We can be certain, therefore, that some versions of this story were in widespread circulation amongst the Norse even *before* the Viking Age.

The Old Norse name of the mead, which is traditionally translated into English as "Mead of Poetry," is Óðrœrir, "Stirrer of óðr" – and óðr, you might remember, is the root of Odin's Old Norse name (Óðinn). The mead should therefore surely be understood as not only a possession of Odin's, but also a central attribute of his character and an extension of his very nature.

## THE MEAD OF POETRY

After many long and tumultuous yet inconclusive battles, the Aesir and the Vanir arrived at the same bitter conclusion: victory was impossible, because both sides were equal in might and in skill. So they decided to end their conflict peaceably and with mutual accord. To make their treaty official and to preserve a reminder of it for posterity, the two tribes of deities spat into one communal vat. When their spittle mingled, it fermented and formed a new divine being who belonged to both tribes yet neither. Since he combined all their powers, he was the wisest being in all the cosmos. No one could find a question to put to him for which he didn't immediately have a perfect, irreproachable answer. They called him Kvasir, "Fermented Berry Juice."

Kvasir traveled throughout the cosmos dispensing his knowledge to anyone who had need of it. One day, he came to the abode of two dwarves, whose names were Fjalar, "Deceiver," and Galar, "Screamer." The dwarves feigned a desire to speak to Kvasir in private about a matter that was troubling them deeply. Once the god was inside their home and out of sight of anyone else, they cruelly murdered him. They drained his blood into a large container and brewed mead with it. They named their prize mead Odroerir, and anyone who drank of it became a formidable poet or scholar.

When Kvasir went missing, the gods retraced his journey and inquired as to where he had last been seen. When they heard that Fjalar and Galar had been his final hosts, they went straight to their dwelling and demanded to know what had become of him. The dwarves responded with a contemptuous smirk and an assertion that Kvasir had been too wise for his own good, and had choked on his overabundance of wisdom.

Kvasir wasn't Fjalar and Galar's only victim, however. Soon thereafter, the pair invited the giant Gilling for a pleasant trip out to sea in their boat. Knowing that Gilling couldn't swim, the dwarves pushed him overboard once they had rowed a good distance from shore, and watched him drown just for the sport of it.

Afterwards, they rowed back to land and reported Gilling's death to his wife, painting it as a tragic accident for which they bore no responsibility. They asked the giant's sobbing wife if she would like to see the spot where her husband had died, and she said yes. One of the dwarves found a pretext to go outside the house of the giantess before the others, whereupon he picked up an enormous millstone and carried it up to the giantess's roof. When she walked through the doorway on her way out, the dwarf dropped it on her head, and she, too, died. The two dwarves agreed that this had been absolutely necessary, because the sound of her weeping had been unbearably annoying.

But Fjalar and Galar forgot to get rid of the last remaining member of Gilling's family: his son Suttung, "Heavy with Drink." When Suttung found out about the manner of his father's death, he flew into a rage, grabbed the dwarves, and waded out at low tide to a reef that would be submerged when the tide came in. There he dropped Fjalar and Galar, intending for them to be drowned just as they had drowned his father. The dwarves pleaded with Suttung to spare them, but the furious giant remained impervious to their desperate entreaties. Until, that is, they offered him something even more valuable than his revenge: the Mead of Poetry. The giant carried them back to their home, where they quickly took out the mead and presented it to Suttung. So, for a second time, the fermented saliva of the gods became the occasion for a reconciliation between warring parties.

Suttung poured the precious drink into three vats and hid them deep beneath the mountain Hnitbjorg, "Pulsing Rock," and appointed his daughter Gunnlod, "Invitation to Battle," to keep watch over them in that dim, damp chamber.

The far-seeing Odin watched all of this happen from his throne in Asgard. He felt that the mead rightly belonged to the gods, since the being from whose blood it had been brewed was one of them and had been murdered in cold blood. He also craved the powerful elixir in order to expand his own already prodigious abilities. So he came up with a devious plan to obtain it.

Odin left Asgard and came to a field where nine thralls were mowing hay. He walked up to the farmhands with a whetstone in his hand and asked them if they would like their scythes sharpened. The men had been working all day and their blades were dull. They welcomed the offer. Odin sharpened their blades, and the men returned to their work. They immediately found that the scythes cut better than ever before. The grass gave way effortlessly as soon as the blades touched it. The men were amazed, and asked Odin if they could purchase the whetstone from him. Odin said he was willing to sell it, but warned that the price would be steep. The workers insisted that they were still interested, so Odin threw the whetstone into the air a little above the thralls' heads. In their scramble to catch it, each cut the throat of another with his scythe, and all died there in the field.

These had been the farmhands of the giant Baugi, the brother of Suttung. Odin, disguised as a simple traveler and calling himself Bolverk, "Worker of Malice," knocked on Baugi's door and asked for lodging for the night. Over dinner, Baugi told Odin of his anxiety over who would cut his hayfields, now that his workers had all mysteriously killed one another. Odin seized his chance and offered to do the work of all nine of the men if, as his payment, he was given one sip of Suttung's mead. Baugi protested that he had no say in what Suttung did with his mead, and that his brother was determined to hoard it all for himself. But eventually Baugi agreed to Odin's terms, and said he would go with his new worker to help him obtain his payment – once, that is, Odin had kept up his end of the bargain.

So Bolverk set to work. By the end of the summer, he had completed the harvest, the work of nine men, and he went to Baugi and asked for the fee he had been promised. The two went to Suttung's house. Baugi, with some embarrassment, told his brother of the deal he had made with his talented, industrious worker. But Suttung flatly refused to grant either of them even a drop of his cherished liquor. Baugi was ready to turn back in defeat, but Bolverk insisted on getting the payment his employer owed him, and suggested an alternative method to obtain it.

The two made their way to Hnitbjorg, where the disguised god drew an auger out of his cloak and handed it to the giant. The strong Baugi bored and bored, and after a great deal of time had passed, he pronounced the hole complete. To make sure that Baugi was telling the truth, Bolverk blew into the hole. Chips flew back into his face. Baugi was either mistaken, or was trying to deliberately deceive him. The now-suspicious Bolverk told Baugi to keep drilling until he had finished his task. This time, when Baugi said he was finished and Bolverk blew into the hole, he blew the remaining chips through to the other side, and he knew that the hole was truly complete.

If Baugi had harbored any doubts as to the divine identity of his guest worker, they were laid to rest when Odin transformed himself into a snake and slithered through the auger hole. Baugi jabbed the auger in after him, but Odin, who had anticipated such treachery, was too quick for him. Odin made it into Gunnlod's cave, and Baugi stormed away in anger.

When Odin came to Gunnlod, he used all his charms on her, and she became smitten. He agreed to sleep with her for three nights if she would give him three drinks of the mead in exchange. Even though she knew she was betraying her father, she was so overwhelmed with lust for Odin that she consented to the bargain. After three nights, Odin downed the contents of all three of the vats of mead in three enormous gulps, shifted his shape into that of an eagle, and flew out of the cave and toward Asgard.

Suttung saw the eagle fly out of the mountain, and guessed what had happened. He, too, transformed into an eagle and took off in close pursuit of the god.

When Odin approached Asgard, his fellow gods set out several large vats into which he could regurgitate the mead. He made it to his fortress just in time and disgorged the contents of his stomach. Since then, he has given out drinks of the Mead of Poetry to those great men and women whom he has deemed worthy of such an invaluable gift.

But to avoid being caught by Suttung, Odin had had to spit out the mead in great haste, and a few drops accidentally fell from Asgard to Midgard without Odin intending them to do so. From these paltry droplets have come the abilities of all the mediocre artists and intellectuals that have since clumsily attempted to ply their crafts.

# CHAPTER 17:
# THE TREASURES OF
# THE GODS

The tale of how the gods came to possess some of their most characteristic belongings – Thor's hammer, Odin's spear, Frey's ship, and Sif's hair – is told only in Snorri Sturluson's *Prose Edda*. Everything in the story is consistent with other, better corroborated aspects of Norse mythology and religion, but there's no direct evidence for the particulars of the narrative outside of Snorri. Therefore, there's little basis for evaluating to what degree the tale is an invention of Snorri's and to what degree it derives from an authentic Viking Age myth.

## THE TREASURES OF THE GODS

Thor's wife, Sif, was admired by all for her dazzling golden hair. Loki, that incorrigible maker of mischief, sliced off all of it one day for no other reason than his delight in naughtiness. When Sif's fearsome husband found out what had happened, he flew into a rage and seized Loki, intending to break every bone in his body. But Loki pleaded with Thor, promising the thunder god that if his life were spared he'd have the dwarves forge for Sif a head of hair made of real gold, but which would grow like real hair. Thor let the panting Loki drop to the floor, and agreed to let him live on the condition that he fulfilled this promise.

So Loki made his way to the subterranean home of the dwarves, and found the dwelling and forge of the master craftsman Ivaldi and his sons. They took pride and care in crafting not only the golden hair, but also the ship Skidbladnir, which was so big that it could carry all of the gods and their weapons at once, yet could be folded up and fit into a small bag, and always had a favorable wind; and the spear Gungnir, "Swaying," which never failed to hit its mark.

Loki had accomplished his task, but he hadn't fully satisfied his itch for prankishness. So he went to the dwarf Brokk, "Metalworker," and bet his head that Brokk's famed brother Sindri, "Sprayer of Sparks," couldn't fashion three objects on par with the three that Ivaldi and his family had just made. Brokk and Sindri accepted the challenge.

Sindri laid a pigskin bellows on the hearth and instructed his brother to blow into it. Sindri worked for a long time with intense concentration until a fly (who was no other than Loki in disguise) landed on his hand and bit him. But the fly's interference was unsuccessful, for shortly thereafter, Sindri lifted out of the hearth Gullinborsti, a stout boar whose mane and bristles were made of gold so bright that it provided light in darkness, and who could run faster and longer than any horse. Then Sindri placed a block of gold in the hearth and told Brokk to keep blowing while he went out for a little while. Brokk breathed into the pigskin steadfastly, but before too long, a fly buzzed around his head, settled on his neck, and bit him hard. Yet still he kept blowing, and soon Sindri returned and took out of the fire Draupnir ("Dripper"), a splendid arm ring from which eight more rings of equal weight fell every ninth night.

Then Sindri placed iron in the hearth, and bade his brother to blow especially carefully and steadily this time, because the project was especially sensitive and would be spoiled if he were to falter. The fly seized his chance and stung Brokk's eyelid, causing blood to flow into his eyes. Brokk left his position to wipe his face and swat the fly away, which proved to be just long enough for the bellows to go flat. Sindri's face was grave, and he said that this misstep had come close to ruining the undertaking. Luckily, however, it was still salvageable, and before long, Sindri pulled a hammer out of the fire. He handed the hammer to Brokk, along with the ring and the boar, and sent him off to Asgard to claim the payment they were due from Loki.

When Loki and Brokk both arrived in Asgard, the gods sat in council and allowed Loki to present what he had obtained first. He laid before them the shining hair, which went to Sif; the ship, which went to Frey; and the spear, which went to Odin.

Then it was Brokk's turn. The dwarf presented the ring to Odin, the boar to Frey, and, at last, the hammer to Thor. This hammer, the dwarf proclaimed, had abilities that rivaled those of any of the other gifts the gods had received that day. Like Odin's spear, the hammer always hit its mark. Not only that, but when thrown it would return to its owner's hand after striking his foe. Nevertheless, Brokk had to admit that the hammer had a defect on account of the fly's interference: it was short in the handle.

The gods decided that despite the hammer's flaw, it was the best of all of the wondrous pieces of workmanship they had been given that day, because it gave the gods their best defense yet against the giants. On that basis, they decreed that Brokk had rightfully won his bet with Loki and was entitled to his head.

As before, Loki protested and offered to redeem himself, but the dwarf declared that the trickster had already caused enough grief and would be given no respite. Loki then dared Brokk to catch him, and took off running. He was promptly caught by Thor, however, and returned to the dwarf. Just as Brokk was about to chop off Loki's head, the wily god thought of a way out at last. "I promised you my head," he admitted, and then added slyly, "but not my neck. My neck you must leave intact." Brokk was enraged, but had to concede that Loki had a point. So he took an awl and string and sewed Loki's lips together, taking care to inflict as much pain as possible, which he thought a fitting vengeance for the grief Loki's words had caused him.

# CHAPTER 18:

# HOW ASGARD'S WALL

# WAS BUILT

The tale of how the gods' heavenly fortress became fortified is told only by Snorri in the *Prose Edda*. Snorri quotes two stanzas from *The Prophecy of the Seeress* as a source, but those verses are extremely vague, and contain nothing that definitively connects them to Snorri's story. Nevertheless, Snorri's narrative reflects Viking Age cosmological and moral conceptions in such detail that the story is almost certainly at bottom an authentic product of the Viking Age, and Snorri is likely justified in connecting those cryptic lines from *The Prophecy of the Seeress* to his tale.

## HOW ASGARD'S WALL WAS BUILT

When Odin and the gods first built Asgard, it lacked any wall to protect it from invading forces. This absence caused the gods no small worry, because the giants posed an ever-present threat.

One day, a stonemason of the giants appeared before the gods and offered to remedy this situation. However, his demands were harsh: if he could complete the wall in three seasons, his payment would be the sun, the moon, and the hand of Freya in marriage. The gods, fearful at the prospect of losing the beings that brought light, warmth, and fecundity to their world, bargained with the mason.

For obvious reasons, Freya was adamantly against the deal. But Loki argued on the craftsman's behalf, and eventually the following terms were reached: the mason would have to finish his work in only one winter, and if, by the first day of summer, so much as one stone had yet to be laid, he would forfeit his entire payment. He was to be helped by no one save his stallion, Svadilfari, "Unlucky Traveler." Surely, the gods thought, such a feat was impossible, and they'd get at least part of a wall without having to pay anything in return. All swore oaths to uphold the terms of the deal and to ensure the giant's safety in Asgard. The latter was a condition upon which the mason insisted, since the mighty Thor held such hatred of his kind.

On the first day of winter, the giant went to work. By night he used his horse to carry huge boulders to the building site, and by day he placed them on the wall. All the gods marveled at the strength and skill of both man and beast, not to mention how quickly the edifice was being erected. As summer drew closer and closer, the gods grew more and more worried that the impossible was becoming possible: the mason was on track to complete his work in time, and Freya, the moon, and the sun would be lost to him.

When summer was only three days away, the wall was so strong and high that it would be unassailable if any of the foes of Asgard mounted an assault against it. It was still incomplete, but only technically. The terrified gods spoke of breaking the oath they had sworn to the giant mason, and of killing him before he was able to finish his work. But Thor was away in the east fighting other giants at the time, so their best giant-slayer was unavailable for the purpose.

Though all of the gods were to blame for this sorry state of affairs, having all sworn the same oath, they did what we humans so often do in situations of this sort: they found a scapegoat. Loki, they recalled, had gone out of his way to argue on the giant's behalf. Therefore, their collective panic reasoned, he was uniquely responsible for this terrible state of affairs. They resolved to put him to death.

But the ever-wily Loki swore that he could turn this desperate situation into a victory for the gods, even at great cost to himself, if only they would let him live. The gods agreed and released him on the condition that he make good on his pledge.

Night fell. The giant and his stallion went on their way to procure the final stones they needed to build the gate in the wall. Just outside of Asgard, as they passed through a forest, a mare appeared in the path before them and whinnied to the stallion. Then she bounded away into the wood. The aroused stallion snapped his reins and leapt into the forest in pursuit of her. The furious giant charged in after them, but found himself unable to keep up. Soon he had lost their track altogether.

By dawn, the entire night's work had been lost. The giant surveyed the gap in the wall where the gate should be and realized that there was no way he could finish in the scant time he had left. He flew into a murderous rage, bellowing and shaking the ground. He was about to smash the wall he had so laboriously constructed over the past several months and kill anyone inside whom he could get his hands on, when Thor returned from the east. The thunder god wasted no time in raising his hammer and paying the giant the wage he felt he was now due. With one blow, the giant's skull burst into crumbs, and his spirit tumbled down to Hel.

Meanwhile, a foal was growing inside Loki. And, in due time, Loki gave birth. The gray, eight-legged horse grew into the finest and swiftest stallion in all the cosmos. He was named Sleipnir, "The Sliding One," and he would go on to faithfully transport Odin all over the universe on that god's countless shamanic errands.

# CHAPTER 19:

# ODIN'S DISCOVERY OF

# THE RUNES

The word "rune," Old Norse *rúna*, referred to the characters of the ancient Germanic alphabet(s). But it also meant "mystery."[1] The runes were not *merely* letters; they were symbolic encapsulations of some of the most potent forces in the cosmos. Simply writing with them could be an inherently magical act, whereby the forces behind the symbols would bring to pass whatever had been inscribed. The knowledge of the runes therefore imparted immense power to whomever possessed it.

The Norse believed that the runes had originally been discovered by Odin, who then taught them to a select few humans.

The story of how Odin discovered the runes is one of the most widely attested of all the stories that have come down to us from the Viking Age. The main version of the story comes from stanzas 138-141 of the Eddic poem *The Sayings of the High One* (*Hávamál*), a section that has little to do with the earlier part of the poem (a compendium of earthy wisdom) and clearly belongs to a different poem (stanzas 138-164) that was combined into the same manuscript, probably at a relatively late date. However, the scene described in these verses influenced depictions of Christ's crucifixion in Viking-controlled England, the Shetland Islands, and elsewhere. Songs from those areas contain lines that are almost the same, word-for-word, as lines from this section of *The Sayings of the High One*.[2]

Therefore, we can be certain that this tale not only comes from the Viking Age, but that the very wording of the relevant stanzas from *The Sayings of the High One* is based on the wording of pre-Christian religious poetry. These poems were quite widespread throughout the Viking world.

Odin's ordeal in this tale has often been interpreted as a shamanic initiation.[3] While it's impossible to know for sure whether or not this was the case due to the lack of descriptions of such rituals in the Old Norse sources, the scene contains virtually all of the hallmarks of a classic shamanic initiation, so the suggestion is highly plausible.

## ODIN'S DISCOVERY OF THE RUNES

Odin was willing to bring upon himself unimaginable pain and suffering if it served to further his relentless pursuit of knowledge, wisdom, and power. One day, while sitting on his throne in Asgard, from which he could see nearly anything that occurred in the entire cosmos, he gazed longingly at the runes the Norns had inscribed in the trunk and roots of the great tree that held Asgard in its highest branches. He was seized by an insatiable desire to acquire for himself this power to write an idea and make it manifest.

When Odin bent his will toward a goal, he let no obstacles stop him until he had acquired the object of his desire. In this case, he knew that this would entail nothing short of his own death – and rebirth.

The customary method of sacrificing a human to Odin was to have the victim be both strangled and stabbed at the same time. So Odin did the same to himself, hanging himself from Yggdrasil and stabbing himself with his spear Gungnir. It was a double "self-sacrifice:" a sacrifice not only *of* himself, but also *to* himself.

For no less than nine days and nights, Odin dangled from the tree, his nearly-dead body swaying in the piercingly cold wind. No one was able to offer him any food, nor any drink. His mind, more dead than alive, maintained only one thought in it: the runes.

Then, at last, they came to him and filled his mind. He saw their forms, grasped their secrets, and received nine chants of power that would enable him to put them to use. With a bloodcurdling scream of exultant joy, he cut himself free and fell to the ground. His nine-day fast ended when he was revived by a drink from the Mead of Poetry.

From that day, his life became like a seed that had been fertilized. One discovery led to another, and one accomplishment led to another. He acquired powers that others thought beyond the means of even the gods, and it seemed that nothing but unyielding fate stood in his way.

# Chapter 20:

# Why Odin Is One-Eyed

The motif of Odin having only one eye is found frequently not only in Old Norse literature, but in archaeology as well.[1] This was inarguably a genuine Viking Age conception.

The story of how Odin lost one of his eyes – no sources say whether it was the right eye or the left eye, and the question is probably beside the point – is never told in "full" in the literary sources. Snorri references its central act in the *Prose Edda*, and cites a stanza from *The Prophecy of the Seeress* along the way. That stanza, like many from that poem, is very vague, and it's not absolutely certain that it even refers to the story Snorri claims it does.

Nevertheless, this story, all but the gist of which is now lost, is in keeping with depictions of Odin in more reliable tales, especially that of his discovery of the runes. It's likely a truly pre-Christian story, but there's insufficient evidence for us to be able to make that claim with certainty.

## WHY ODIN IS ONE-EYED

One of the wisest of all beings to have ever lived was Mimir, a solitary god – or was he actually a giant? – who dwelt by the well at the base of Yggdrasil. The waters of that well were full of magical properties, and much of his legendary wisdom came from his daily ritual of taking a drink from those murky depths.

Odin, who lusted insatiably for ever greater wisdom, one day rode Sleipnir down Yggdrasil's trunk to its base and to Mimir's dwelling there. He found Mimir sitting at the edge of the misty pool, sipping from his drinking horn, with the expression of one deep in thought. When Mimir looked up from his reverie long enough to notice Odin, he finished his drink and went to greet the god. "What brings you here?" he asked, knowing that Odin went nowhere idly. Odin answered that he wanted to partake of the source of Mimir's wisdom – to have a drink from the well.

"Ah," said Mimir with a hard smile, "and what will you give to the guardian of the well in return?"

"What kind of payment do you demand?" asked Odin, a bit of nervousness showing from beneath his resolute demeanor.

The old warden of the waters replied, "Something of equal or greater value to me, naturally. You know that I, too, am a great lover of wisdom, so something that would increase my own store would be most fitting. You are known for your ability to see far and wide, like a bird of prey. How about one of your eyes, then?"

Odin closed his eyes and breathed deeply for a moment, shocked by the steepness of the price. But he knew what his answer would be even before he had consciously made up his mind. He reached up, dug his fingers into one of his eye sockets, carved out the eye it contained, and handed it to Mimir. As blood spurted from the wound and Odin reeled in stabbing pain, Mimir handed him a full drinking horn with a gesture of solemn honor and admiration.

Mimir placed Odin's eye in the well, and its own immense wisdom and powers infused the waters from which Mimir continued to drink every day.

# Chapter 21:

# The Binding of the

# Wolf

The tale of the birth and capture of the great wolf Fenrir comes only from Snorri's *Prose Edda*. *Loki's Taunts* (*Lokasenna*), one of the poems in the *Poetic Edda*, briefly alludes to the god Tyr having lost a hand to Fenrir, but says nothing more about how this occurred.[1] The motif of Fenrir being chained and breaking free at Ragnarok is found throughout Old Norse literature, however. Snorri's tale likely has a basis in ancient lore, but the origin of the details of the story is anyone's guess.

## THE BINDING OF THE WOLF

Loki had many children with many different mothers – and fathers. With the giantess Angrboda, "Distress-Bringer," he had three. One was Hel, "Grave," the ghastly goddess who presided over the underworld. The second was Jormungand, "Mighty Beast," the great serpent who festered beneath the ocean, his elongated body encircling the land. And the third was Fenrir, "Marsh-Dweller," an enormous and ravenous wolf.

When they were first born, however, these children of Loki had not acquired these roles that they would later assume. Angrboda suckled them in Jotunheim, the land of the giants, and at first they seemed scarcely more dangerous than any other giants. But as they grew – and as the gods got wind of ominous prophecies that foretold that the doom of the cosmos would one day come through these fell creatures – the deities assembled together to address the peril that loomed before them. Odin ordered the three to be brought before him. As soon as he saw how prodigiously they had grown since the last time he had laid eyes on them, and how much more dreadful each of the monsters seemed than before, he immediately cast two of them into remote regions from which they could do the gods relatively little harm, at least for the time being. Hel he sank into the underworld, which is how she received her position as the ruler of the dead. And Jormungand he threw into the ocean, which in time he almost outgrew, to the point that he had to wrap himself around the entire land mass in order to fit.

Fenrir, however, inspired so much fear in the gods' hearts that they decided to rear the pup themselves in Asgard, where they could keep an eye on him. Of all of them, only the brave Tyr dared to go near enough to his pen to give him the ever more massive slabs of meat that he required every day to keep him fed. Eventually, however, the wolf grew so grotesquely large that the divinities could no longer bear to maintain him so close to them. They thought of killing him, but couldn't bear the thought of desecrating their holy stronghold with bloodshed. So they hatched a plan to disarm him.

They presented Fenrir with a strong chain, and proposed a game to him: they would tie him in the fetter and let him break free to demonstrate his incredible strength. The wolf scoffed at what seemed to him like a puny string, and agreed to play. As soon as he was bound, he gave a half-hearted struggle and easily snapped the chain. Then the gods had another chain forged, one that was stronger by half than the first chain, and presented this to Fenrir on the same terms. The wolf thought the task of escaping from this bond to be more daunting than the previous one. But he wanted the whole world to know his strength, so he accepted the risk and agreed to a second round of the game. When the fetter was placed around him, he struggled mightily for a long time, but in the end tore through this chain, too, and gloried in his feat.

After this formidable accomplishment, the gods began to worry that they might never successfully bind the wolf. Their only hope was to have the dwarves, those master craftsmen, build the most exquisite chain that anyone had ever seen. They sent Frey's emissary, Skirnir, to the land of the dwarves to explain the situation and enlist their aid in neutralizing this cosmic terror. The result of this mission was the fetter Gleipnir, "Open," which the dwarves made from the sound of a cat's footsteps, a woman's beard, the roots of a mountain, a bear's tendons, a fish's breaths, and the spittle of a bird. These are things that no one has ever encountered – and which, therefore, can never be put to the test.

The gods took Fenrir with them to a remote, marshy island in the middle of a wide lake. There, the gods presented the third chain to Fenrir. The wolf appraised it with puzzlement. It looked like a tiny silk cord, so thin that it was almost invisible. The beast suspected trickery, but knew that he would be called a coward, and his reputation ruined, if he refused. So he declared that he would agree to be bound with this manacle, but only if one of the deities would place his or her hand in the wolf's mouth as a pledge that they weren't trying to deceive him.

The deities were astonished and afraid. They should have expected such a demand from the wolf, and perhaps in their hearts they had. But now that the time had come for one of them to sacrifice a hand to uphold a false oath, or for all of them to refuse and allow the wolf to know their plot and arouse his anger, they all demurred. All, that is, except Tyr, who agreed to the wolf's terms. He stuck his trembling hand in the beast's hot, wet mouth, and felt his razor-sharp teeth laying lightly on his wrist.

Gleipnir was tied around Fenrir, and the contest began. Fenrir struggled with all his might. But the more he struggled, the tighter the fetter wound itself around him. In the end he found himself unable to break free. All of the gods were doubled over in laughter at the wolf's sorry predicament – except for Tyr, who duly lost his hand.

The gods tied a heavy chain to Gleipnir, then tied the chain to a great boulder, then drove that boulder into the ground with an even greater one, pinning the wolf in place. When he opened his mouth to try to bite his captors, they thrust a sword between his jaws to hold them agape and unable to clamp down. He howled ferociously and unceasingly, and his saliva began to form into a gushing river. And there has he laid throughout the eons, striving futilely against his imprisonment. But at Ragnarok, the prophecies foretell, he will win his freedom at last, and shall have his vengeance upon the gods and their world.

# Chapter 22:

# Thor Fishes for the

# Great Serpent

Thor's attempt to hoist his arch-enemy Jormungand out of the ocean and slay him forms the backbone of one of the oldest and best-attested Norse myths that has come down to us. No less than four literary sources tell the tale in "full," although the details naturally differ between them. These include two Viking Age skaldic poems: Bragi the Old's *Poem of Ragnar* (*Ragnarsdrápa*) and Ulf Uggason's *House Poem* (*Húsdrápa*). The tale is also contained in *The Poem of Hymir* (*Hymiskviða*), which is one of the pieces in the *Poetic Edda*, and is given a lengthy treatment in Snorri's *Prose Edda*.

Archaeology furnishes us with additional corroborations in the form of scenes from the story visually depicted on large picture-stones, most notably the Altuna stone in Sweden and the Gosforth stone in England.[1]

Therefore, in the surely accurate estimation of philologist Rudolf Simek, "a knowledge of the myth can be assumed for the whole of Viking Age and medieval Scandinavia."[2]

## THOR FISHES FOR THE GREAT SERPENT

Thor traveled to Jotunheim, the wild, forbidding land at the outer edge of the cosmos, on numerous occasions. Often, he went with the sole intention of killing giants, in which case he needed no disguise. But sometimes, his goal involved enlisting the aid of particular giants along the way. Such undertakings called for assuming a character so that the giants whom he met wouldn't recognize him for who he was: the foremost enemy of their kind, who had killed more of them than any other being in the universe by far.

Once, Thor journeyed to the land of the giants in hopes of obtaining what was, to his mind, the greatest prize out there to obtain: the head of Jormungand, that grisly son of Loki who coiled around all the land in the vast ocean that lay beyond its shores. Due to the delicate nature of this mission, which would involve lodging with the giants themselves on his way to the far side of Jotunheim, Thor prudently decided to don a disguise – in this case, that of a simple young man from Midgard.

The humble lad made it to the house of the giant Hymir, who dwelt on the rugged, weather-beaten coast, and he stayed there overnight. In the morning, his host, who was a fisherman by trade, prepared to row out to sea. Thor announced that he wanted to be a helpful guest, and to go with him to fish. But Hymir scoffed at the offer, saying that the youth would freeze to death before the end of the day's work. Thor was so incensed that he had to summon all his strength to resist the urge to pull out his hammer and smite the giant right then and there. But he turned his desire down, and instead calmly insisted to the giant that he would not freeze, and that furthermore he wanted to row farther out and stay longer than the giant was accustomed. Hymir laughed at what he thought was just a brash, foolhardy boy, and agreed to let him come.

Thor asked Hymir what they would use as bait. His host replied that if he was so confident in his abilities as a fisherman, he should go get his own bait. So Thor walked out of Hymir's house and into the pen where the oxen were kept. He grabbed the largest ox, a humongous bull, and beheaded him.

When he reached the shore with the ox's head under his arm, he found that Hymir had already pushed the boat out. He splashed over to the boat, climbed into the stern, grabbed two oars, and started to row. Hymir was startled by how fast his guest was able to row. Before

177

long, they had reached the area where Hymir usually stopped to fish. "That's enough rowing," he called to his companion in the stern. "We're here."

But Thor kept rowing, and rowing, and rowing. The shore receded further into the distance, and then disappeared altogether. Hymir commanded his guest to row no further, lest they draw near to the dreaded serpent that dwelt in these deep waters. But Thor replied that he intended to go out just a little further, and, over the giant's protestations, he did so. By the time Thor reached the point where he was content to stop rowing, Hymir's fear chilled him more than the cold, hard wind that blew relentlessly over those waters. He marveled at how such a mediocre-looking youth not only had the stamina to make it out this far, but the courage to do so as well.

The disguised god laid down his oars. He readied a strong fishing line and tied an enormous hook to its end. On the hook, he placed the ox's head. Then he cast his line and waited.

After a while, the two began to hear a faint rumble coming from all around them. As it grew closer, it became louder and more fearsome. The boat trembled, and the fishing gear in the bottom clanked and clattered as it was tossed to and fro. Then there was a great crash as the serpent snapped at the bait, and then the whole ocean seemed to jerk away as the snake clamped down on the hook and tried to free himself. Thor braced himself and began to reel in his line with all his might. His feet broke through the bottom of the boat, but still he pulled and pulled. At last, Jormungand's head began to rise from the waves. His burning eyes stared implacably into those of Thor, who glared back at him with a face of utter enmity and determination. The snake spat venom, and the god swerved to avoid it. Thor raised his hammer and prepared to deliver the death blow to his enemy.

But the prophecy that neither the monster nor the god were to slay each other until Ragnarok had to be fulfilled. Hymir had been cowering in fear at the far corner of the boat this whole time, but when he saw the beast's head before him, he could bear this mortifying scene no longer. With one swift, anxious motion, he swiped at the line with his fishing knife, slicing through it and cutting Jormungand free. The bleeding ghoul wasted no time in diving to the bottom of the ocean, where Thor couldn't reach him.

Thor's rage was now greater than ever before, and he lunged at the giant who had prevented him from smiting his arch-foe. With one mighty blow to the head, Hymir was knocked overboard, and fell face first into the waters. When the soles of the giant's feet had disappeared into the cold murk, Thor abandoned the waterlogged boat and waded to shore.

# CHAPTER 23:

# THE KIDNAPPING OF

# IDUN

The obscure goddess Idun "stars" only in this one myth. The tale of her kidnapping and rescue comes from the tenth-century skaldic poem *Autumn-Long* (*Haustlöng*) by Thjodolf of Hvin, as well as Snorri's version from the *Prose Edda*, which is based on Thjodolf's poem but adds a considerable amount of material that can't be found in it. Numerous kennings and other brief allusions in skaldic poetry demonstrate that several different versions of this tale were in circulation in pre-Christian times.[1] Most of the otherwise unattested elements in Snorri's version probably come from one or more of these now-lost variants.

The rejuvenating food that Idun kept is usually referred to as "apples" in modern literature on Norse mythology. However, it's virtually impossible that this was originally the case, since apples were only introduced into Scandinavia in the Middle Ages. The Old Norse word used to refer to her fruit, *epli*, was a generic word for any fruit or nut, so it's unclear which species Idun's produce was thought to be.[2]

## THE KIDNAPPING OF IDUN

Odin, Loki, and Hoenir went on a journey that took them through a barren, mountainous land. They could find little food to eat, and they were hungry. Then, when they rounded a certain mountain crest and caught sight of the valley below, they saw that a herd of oxen was grazing in the valley. Here, at last, was enough meat for a proper meal! They cut the throat of one of the oxen, made camp, and started cooking the meat on their fire.

After what seemed to them like sufficient time to cook the meat, they took it out of the fire. To their great surprise, it was still as cold and uncooked as it had been when they put it in the fire. So they put it back in, rearranged the embers around it, and chatted for a while. When they took the meat out for a second time, it was just as raw as before. They were quite perplexed by this, and discussed what might have been going on.

In the midst of their deliberations, a low, cruel voice addressed them from above, saying, "It is I who have rendered your fire useless." Startled, the three gods looked up, and saw an exceptionally large eagle sitting on the bare branch of a gnarled, dead tree. The eagle said to the three, "If you will give me a share of your meat, I will release my magic and allow your fire to cook." After briefly consulting with each other, the three gods agreed to the terms of this mysterious bird. The eagle then flew down from the tree, alighted by the meat, and began selecting his portion. When he had finished, he had set aside all the choicest parts of the ox for himself. This perturbed the temperamental Loki, who picked up a thick stick that was lying beside him and struck at the eagle with it. But the branch stuck to the bird's back, and Loki's hands stuck to the branch. The eagle flew off, with Loki helplessly bound to him.

The sorcerer bird darted over the bleak terrain just low enough to the ground that Loki's legs slammed into trees, boulders, and mountainsides. Loki felt like his body was about to rip apart. At last, fear and pain overcame his rage, and he begged his captor to let him go. The eagle chuckled, and said sternly that he would not. Loki cried and pleaded, and the bird finally said to him, "Well, there is one thing you could do to secure your release, but one thing only. I have seen how you gods are nourished by the succulent fruits that are kept by the beautiful goddess Idun. Because you eat that fruit, you never grow old, nor die of age. Swear an oath to me here and now that you will bring me both Idun and her fruit, and I will set you down." Desperate, Loki swore the oath, and was returned to his companions.

Loki and the eagle had agreed that at a certain time, Loki would coax Idun out of Asgard, and the eagle would be there to carry her off. Loki followed through with his end of the bargain, and led Idun to believe that he had found a grove outside of Asgard's walls where there grew fruits even more marvelous than hers. He offered to show it to her, and suggested that she bring her basket of fruit so that she could compare hers to the ones that grew there. She could scarcely believe the tale, but couldn't pass up such an opportunity. When the two had gone a sufficient distance from the gods' stronghold, the eagle – who was none other than the giant Thjazi – swooped in, snatched up the goddess, and carried her away to his home in Thrymheim, "The Home of Thunder." Thrymheim was an icy land high in Jotunheim's mountains where nothing ever grew and no birds ever sang.

Without Idun and her rejuvenating fruits, old age began to creep up on the gods. Their skin wrinkled, their hair turned white and started to fall out, and their bodies became frail and diseased. They held a council to decide what to do about this. When they attempted to retrace where and when Idun had last been seen, it became clear that it was when she went out of Asgard with Loki. "Ah, of course," the deities sighed, practically in unison, embarrassed that they hadn't thought to consider the possibility of Loki's involvement sooner.

Loki was seized and dragged before the assembly, where he was threatened with a slow, torturous execution if he didn't retrieve Idun and her fruit himself. Terrified, he immediately agreed to get her back, and he instantly thought of a plan by which he could do so. Freya owned a set of hawk wings that enabled their wearer to transform into a hawk, and Loki said he would need these. Freya – perhaps the most anxious of all about her diminishing beauty – granted his request.

Loki put on the hawk wings and took off in flight to Thrymheim. When he arrived at the home of Thjazi, he found that the giant was away at sea on a fishing trip, and Idun was alone in his house. He changed her shape into that of a nut, picked her up in his talons, and sped away to Asgard.

A short while later, Thjazi returned from his fishing trip. When he found Idun missing, he surmised what had happened. Though tired from his trip, he wasted no time in donning his eagle plumes and taking off for Asgard. The sound of his wings swooshed and boomed through the air.

When the deities spied the hawk flying toward Asgard with the nut in his claws, and the mighty eagle in pursuit, they spread out piles of sawdust and kindling along the fortress walls. The moment Loki had passed the walls safely, they threw torches on the fuel, and huge flames immediately shot up high into the sky. Thjazi tried to turn back, but his furious momentum proved to be his downfall. He flew straight into the flames, which burned off all his feathers, and he fell to the ground inside Asgard. The gods gathered around his squirming and badly burnt body, and finished him off. Both youth and the precious Idun were restored to the gods.

# Chapter 24:

# The Marriage of

# Njord and Skadi

The plot of the story of the marriage between the summery, fun-loving god Njord and the stern, wintry giantess (and honorary goddess) Skadi picks up where the plot of the story of the theft of Idun left off. This tale comes only from Snorri's *Prose Edda*. While the myth's contents are certainly in keeping with tales we know for sure date from the Viking Age, the lack of independent corroboration of many of the details of Snorri's narrative makes it difficult to say with certainty to what degree it's an authentic product of pre-Christian times, and to what degree particular elements may have been created by Snorri.

## THE MARRIAGE OF NJORD AND SKADI

While the gods were feasting in celebration of their slaying of the giant Thjazi and the return of Idun to their halls, an uninvited guest stormed into their merrymaking.

It was the giantess Skadi, the daughter of Thjazi, who had arrived with armor and weapons to avenge the death of her father. The gods were patient with her, and after many conciliatory words, they convinced her to accept compensation instead of seeking vengeance.

Their payment came in three parts. First, Odin took Thjazi's eyes and ceremoniously cast them into the night sky, where they became two stars.

Second, the gods set out to make Skadi laugh. After many feats were tried, none succeeded in bringing a smile to the stony face of the giantess. At last, Loki tied one end of a rope to a goat and the other end around his testicles and began a game of tug of war with the goat. Each screeched and howled in turn, until at last Loki fell over into Skadi's lap. The giantess's mood thawed, and she couldn't help but giggle.

Third, Skadi was to be given a god of her choosing in marriage, but she was to select him by the sight of his legs and feet alone. She picked the fairest pair of legs she could see, thinking them to be those of Balder. However, as it turned out, they were those of the sea god Njord.

Skadi and Njord had a magnificent, lavish wedding fitting for a god and his bride. Afterwards, the newlyweds had to decide where to live, and found the festive mood of their wedding already giving way to contention. Njord's home was Noatun, "The Place of Ships," a bright, warm land on the beach. Thrymheim, Skadi's home, couldn't have been more different: a dark, foreboding place in the highest mountain peaks where the snow never melts.

The pair first spent nine nights in Thrymheim. When this time had passed and they made their way down from the mountains, Njord declared that, although brief, his time in Thrymheim had been loathsome. He had been particularly dismayed by the sounds of the wolves, to which he overwhelmingly preferred the songs of the swans to which he was accustomed.

After the two had slept for nine nights in Noatun, Skadi had similar opinions to express regarding the sunny home of Njord. The cries of the seabirds had been unbearably abrasive to her ears, and she had found it impossible to sleep. So she departed for the mountains, and the two parted ways.

# CHAPTER 25:

# THOR AND GEIRROD

The earliest surviving source for the myth of Thor's journey to the court of the giant Geirrod ("Protection from Spears") in Jotunheim is the tenth-century skaldic poem *Poem of Thor* (*Þórsdrápa*) by Eilif Godrunarson. Snorri, using Eilif's poem as his main source, retells the tale in the *Prose Edda*. Elements from the narrative are included by Saxo Grammaticus in his *History of the Danes*, and a fourteenth-century Icelandic short story called the *Tale of Thorstein* (*Þorsteins Þáttr*) recounts another version of the tale.[1] Since we possess no less than four different versions of the tale, and since one of them comes from the later part of the Viking Age itself, we can be certain that this is indeed an authentic Norse myth.

## THOR AND GEIRROD

Frigg, like Freya, owned a fine set of hawk wings that had the power to transform their wearer into that bird of prey. One day, Loki, in his usual prankish mood, stole them and put them on. In his assumed form, he gallivanted around the land of the giants, enjoying the thrill of the bracing wind in his wings and the sight of mountain beyond mountain beyond mountain below.

When he flew near the hall of Geirrod, a giant chieftain, curiosity overcame him. He flew in through a window and alighted on a wooden beam so that he could watch and hear what was going on inside. But Geirrod spotted him and ordered one of his men to capture the regal-looking bird. Loki took great pleasure in flitting through the great hall, maneuvering around the many beams and poles that held up its towering walls and ceilings. He would land and wait for Geirrod's man to shimmy up the nearest pole after him, then take off at the last instant before he could be grabbed. But after doing this countless times, he at last found his feet stuck to the wood as if by magic, and he was caught.

He was taken before Geirrod, who noted a sparkle of peculiar intelligence in the bird's eyes. Suspecting that the hawk was actually another giant or a god in disguise, Geirrod locked him away in a trunk and starved him for no less than three months.

When he was finally taken out of the trunk, Loki – still in his hawk form – was at the brink of death. He was in no position to continue playing games. So when Geirrod asked him who he really was, he answered, and answered honestly.

This delighted Geirrod, for now the already-great chieftain had a chance to become even greater. He told Loki sternly that there was one condition upon which his life would be spared, and one alone: he would coax Thor, the foremost enemy of Geirrod's kind, to come to the chieftain's hall without his hammer, his belt that doubled his strength, or any weapon or armor of any kind. Loki, having little choice, agreed, and was released.

When he arrived back in Asgard, Loki conjured up a cunning rationale to obtain Thor's consent to accompany him on a trip to Geirrod's court unarmed. Along the way, they spent the night at the house of a giantess named Grid, "Greed." When she heard what the destination of her guests' journey was, she became tense. She warned them that Geirrod was crafty, and dangerous to have dealings with. Alarmed that her guests were traveling to Geirrod's hall unarmed, she equipped Thor with several of her own possessions, which she assured him would serve him well: her own Belt of Might, a pair of iron gloves, and a metal rod.

After thanking Grid and departing from her house, the two came to the River Vimur, "Frothing," and had to cross to the other side of the torrential current. Thor put on the Belt of Might that Grid had given him, and Loki clung to Thor by that belt. When the pair had reached the middle of the river, the waters began to rise and the current became even stronger than before. Thor was now in up to his shoulders, and even with his Belt of Might, he had to fight hard to maintain his footing. Looking around to see what might be causing the sudden blast, he spied the giantess Gjalp, "Roarer," a daughter of Geirrod, standing upstream from them. She straddled the river, with one leg on one bank and her other leg on the opposite bank, and she was urinating into the water, doubling its flow. Thor recited the proverb that "a river should be stemmed at its source," picked up a hefty rock, and hurled it at the gushing giantess. His aim was true, and she fell down dead in her own discharge.

Thor then lunged toward a rowan tree growing by the bank of the River Vimur, grabbed onto it, and pulled himself out of the raging torrent. After this, to commemorate the rowan's role in saving the thunder god's life, its species was called "Thor's rescue."

When Thor and Loki arrived at Geirrod's hall, their host showed them to the barn where goats were kept. There would be great entertainment there, he promised. Once inside, they found that there was a single seat, and Thor was invited to sit on it as the guest of honor. Just when he had gotten comfortable, however, the chair began to rise toward the ceiling. An instant before he would have been crushed between the chair and the rafters, he took out the rod that Grid had given him and pushed against the ceiling with all his strength. Two hideous snapping sounds followed, and then a cacophony of wild shrieks before the chair tumbled to the ground with a great thud. Two of Geirrod's daughters, as it turned out, had been lifting the chair up from beneath, and when Thor forcibly stopped its rise, he had broken both their backs. As the two lay on the floor, helplessly writhing in unbearable pain, their father invited the guests into his main hall to play games.

Bright, warm fires glowed from the sides of the chieftain's otherwise dark hall. Geirrod's face glowed eerily in the dim, shifting light as he proposed a wrestling match between himself and Thor. Naturally, the champion of Asgard accepted. When the fight began,

Thor threw himself at Geirrod with utter abandon. But Geirrod swerved to avoid him. In the same motion, he bent down and grasped a pair of tongs. With these, he picked up a bar of glowing hot iron from the fire and hurled it at his opponent.

But Thor caught the bar in the iron gloves he had been given by Grid. When he raised his arm to throw it back at his assailant, Geirrod ducked behind an iron pillar in hopes of saving himself. But the thunder god's arm launched the blazing bar through the iron pillar, through Geirrod's body, through the side of the hall, and into the ground outside, where, at a great depth, it finally came to rest. Thus died Geirrod the giant.

# CHAPTER 26:

# THE THEFT OF FREYA'S

# NECKLACE

Only a fragment of one late version of this myth survives. It comes from the *Tale of Sorli* (*Sörla Þáttr*) in the *Flat Island Book* (*Flateyjarbók*), a compendium of sagas written in Iceland in the fourteenth century. Due to the centuries that had elapsed between the composition of the *Tale of Sorli* and Viking religion as a living practice, the narrative in its present form has undoubtedly been "corrupted" by the addition of elements that weren't found in any version of the story from the Viking Age. (In the retelling below, I've made a few minor changes to "restore" the most blatantly Christianized moments to a hypothesized more original form.) However, the basic outline of the story is alluded to elsewhere in the sources, and the actions of the characters are generally consistent with their portrayals in earlier, more reliable sources, so we can conclude that the story is ultimately woven around an authentic Viking myth.[1]

Based on the passing references to this tale in other Old Norse sources, it seems that one of the now-lost parts of the narrative featured a fight between Loki and Heimdall over possession of the necklace.[2]

Another noteworthy aspect of the version of this story in the *Tale of Sorli* is that the somewhat artificial and strained splitting of Freya-Frigg into two separate goddesses, and Odin-Od into two separate gods, is absent here. Freya is said to be Odin's wife – a "rationalistic" gloss that may suit our modern taste for the elimination of redundancy.

## THE THEFT OF FREYA'S NECKLACE

While out walking one day, Freya happened to come upon a craggy boulder that was known to be an entrance to the winding caverns where the dwarves lived. On this particular day, the rock had been left askew, and she snuck a peek down into their subterranean forges. She couldn't help but notice that four dwarves were forging a gorgeous golden necklace. It was almost completed, and had already been inlaid with the finest, most brilliant jewels she had ever seen. Before she knew it, she had made her way down into the cave and had struck up a conversation with the smiths about their work.

The four dwarves were named Alfregg, "Accomplished;" Dvalin, "Short;" Berling, "Short Beam;" and Grer, "Bellower." They refused Freya's offers to purchase their handiwork with gold, silver, and other treasures. But when the exasperated and covetous goddess asked if there was anything, anything at all, for which they'd be willing to sell the necklace, the dwarves smiled knowingly at one another, and then back at Freya. They would only give her the necklace, they said, if she would spend one night with each one of them in turn. As repulsed as Freya was by the grimy, sooty, and just plan ugly dwarves, her lust for the necklace overcame her aversion to such an unwelcome deed, and she consented to the dwarves' terms.

Four days later, Alfregg, Dvalin, Berling, and Grer handed her the necklace, which was called Brisingamen. She took it back with her to Asgard and acted as if nothing out of the ordinary had happened. But the scheming Loki found out about Freya's necklace, and how she had come to be in possession of it. He told this to Odin, who commanded Loki to pilfer the necklace from his wife and bring it to him. Loki protested, saying that Freya's bedroom was impenetrable due to how jealously Odin himself had her guarded. But this only angered the chief of the gods, and he repeated his command to Loki, this time more sternly than before. Loki gave in, and sulked away. After a great deal of wayward brooding, however, an idea finally came to him.

Night fell. Loki took on the form of a fly and slipped through an almost imperceptible crack in the door to Freya's chamber. Inside, he found Freya and all of her servants sleeping soundly. But the goddess was sleeping on her back with the necklace around her neck, and the clasp was underneath her. So Loki turned into a flea and bit the goddess on the neck. This woke her up just enough that she turned onto one side, exposing the clasp. Loki changed back into his regular form, delicately peeled the necklace off of her neck without waking her, and tiptoed out of the room through the door without waking anyone.

Freya awoke in the morning to find that her door was ajar and her precious necklace was gone. When she deduced what had happened, her shock turned to anger. After throwing on a robe, she stormed into her husband's court and demanded that he return the Brisingamen to her. But Odin was unmoved, and said that because of the manner in which she had obtained the necklace, she didn't deserve to ever have it back. "Unless," he added, feigning the sudden arrival of the idea, "you can pit two kings, each with twenty other kings in their service, against each other. Enable great heroes to arise among men, and fill the ranks of my armies in Valhalla."

Freya agreed to these terms. Before long, she had incited the kings to battle, and a mighty feud ensued that claimed untold lives. The Brisingamen, unparalleled among all pieces of jewelry, became Freya's once again, and she wore it proudly from that day on.

# Chapter 27:
# Odin's Exile

We've seen how members of Norse society might be outlawed for committing especially serious offences against others. Odin, you may recall, was the patron god of outlaws. This was probably at least partially because, on at least one occasion, Odin himself was banished from Asgard by the other gods.

The sources provide us with no less than three (all very brief) accounts of the myth of Odin's exile: one in Snorri's *The Saga of the Ynglings*, and two from Saxo's *History of the Danes*. All three versions are radically different from one another – they have scarcely more in common than the general theme of the chief of the gods being banished from the kingdom over which he ruled. This diversity is hardly surprising for myths that were originally passed down orally, but it does present problems for those who want a "canonical" version of any given myth.

The retelling below is my own composite version. It selects pieces from each of the three variants and stitches them together to form a single coherent narrative. I've tried to include the elements that seem most in keeping with motifs and attitudes that run throughout the sources, and to exclude those that have a ring of medieval folklore, fantasy, and misunderstanding. Perhaps this version is therefore actually closer to the versions the Vikings told amongst themselves, but perhaps not.

# ODIN'S EXILE

The gods got together and decided to honor their illustrious ruler by erecting a statue of him in Asgard. They commissioned the dwarves to craft it, and those expert smiths did a marvelous job. It was a spitting image of the chieftain of the gods, emphasized all of his most flattering aspects, and had a powerful air of the wisdom, insight, and warlike prowess for which Odin was so famous. The entire statue, from the top of its head to the base upon which it stood, was covered in gold. When the gods presented it to Odin, he was deeply proud and grateful, and had it placed at the entrance to his court.

But Odin's wife, Frigg, was as great a lover of gold as she was of her husband. She yearned to possess such an enormous amount of the precious metal for herself. One night, she had several smiths steal the statue and melt down all of its gold to make jewelry for her. When Odin found the statue missing the next morning, he flew into a rage, and when he found out what had happened, he had all of the smiths executed by hanging. Then, once the statue had been rebuilt, he cast secret seid spells over it so that whenever someone touched it, it would cry out.

Frigg had been disgraced by the exposure and failure of her thievery, and she burned for revenge against her husband. First, she slept with one of her male servants, and made sure that everyone knew about it. Then, she convinced him to destroy Odin's statue once and for all and hide the gold that adorned it.

By then, the gods' opinion of Odin had changed. His wife had put him sorely to shame; what wife of a true man would rather sleep with a servant than her husband? Odin's own actions had brought shame upon him as well. He had been shown to be weak and ineffective in his failure to prevent the statue's destruction – that, too, was unbecoming of a true man. And he had resorted to seid to further his aims, as he had on countless occasions before – and that was *certainly* unbecoming of a true man.

The gods decided that their leader's manly honor had left him, and that he was no longer fit to be their king. So, at a council they called for the purpose, they banished him from Asgard.

This was hard news for Odin, but he took it well. After all, he had been absent from his throne for long stretches at a time before, while traveling far and wide throughout the cosmos on his countless quests for knowledge. So he did the same on this occasion, and put his ill fortune to good use.

Years passed. Odin lodged with his many friends in all the worlds held in the branches and roots of Yggdrasil, learned much from them, and accomplished many great feats along the way.

But one day, word reached him that his brothers, Vili and Ve, had taken over his position in his absence. They had divided up his possessions between them, but had chosen to share his wife. Ah, Frigg – her unfaithfulness, her jealousy, and her affronts to his honor seemed so distant as to be trivial, and when he thought of his beloved wife, the only image that filled his mind was that of her gorgeous face smiling at him. He began making preparations to reclaim his kingdom.

With his sword in one hand and his sorcerer's staff in the other, Odin fought his way back into Asgard, deposed Vili and Ve, and retook his throne. After this shining display of his power, the gods had little reason to doubt his right to rule their realm. So he resumed his old position, and savored Frigg's embraces once again.

# Chapter 28:

# Frey's Wooing of

# Gerd

The myth of Frey's violent wooing of the giantess Gerd comes from *The Song of Skirnir* (*Skírnismál*), one of the poems in the *Poetic Edda*. Scholars are divided on the age of the poem, and no particularly convincing theory has been put forward so far. However, other pieces of Old Norse literature allude to parts of the plot of this story, so we can be certain that it's at least based on an authentic Viking Age myth.[1]

The eleven golden fruits that Frey's emissary, Skirnir ("Shining"), offers to Gerd in hopes of winning her hand voluntarily might be some of Idun's fruits that confer perpetual youth, but there's nothing in the text that says that definitively.[2]

### FREY'S WOOING OF GERD

Frey once sat in Odin's throne for a day while its usual occupant was elsewhere. He thought it would be amusing, and that surely no harm could come of it.

The majestic seat had a commanding view of the entire cosmos. Frey watched what was going on in each of the many lands in the universe, and found it to be quite an entertaining and illuminating way to spend his day. When he gazed into the land of the giants, however, his eyes grew wide, and he could barely breathe. A fluttering sensation filled his belly and his chest. There, in that otherwise so dreary and foreboding terrain, he watched as the most beautiful maiden he had ever seen strolled through her father's fortress on her way to her bedchamber. Her skin seemed to glow with all the radiance of the sky. Frey was stricken with a debilitating love-sickness, and refused to let anyone see him for days.

Frey's father, Njord, grew worried about his son when he failed to emerge from his quarters for many days in a row. So Njord sent Skirnir, one of Frey's servants, to see what was troubling him.

In a gentle tone of voice, Skirnir said to Frey, "Remember when we were young, how we grew up together, and could always trust each other? Surely, old friend, you can still confide in me now. I want to hear the source of your sorrow, in hopes that I might be able to relieve you of some of it."

After much hesitation, Frey sighed and responded, "I know that you mean well. But I don't think you'll understand the anguish I'm going through." Then he told him about the maiden he had seen from Odin's throne, her appearance, her walk, and how he pined for her with every fiber in his body. He couldn't sleep, and he couldn't eat; he could do nothing but sit and long for her. Sighing again, he finished: "But there's no way that she, a giantess, and I, a god, could ever be together."

Skirnir, deeply moved by his friend and master's story, stood up boldly and said, "If I can help it, there will be a way. Lend me your best horse and your sword that fights by itself and never fails to slay its target, and I shall go to the stronghold of Gymir, her father, and win her hand on your behalf." Frey didn't believe that Skirnir could succeed, but he saw how badly his loyal friend wanted to help him. So he granted Skirnir's requests and sent him off.

Skirnir rode long and hard over dark, wild hills until at last he spotted the imposing fortress of Gymir in the distance. As he approached, Gerd felt the ground tremble and the walls of her bower quake. A thunderous crashing sound drew nearer and nearer. She ran out and fearfully asked one of her servant girls who was approaching. The girl told her that it was an unknown man, likely a demigod, who had just dismounted and let his horse graze. Gerd told her to let the fellow in so she could question him.

Skirnir entered the hall, and found Gerd there to greet him. Her face was stern. "Who are you?" she asked. "Are you an elf? A god? How did you ever get to our remote stronghold?"

"I am not an elf, nor a god," answered Skirnir. Evading her question and getting right down to his business, he pulled eleven round, golden fruits out of his sack and presented them to her. "These will be yours," he said, "if you will consent to be the bride of the great Frey." A look of scorn came over Gerd's face, and she flatly refused the offer, saying that nothing in the world could cause her to desire to marry Frey.

Skirnir then pulled out of his satchel something even more magnificent: Draupnir, that golden ring of Odin's from which eight more golden rings fall every ninth night. "This was burned on the pyre of Balder," Skirnir told her, "and it will be yours to keep if you accept my master's offer." Gerd refused the ring, too, saying that her father had more gold than she could ever wish for.

Skirnir's face darkened. He took the unerring sword out of his bag and flashed it in Gerd's face. "See this sword?" he asked her. "By it, your father shall fall." Then he held up his magic staff and began to intone a curse upon the giantess: "With this staff, grimmer than any sword, I strike you. Your will shall be bent to mine. You shall become so hideously ugly that you will be famous for it. You shall know nothing but sorrow, loneliness, and rage all the rest of your days. Though your face shall be grisly, and your loins as dry as a thistle, you shall burn with unquenchable, maddening lust. You shall crawl to men and beg them to lay you, but none will have you. Three of the most loathsome runes I am now about to write for you, and all of this shall come to pass - but if you would change your mind, and accept my master's offer, I could leave all three unwritten."

Gerd's demeanor transformed abruptly. "I never would have thought it possible," she said, "but I am filled with longing for Frey. Take my words to him as you would a cup of fine mead to his lips, and tell him that I will come to him after nine nights, and we shall be married."

When Skirnir arrived back in Asgard, Frey ran up to him and said, "Before you even get off of the horse, tell me, what did she say?" Skirnir told him, taking care to leave out the part about the threats and curses. "Ah," sighed Frey contentedly. "I don't know how I will be able to bear even one night without out her now. Two will be torture. And the third? Half of any one of these nights will feel like a month to me."

But Frey made it through the nine nights, and on the following morning, he and Gerd were married in a lush, leafy grove.

# Chapter 29:

# The Ordeal of the

# Hooded One

This tale comes from the poem *The Song of the Hooded One* (*Grímnismál*) in the *Poetic Edda*. The poem's primary aim is to didactically convey cosmological lore in a manner that's about as close to an encyclopedia as you can get in poetry. Its presentation is remarkably systematic for a pre-Christian poem, yet contains no trace of direct Christian influence. Therefore, *The Song of the Hooded One* was likely composed during the late Viking Age or very early medieval period, when the Norse religion was dying out, but was still practiced by a substantial proportion of the Norse people.[1]

Even though the main intent of the poem is to dispense cosmological knowledge, the fairly well-developed framing story is quite possibly a traditional Norse myth. In my retelling of it below, I don't repeat much of the exhaustively detailed cosmological lore. That's because the central points of that lore have already been discussed in Part One, and because its content – apart from its sheer volume – isn't particularly relevant to the storyline, which is what concerns us here in this present chapter.

## THE ORDEAL OF THE HOODED ONE

A king named Hraudung had two sons, Agnar and Geirrod. (Geirrod was unrelated to the giant of the same name.) On an autumn day when Agnar was ten years old and Geirrod eight, the two boys were fishing at sea in a small boat. A strong wind arose and blew them far from the shore. At dusk, they made it to land – but only when their little boat, driven by the furious wind, crashed and splintered against rocks they had never before seen.

They found themselves in a vast wilderness, which in the twilight appeared to them as one looming darkness, unbroken except for a single tiny, orange light in the distance. Drenched, shivering, hungry, and scared, they made their way towards the lone point of light. As they approached, it turned out to be firelight coming from the window of a peasant cottage. They knocked on the door, and were relieved when they were welcomed in by the old man and woman who lived there. For the rest of the winter, the two boys stayed in the cottage and were looked after by the elderly couple. The woman took a particular interest in caring for Agnar, and the man mostly concerned himself with Geirrod. The old man prided himself on his wisdom, and taught some of it to Geirrod over the course of the season.

When spring came, the couple gave the boys a boat and told them how to make their way back to their father's house. The old man whispered something in Geirrod's ear, and the brothers at last set out for their home. Geirrod was in the front of the boat, and Agnar in the back. When they had almost reached the shore, Geirrod leapt to land and pushed the boat back into the waves, cursing his brother and leaving him to helplessly drift back into the open ocean.

Geirrod strutted up to the opulent, fortified mansion where his family lived – a far cry from the humble peasant cottage, he thought. When he arrived at the door, the entire household was overjoyed to see him alive – all, that is, except his father the king, who had died over the winter. Since Agnar was dead – or so Geirrod had told everyone, feigning grief – Geirrod was crowned king.

Many years later, when Geirrod and Agnar were grown men, Odin and Frigg sat in their throne room in Asgard, looking out over the world. Odin pointed to Geirrod's kingdom in Midgard, and said to his wife, "See what has become of Agnar, your foster-son? He dwells in a cave and fathers children with giantesses. But look at my foster-son, Geirrod. He is a king, and has won for himself wide renown."

Frigg shot back, "Your Geirrod is the most miserly king who has ever reigned among men. When he has too many guests for his liking, he tortures them to death!"

Odin was incensed at the suggestion that his foster-son had turned out to be such a stingy and dishonorable man. So he made a bet with Frigg that if he were to go to Midgard in disguise and seek lodging with Geirrod, he would be treated as hospitably as he had treated Geirrod those years ago in the forest.

Soon thereafter, a stranger appeared in Geirrod's realm. He wore a dark blue cloak and called himself Grimnir, "Hooded One," but would say nothing more about who he was, where he had come from, or why he was there. No dog would dare to even bark at him. Frigg had sent a messenger to Geirrod's court to tell the king that a magician full of malice was on his way to the kingdom, and that the king would know the man by his suspiciously good treatment by the dogs.

When Grimnir came to Geirrod's court, the king had him arrested and tortured. Wanting to know who this mysterious stranger was, Geirrod tied him up between two roaring fires until he would talk and reveal his true identity. Grimnir sat between the two blazes for eight nights, as silent as the grave.

Geirrod had a ten-year-old son named Agnar after his forsaken brother. On the ninth night of Grimnir's ordeal, the boy brought the stranger a horn full of mead. Pressing it to the man's lips, Agnar said to him, with compassion in his voice, that it was profoundly unjust for his father to inflict such pain upon someone for no reason.

Grimnir drank the horn to the dregs. The fires came so close to him that his cloak began to burn. Then, at last, he spoke:

"For nine nights have I sat here between these fires, and no one in all of Geirrod's kingdom has brought me anything to eat or drink but little Agnar. I tell you now, no one will ever receive a greater payment for a single drink than he!"

Then he began to regale the king and all who were present with an enormous hoard of lore about every corner of the cosmos. The assembled crowd was astonished, and they wondered amongst themselves who could possibly know so much about so much. Gradually, it dawned on their horrified minds that only one being in the entire universe could pull off the feat they were seeing unfolding before their eyes: it could be none other than Odin, foremost of the gods, whom they had been so cruelly torturing for so long.

Toward the end of his speech, Odin listed dozens of his names, saying, "I have never been known by just one name among men, nor among anyone else." After reminding those gathered there of just a few of his great deeds, he turned to Geirrod, who finally saw that this stranger was the old peasant who had cared for him in the woods those many years ago. Now, those same kindly eyes glared right into him with pure hatred and contempt. "Geirrod," Odin snarled, "you are drunk. Your stupor has cost you more than you know, and more than you will ever be able to bear. I once saved your life, but never again will you receive any aid from me. In fact, I see in my mind your sword, and it drips with your blood. Your reign is over, and the reign of your son Agnar has begun."

The terrified Geirrod stood and ran to Odin with his sword in his hand, hoping to earn the god's mercy by cutting him free. But the sword slipped from his hand, and in that same instant he tripped. The sword was caught between the floor and his chest, with the blade pointing up, and it pierced him straight through.

Everyone present rushed to Geirrod's side to attend to him, but he was already dead. When they looked up, they saw that there was only empty space between the two fires, and the ashes of a dark blue cloak between them. The prisoner had vanished.

Agnar's reign was long, and songs about him were sung for countless generations.

# Chapter 30:

# Gefjun Plows

# Zealand from

# Sweden

The island of Zealand ("Sjaelland" in Danish) lies in the Baltic Sea between Denmark and Sweden. Politically, it's a part of Denmark, and the Danish capital, Copenhagen, is located on the island.

According to this story, Zealand wasn't always located where it is today. Instead, it used to be part of the Swedish mainland, and was dragged into the ocean by the goddess Gefjun in ancient times.

The tale of how this happened is given by Snorri in two of his works: the *Prose Edda* and *The Saga of the Ynglings*. The basic outline of the story is the same in both versions, but some of the details differ. To support his claim to authenticity, Snorri cites a stanza from a poem by the ninth-century skaldic poet Bragi Boddason.[1] Because of this corroboration, we can be reasonably sure that Snorri's tale is at least based on a myth from the Viking Age.

## GEFJUN PLOWS ZEALAND FROM SWEDEN

Long ago, when King Gylfi reigned in Sweden, a female minstrel wandered into his court. She entertained the king and his men long and well with all manner of songs, dances, and tales. At the end of her act, the king was in such a pleasant mood that he offered her a plot of land of whatever size four oxen could plow in a single day and night.

Had King Gylfi known that this minstrel was none other than the goddess Gefjun in disguise, he probably wouldn't have made such an offer. Gefjun summoned the four sons she had borne by a giant and transformed them into oxen. Each ox had four heads and eight moonlike eyes. Gefjun yoked them to a plow, which she dug into the land of Zealand. With their legs in the ocean, they grunted and sweated as they towed the vast plot of land westward into the water, where it became an island under the control of Denmark. The king could do nothing but helplessly watch as he lost a huge portion of some of the finest land in his kingdom. Gefjun, fittingly, became the island's patron goddess.

# Chapter 31:

# Thor's Duel with

# Hrungnir

This myth is found in the skaldic poem *Autumn-Long* (*Haustlöng*) by Thjodolf of Hvin, as well as in Snorri's *Prose Edda*. Snorri uses Thjodolf's poem as a source for his account, but adds material that isn't found there or in any other source that we possess. We don't know where Snorri's additions come from – lost skaldic poems, late and unreliable poems, Snorri's own imagination, or somewhere else? Nevertheless, the basic outline of the story is well-attested in *Autumn-Long* and in brief references in other skaldic poems, so we can be sure that this is, at bottom, a genuine Viking Age myth.

## THOR'S DUEL WITH HRUNGNIR

One day, Hrungnir, the strongest of the giants and their best fighter, saw a stranger riding toward his house deep in the somber mountains of Jotunheim. The man's golden helmet shimmered in the midday sun, and his eight-legged horse galloped effortlessly through the air between the mountains, and over the water of the lagoons that punctuated them. When the stranger came near Hrungnir, the giant called out to him, saying that his steed was a wonder to behold. Then Hrungnir asked the man, whose face was hidden beneath his golden helmet, who he was. The visitor – who was none other than Odin – didn't answer his question, but instead challenged the giant to a bet. "I would wager my head," he declared, "that there is no finer steed than mine in all of Jotunheim."

Hrungnir was insulted, and angrily replied that although the stranger's horse was fine enough, it was no match for his own horse, Gullfaxi, "Gold-Mane." To back up his claim, Hrungnir mounted Gullfaxi then and there and galloped after Odin and Sleipnir. The two raced furiously over the craggy tundra and glaciers of the mountain heights, and the green valleys in between them. The landscape changed to flat pastures and crop fields with pockets of woods at their margins, and still the two horses sprinted on, almost neck and neck with each other, along the winding dirt roads and past the occasional bewildered peasant. Hrungnir's attention was so absorbed in the match that he hardly noticed the changing scenes around him until he and his opponent had gone past the gate of Asgard and into its shining halls. Odin dismounted and invited his formidable challenger to share a drink with him.

Seemingly from his first sip inside the gods' ornate feasting hall, Hrungnir became boastful and bellicose. He ordered all of Thor's drinking horns to be brought before him, and he drank from each one in turn, mocking that famous slayer of his kind with every gulp. Soon, he became so belligerent that he threatened to rip Asgard apart and throw it into the ocean, sparing only Valhalla, Freya, and Sif, which he would carry off to Jotunheim to keep as his possessions. He would kill all of the other deities, too – but first, he would drink all of their ale. And it seemed that he was already making good on this last threat.

Thor had been gone on a raid in Jotunheim, but he arrived back in Asgard that evening. When he entered the feasting hall and saw what was going on there, he lifted his hammer and charged at Hrungnir. But the giant protested, pointing out that he had been invited in by Odin, and was therefore entitled to protection as the gods' guest. Thor swiveled sharply to his father, who sullenly nodded his head to confirm that the giant had spoken the truth.

Turning back to Hrungnir, Thor glared at him and bellowed, "You dog of a giant, you will soon regret that you ever accepted that invitation."

But Hrungnir fired back in a taunting tone of voice, "Ah, great and mighty Thor, it would be awfully cowardly for you to kill an unarmed man, now wouldn't it?" Hrungnir's ensuing giggle was caught by a burp, which the giant tried to pass off as simply clearing his throat.

Instead, the giant proposed that the two fight each other in single combat, when Hrungnir had had a chance to return home, get his weapons, and prepare himself. Thor accepted the challenge.

By the time Hrungnir had made his way back to Jotunheim, word of his impending duel with Thor had spread. It seemed like every last giant made a point to seek out Hrungnir to wish him well or to offer him whatever assistance they could. The stakes, after all, were awfully high: either the giants' strongest warrior or their strongest adversary would be slain. In order to provide their hero with the best helper they could, the giants constructed a man of hard clay who was nine miles tall and three miles wide, with the heart of a mare beating inside his chest. They called him Mokkurkalfi. Hrungnir's own heart was notorious: it had three corners, was made of stone, and was covered in spikes. When Hrungnir entered the ground where the duel was to be held with a huge shield made of thick stone like his heart, swinging in his arm a whetstone the size of a cow, and with Mokkurkalfi by his side, he was a fearsome sight to behold.

Thor's assistant, Thjalfi, arrived at the site before the god himself. He approached the roaring giant, appraised his posture, feigned a sigh, and said to him, "Just so you know, if I were you, I wouldn't be holding my shield out in front of me like that. Thor's going to arrive any minute now, and when he does, he'll be coming up from the ground right below you." Hrungnir took Thjalfi at his word, placed his shield underneath his feet, and stood on it.

The sky darkened. Lightning flashes appeared in the distance and approached closer and closer. The crack of their thunder grew louder and louder. Finally, the thunder growled right above Hrungnir's head. Thor leapt out of the clouds. Hrungnir wet himself.

The thunder god hurled his hammer at the head of the giant, who responded by throwing his whetstone at the hammer. The two weapons hit each other in the middle of their flight. At the hammer's touch, the stone burst into two pieces. One of them fell to the ground and shattered, which is where all the flint rocks on earth have come from. The other struck Thor in the forehead and lodged there, knocking the god on his back. But the hammer, after breaking the whetstone, shot straight into its original target. Hrungnir's skull exploded into tiny crumbs, and the headless corpse of the giant fell forward onto Thor. One of the legs fell across his neck, pinning him to the ground. Thjalfi felled Mokkurkalfi without much difficulty, then ran over to his master and attempted to pull the leg off of him. But, though he tugged and heaved as hard as he could, he was unable.

When the gods heard of Thor's predicament, they all rushed to his side, and every one of them tried to lift the leg off of him. But none had any more success than Thjalfi until, at last, Thor's son Magni, "Strong," arrived. Magni had been born just three nights earlier, but when he put his chubby baby hands on the giant's leg, it gave way instantly, and Thor was released. Magni cooed with delight, and then said to his father, "It's a pity that I didn't come sooner. I could have smote Hrungnir with just my fist." Thor praised his boy profusely, and as a reward, he gave him Gullfaxi, Hrungnir's steed. This angered Odin, who had badly desired for himself that horse that had almost outrun his own Sleipnir.

But there was still the matter of the whetstone lodged in Thor's head to attend to. So Hrungnir's slayer made his way to the home of the famous sorceress Groa, "Thriving." Groa chanted her songs over the whetstone, and Thor began to feel the stone lightening and loosening in his forehead.

Jubilant at the prospect of the stone coming out, Thor immediately told Groa what he was going to do to reward her for her work. Her husband, the famously brave Aurvandil, had been presumed dead. But Thor told her that he had found Aurvandil alive in Jotunheim and carried him back to Midgard in a basket. As proof that his story was true, Thor pointed out that a new star had recently been observed in the sky; this, he said, was Aurvandil's toe, which had stuck out from the basket, had become frozen, and had needed to be cut off. Thor had then slung the toe into the sky where it became this new star, which he named Aurvandil's Toe. And it would not be long, Thor said, until her husband would come home to her.

But Thor, in his excitement, had gone too far. Groa was so overjoyed that she forgot the words to her charms. So the stone remained fastened in Thor's forehead from then on. And to this day, if you throw a whetstone across the floor, the one in Thor's forehead stirs, and causes him a great deal of pain.

# CHAPTER 32:

# GRAY-BEARD THE

# FERRYMAN

This tale comes from the poem *The Song of Gray-Beard* (*Hárbarðsljóð*) in the *Poetic Edda*. There's no particular sign of Christian influence on the poem, and it probably comes from the Viking Age. The poem could have been composed by a learned devotee of Odin out of a desire to mock the simple Thor and his low-class followers.[1] It's unknown to what degree the poem relates a "traditional" myth, and to what degree the storyline is the invention of an individual poet. The poem references a number of myths along the way, some of which we know from other sources (and which are retold in other chapters of this book), and some of which are now lost (or possibly invented by the poet).

## GRAY-BEARD THE FERRYMAN

While on his way back from one of his many journeys to Jotunheim, Thor reached a deep fjord. He could see a man standing by a boat on the far shore, and he called out to him, "Ferryman, who are you?"

The ferryman mockingly returned the question. "Who are you, peasant?"

Though taken aback, Thor chose to ignore the slight and to offer the man with the boat a reward for bearing him to the other side of the water. He pointed to the basket he was wearing on his back and said,

211

"This thing is full of fresh herrings and porridge. If you help me across, I'll give you as much of my provisions as you can eat."

But the stranger on the far shore ignored this offer, and continued to insult his potential customer. "Look at you!" he scoffed. "You're barefoot, and what clothes you have are just tattered rags. You look like a beggar. The man who built me this boat was a great hero, and he told me - wisely - to give passage only to those who are worthy, and to people whom I myself know. You, as far as I can tell, are neither. If you want to have any chance of being ferried across this fjord, you'd better tell me your name."

Thor rolled his eyes and sighed. "All right, I will tell you my name, though it might put me in danger. I am the son of Odin, the brother of Meili, and the father of Magni. The man with whom you now speak is none other than Thor. And now, why don't you tell me your name?"

"I am Harbard," he said. The name - unbeknownst to Thor - was one of Odin's, and it meant "Gray-Beard." "But I didn't want to reveal my name to you until I knew yours. You give every appearance of being quite a disreputable fellow, and it's always well to be on one's guard around such folk as you."

By now, Thor had become so angered by Harbard's taunts that he could no longer retain his composure. Gesturing violently at Harbard, Thor yelled, "If this water weren't so deep, and if I wouldn't get so wet in wading across, I'd come over there right now and give you the payment you deserve for your slanderous words!"

"I will stand right here and wait for you," Harbard replied in a sardonically casual tone of voice. "Not since Hrungnir have you met a more formidable foe."

"Well, I slew him, didn't I?" Thor retorted. "And what were *you* doing at that time?"

Harbard answered the rhetorical question as if it had been asked in earnest. "I was with Fjolvar on the island of Algron for five years. I felled countless enemies and coupled with countless maidens - even the seven sisters, who gave me great pleasure. And what were *you* doing at that time?"

"I dealt Thjazi, that monstrous giant, his death blow. Then I cast his eyes into the heavens and formed stars from them, so that proof of my deed would live forever. And what were *you* doing at that time?"

"Why, seducing sorceresses away from their husbands and making love to them, naturally. Oh, and I convinced Hlebard, that famed wizard of a giant, to give me his staff. Then I used it to steal his wits like I stole those women. And what were *you* doing at that time?"

"Unlike your vile deeds, mine were virtuous and upright. I was off in Jotunheim, slaying yet more giants. If it weren't for me, they would have long ago overrun all of Midgard and all of Asgard, and there would be no men or gods left. And what were *you* doing at that time?"

"I was stirring up strife among men. I have always incited the princes to battle, and never have I attempted to make peace between them. After all, when noblemen fall in battle, they go to Odin; but when slaves perish, they go to Thor."

Thor's anger reached a boiling point. "You *argr* Harbard, if I could but reach across the sound with my arm, I would knock you straight into the grave!"

Harbard chuckled. "Why bother? Your empty threat conceals the fact that you haven't offered a tale of some accomplishment of your own to match the last one I gave. So while I was pitting kings and heroes against one another, what might *you* have been doing?"

Thor glared across the fjord and snorted while thinking of a suitable rejoinder. "I was guarding the river from the sons of Svarang. Though they slung boulders at me, I maintained my post, and in the end, I had them begging me for mercy. And what were *you* doing at that time?"

"In the land of the giants, I stealthily played with that maiden whose skin was white as new linen, and whose arms, neck, and forehead were wrapped in countless fine pieces of jewelry. And what were *you* doing at that time?"

"I was on the island of Hlesey, hacking down the malicious brides of berserkers."

"Are you really boasting about killing women?" jabbed Harbard.

"They were more like she-wolves than women," protested Thor. "They shook my ship, and chased away Thjalfi while swinging clubs made of iron. In any case, what were *you* doing at that time?"

"Raising my banners against your people, and making ready to redden my spear."

"I have never met anyone with a mouth as foul as yours! If I chose to wade the water that separates us, one strike of my hammer would make you howl louder than a wolf!"

"Save your rage for the man who's sleeping with your wife as we speak."

"Now you're just conjuring up whatever lies will offend me most!"

"Everything I've said has been perfectly true. And speaking of truths you don't want to hear, you've put yourself well behind on your journey by standing there and quarreling with me, haven't you?"

"*Argr* Harbard, *you* are the one who has held me here so long!"

"I never thought the great Thor would be prevented from traveling by a mere ferryman."

"Come on. Let's drop this idle chatter. Row your boat over here and carry the son of Odin and the father of Magni across the fjord."

"You're wasting your time standing there on the shore. You will not gain the passage you desire."

"Then at least tell me how to go around the bay, if you won't row me over it."

"To tell you the way is easy, but to go that route is long and arduous. After scrambling over the roots and rocks for a good while, you'll find a hardly more civilized road that will take you to the town at the head of the fjord. There, you'll meet your mother, Fjorgyn, and she will guide you back to Odin's realm."

"Can I reach my destination by nightfall?"

"Well, you've squandered much of the day standing there arguing with me. But if you hurry and don't hurt yourself along the way, I suppose it's possible."

"If I ever meet you again, I will give you the payment you deserve for your slander!" shouted Thor, who still had not discerned the true identity of the man with whom he had been conversing.

Odin replied, "Be gone, and may every foul creature in the world find its way to you!"

# CHAPTER 33:

# ODIN AND BILLING'S

# DAUGHTER

Odin's amorous escapades weren't always as successful as his boasts in *The Song of Gray-Beard* might suggest.

In this story, Odin attempts to woo an unnamed daughter of Billing, "Twin." Since other tales feature Odin courting the daughters of giants, Billing may be a giant. However, no giant with that name is featured elsewhere in the Old Norse sources, but a dwarf named Billing is mentioned in one (and only one) of the manuscripts of *The Prophecy of the Seeress*.[1] Therefore, Billing (and consequently his daughter) was probably either a giant or a dwarf, and either interpretation is more or less as plausible as the other.

This tale is told only in outline in the Eddic poem *The Sayings of the High One*. It's recounted in the context of illustrating a lesson about how awful it is to not obtain the object of one's desire, as well as the untrustworthiness of women. The story could be part of a now-lost myth, but it's also entirely possible that it was invented by the poet of this section of *The Sayings of the High One* in order to provide an example of his point – almost like a cynical Viking morality play.

## ODIN AND BILLING'S DAUGHTER

In the course of his countless quests, Odin once found himself in the hall of the rich and powerful Billing. When he walked by the bedroom of his host's daughter, he happened to catch a glimpse of her beautiful form as she lay in her bed. Though asleep, she was more radiant than the sun. As lavish and ornate as the nobleman's estate was, all of it seemed like empty squalor in comparison with the splendor of the maiden's body.

Odin made an excuse to enter her chamber. Once inside, he tried to win her over with all kinds of honeyed flattery. When he attempted to lie down next to her in her bed, she held her arms out to keep him at bay. "Dearest Odin," she addressed him in her beguilingly sweet voice, "not now. If we try to make love during the day, everyone in my father's court will know about it, and both of us would be in grave trouble. If you want me, come back tonight when all are asleep, and then I shall be yours."

Odin took her counsel. After kissing her soft and supple hand, he left her room, taking care not to let anyone see him. For the rest of the day, he could think of nothing but her. He paced up and down the grounds of Billing's estate, lost in a delirium of lovesickness and fevered anticipation.

Though the sun seemed to take a millennium to set, darkness finally covered the land. Odin tiptoed back up the hallway to the young woman's bedchamber, full of rapturous glee that was hardly mitigated by his caution. But the guards, most of whom had usually gone to bed by this time, were all wide awake and at their posts. When they caught sight of Odin, they brandished their swords and curtly informed him that guests of the master of the house were not permitted in that part of the hall at that hour. Though enraged and in anguish, Odin was forced to turn back without winning his prize.

The next morning, Odin once again made his way to the room of Billing's daughter. This time, the guards were curiously few, and didn't seem to mind his passing. Finding the door to the girl's room ajar, he looked both ways and then slowly and quietly pressed it open. At the door's first creak, furious barking and metallic clanking erupted from within the room. Peering around the door, he found a dog chained to the bed of Billing's daughter, and the woman herself nowhere in sight.

# Chapter 34: Thor and Utgarda-Loki

The tale of Thor and Loki's journey to Utgard (another name for Jotunheim, the homeland of the giants) comes almost exclusively from Snorri Sturluson's *Prose Edda*. In the form in which Snorri has handed it down to us, the story is essentially a medieval fairy tale that freely borrows from some authentic motifs from Viking Age myths along the way. Most of these will be easily recognizable from other parts of this book: Thor journeying to Jotunheim, Loki tagging along, Thor bringing life and prosperity by hallowing something with his hammer, etc. Other elements – the flippant tone that pervades the tale, characters that are straightforward allegories for abstract concepts, the giants being distinguished by being of comically large size, and others – are unlike anything in more reliably genuine Norse myths, but are right at home in medieval literature.

Further evidence of the general confusion of Snorri's narrative can be found in the fact that Loki appears in two different roles in the story. In one, he is Thor's traveling companion. In the other, he is the giant Utgarda-Loki, "Loki of Utgard." Indeed, in Saxo's *History of the Danes*, Thor encounters Utgarda-Loki bound in chains, just like Loki himself was after he betrayed the gods one too many times. Since Loki often takes the side of the giants against the gods throughout the Norse myths, there can be little doubt that Utgarda-Loki is none other than the son of Nal and Farbauti.[1]

Thus, there seems to have once been a Viking Age myth where Thor went to visit the bound Loki. But that's almost the entire extent of the plot that can be inferred from the available evidence. That story is therefore irrecoverable. Other parts of Snorri's narrative may be derived from another myth that recounted one of Thor's many travels to Jotunheim.[2] But if so, then that myth, too, has been lost over the course of the centuries.

In lieu of those older, authentically pre-Christian myths, here's Snorri's fairy tale, which is built on top of their ruins.

## THOR AND UTGARDA-LOKI

While Thor and Loki were traveling far from Asgard in Thor's goat-drawn chariot, night overtook them and they were welcomed into the house of a farmer and his family.

To repay his hosts for their hospitality, Thor offered his goats for supper, knowing that he could bring them back to life afterwards and not be at any loss. Just before the meal began, Thor laid the goats' hides on the floor and instructed his hosts to place the bones on the hides after the meat had been gleaned from them.

The farmer had two children: a boy named Thjalfi and a daughter named Roskva. Despite the thunder god's instructions, Thjalfi broke open one of the goats' leg bones to suck out the marrow before placing it on the hide with the others.

Thor awoke early the following morning, before anyone else in the household. He hallowed the goat hides and bones with his hammer, whereupon the goats sprang back to life. One of them, however, had a lame hind leg. Thor immediately intuited the reason for this, and flew into a rage. The farmer and his family awoke abruptly to Thor's howls and crashes. The thunder god would have slain them all on the spot had the farmer not offered him his children, Thjalfi and Roskva, to be his servants. Thor accepted, and he, Loki, and the children pressed onward on foot, since the goats were in no shape to pull a chariot.

The party's destination was Jotunheim. On the way, they crossed an ocean and a thick, tangled forest. Just as night was falling, they came to a huge hall. They found no one inside, and decided to spend the night there.

In the middle of the night, they were jostled awake by a great earthquake. Running outside, they found a sleeping giant whose snores caused the earth to rumble and shake. Thor clutched his hammer and resolved to smite this sure foe of his. But the giant awoke at the last second and seemed to be cheered, or at least amused, by the sight of Thor and his companions. The giant introduced himself as Skrymir, "Boaster," but said that he already knew the identity of those to whom he was speaking.

Skrymir picked up his glove, the great hall in which Thor and his company had slept during the night, and proposed that he accompany them on their journey. Despite their apprehension, they agreed in the interest of having a native guide. And off they went through dark forests and over steep hills.

At night, they took shelter beneath a mighty, ancient oak. Skrymir had been carrying all of their provisions in his bag, and when the giant fell asleep, the task of opening the bag fell to Thor. But the god found himself unable to untie the giant's knots. This so angered him that he struck the dozing Skrymir in the forehead, hoping to kill him. But the giant awoke calmly and asked if a leaf had fallen on his head.

Later in the night, the giant's snores grew so loud that they echoed through the valleys like thunder. Thor, annoyed by his inability to sleep, and still looking for any excuse to kill the giant, tried a second time to smite him by striking him on the head. But, much as before, Skrymir awoke and asked if an acorn had fallen on his head.

Just before dawn, Thor decided to try one more time to end Skrymir's life. But when the giant woke up, he asked if some birds had roosted above him and shaken some dirt from the branches onto his face.

Skrymir departed from Thor and his companions, and the company pressed onward toward a castle called Utgard.

Around midday, the travelers reached their destination. The gate was locked and no one was there to open it, but Thor and the others found that they could fit through the very large spaces between the bars of the gate easily enough. Once inside, they found a hall where men sat eating and drinking. Amongst them was the king of this castle, the giant Utgarda-Loki, who immediately recognized his new guests and set about taunting them for how small they were in comparison with himself and his people.

Wanting to salvage his dignity and that of his companions, Loki proudly asserted that no one else in this castle could eat food faster than he could. Utgarda-Loki challenged him to prove this boast by entering a contest with one of the men there, whose name was Logi, "Fire." A trough of meat was set before them, with Loki at one end and Logi at the other, and they were to see who could reach the middle first. They met in the middle at the same time, but while Loki had eaten all of the meat between the end and the middle, Logi had eaten the meat, the bones, and even the trough itself! Loki had clearly lost.

Thjalfi, who was a famously swift runner, then offered to race anyone in the castle. Utgarda-Loki led him out to a race track and appointed one Hugi, "Thought," to compete with him. By the time Hugi reached the finish line, he was so far ahead of Thjalfi that he doubled back to meet his opponent. They raced a second time, and once again Hugi beat Thjalfi by a long bow-shot. Still, they raced a third time, but Thjalfi fared even worse; he was still at the midpoint of the track by the time Hugi finished.

Thor then challenged anyone in the castle to a drinking contest, something at which he had no little skill. Utgarda-Loki had one of his servants fetch the kind of drinking horn from which Utgarda-Loki's men were said to drink. When it was placed before Thor, Utgarda-Loki informed him that whoever could finish the horn in one drink was considered a great drinker, whoever could do it in two was considered fair, but no one in his retinue was such a poor drinker as to be unable to finish it in three.

Thor drank mightily, but by the time he had to pause for a breath, the level of liquor in the horn had barely lowered. So he gave it a second try, straining to gulp and gulp until his breath failed him. This time, the level had gone down appreciably, but the better part of the horn still remained. His third drink was even more formidable than the previous two, but in the end, much was still left. By that point, however, Thor could drink could no more, and gave up.

Then Utgarda-Loki suggested that Thor attempt to simply lift his cat from the floor, but Thor proved unable to do even this.

In a rage, Thor challenged anyone in the castle to wrestle with him. Insultingly, Utgarda-Loki appointed an old woman, Elli, "Age," who was one of his servants. But the great god lost even this contest.

After this, Utgarda-Loki decided that there should be no more contests, and the company spent the night there in the castle.

In the morning, they rose and prepared to leave. After Utgarda-Loki had shown them out of the castle, he confided to them what had actually transpired in their contests, saying to Thor, "Now that you have left my castle, I shall see to it that you never enter it again. The knot on my provision bag that you almost succeeded in untying had been wrought in iron. I used magic to deflect the blows you attempted to inflict on me with your hammer; instead of my face, you hit the mountainside, and carved three gaping valleys into it. Had you struck me, I would have been killed then and there."

He continued, "Loki held his own remarkably well in his eating contest, since his opponent was none other than fire itself. So it was with Thjalfi, too – he raced against thought, which nobody could ever hope to outrun. The far end of the horn from which you drank was connected to the sea, and we were actually greatly afraid that you were going to drink it all. When you cross over the sea again, you will see how much you have lowered its level. My cat was actually the Midgard serpent, whom you succeeded in raising out of the ocean and into the sky. And, finally, you wrestled against old age, and took a long, long time to fall. Now, for your sake and for ours, leave, and never come back."

Thor was so angered by this humiliating trickery that he raised his hammer and prepared to slay Utgarda-Loki and smash his castle to pieces. But when he turned to do so he saw no giant and no castle – just a vast, empty plain.

# Chapter 35:

# Odin and

# Vafthrudnir

The story of Odin's wisdom contest with the giant Vafthrudnir, "Entangler," comes from the poem *The Song of Vafthrudnir* (*Váfþrúðnismál*) in the *Poetic Edda*. As with *The Song of the Hooded One*, the main purpose of the poem is to convey lots of bits and pieces of lore, and the narrative that frames the poem serves as a vessel for that lore rather than a story told for its own sake. And as with many of the other Eddic poems, it's unknown to what degree the framing story of *The Song of Vafthrudnir* is a traditional myth, and to what degree it was invented by the poet as a clever way to keep his audience entertained while he educated them.

Scholarly estimates of the date of the poem's composition vary widely, ranging from the tenth century (the later part of the Viking Age) to the thirteenth (well into the medieval period).[1]

The retelling below focuses on the story itself, and mostly leaves out the scraps of lore that Odin and Vafthrudnir recite to impress each other. Almost all of that lore is related elsewhere in this book, so going over it again here would just be redundant. Additionally, from the standpoint of the story itself, the important point is that Odin and Vafthrudnir are both masters of the old cosmology and mythology; as with *The Song of the Hooded One*, the significance of the lore for the plot is its sheer volume, not its content.

## ODIN AND VAFTHRUDNIR

Odin approached Frigg one day in Asgard and told her that he intended to go to the hall of the giant Vafthrudnir, who was famed throughout the cosmos for his wide-ranging and scrupulous knowledge. There, he said, he wanted to see if his own learnedness had at last overtaken that of any other being in the universe. If he could win a contest of erudition with Vafthrudnir, then he could rest satisfied that he had attained that position.

Frigg's eyes had a look of sadness and worry in them. She pleaded with Odin not to go to the house of someone as dangerous as Vafthrudnir. But Odin was resolute, and Frigg knew her husband well enough to know that when his mind was made up, there was nothing she could do to dissuade him. So, after giving him a big, long hug, she told him to be safe and to keep his wits about him.

The ruler of Asgard disguised himself, left his fortress, and fared far over land, water, and air. After many hard days of traveling, he came to the cold, dreary terrain in which the great giant's hall stood. The hall itself was extraordinarily long, wide, and tall, and once inside, he found it to be warm and bright from the many fires that lined its sides.

The guards took him before their master. Odin greeted Vafthrudnir with a hearty hail, and then said, "I have come here to find you, great giant. Tell me, have you won all the wisdom there is to win?"

Vafthrudnir, suspecting a hint of sarcastic mockery in his guest's voice, replied, "And who are you to come here to my high hall and ask me that? I tell you now, unless you prove yourself to be wiser than I, you won't be leaving this place in one piece."

Odin answered that he was called Gagnrad, "Dissuader." In a gentle tone of voice, he added, "my journey to your hall has been long and hard, and a kind welcome from you is what I seek most."

This put Vafthrudnir in a pleasanter mood. "Well, why are you standing there on the floor, then? Come sit with me at my table and relieve your thirst. Then we will know who has more knowledge: the guest or the venerable sage."

But Odin stood where he was, and said, as if quoting a proverb, "When a poor man is the guest of a rich man, he should speak capably or not at all. Nothing is worse to a cultivated man than chatter."

Vafthrudnir's eyes narrowed, and his smile vanished. After a pause, he said, "Very well, then. Stand there where you are before my throne if you so desire." He then launched a volley of questions about the obscure minutiae of the cosmos and its parts. Odin answered each one not only perfectly correctly, but eloquently as well.

Next, it was Odin's turn. His questions wound their way through all kinds of technicalities and paradoxes, but Vafthrudnir didn't miss a beat, and had an answer for each that was more than satisfying.

But Odin had a trick up his sleeve. For his final question to Vafthrudnir, he asked, "And what, wise giant, did Odin whisper in the ear of Balder, before that great son of his was burned on the funeral pyre?"

Vafthrudnir became livid with rage. "Now I see who you really are," he said grimly, "for only Odin himself could know the answer to that question." He clenched his teeth and his fists, and closed his eyes. When he opened them, however, his face had an expression of melancholy acceptance, and he said, "Now for the first time in my life I have lost a contest of lore. But my consolation will be that I lost it to Odin, the most knowledgeable being there is."

# CHAPTER 36:
# THOR THE BRIDE

The story of Thor's having to put on the costume of a bride to appease the giants comes only from *The Poem of Thrym* (Þrymskviða). The tale seems to have been unknown to the skaldic poets, Eddic poets, Snorri, and everyone else who wrote on Norse mythology prior to the twelfth or thirteenth century; they never reference it at all, even in passing. On that basis, as well as its content, scholars typically date the poem's – and the tale's – composition to the twelfth or thirteenth century.[1]

In the words of esteemed Old Norse scholar E.O.G. Turville-Petre, the tale is "a caricature of the noble Thor," the work of a late poet who sought to make fun of the Vikings' religion by casting the quintessentially manly and honorable Thor in a humiliatingly *argr* role.[2] While the story includes some authentic Viking Age motifs along the way – Thor's hammer hallowing a marriage, Freya's necklace, her feather cloak, etc. – we can confidently say that the tale itself didn't exist prior to the medieval period. Not only that, but it is deliberately *antithetical* to the spirit of Viking Age religion.

## THOR THE BRIDE

One morning, Thor awoke to find that his hammer was missing. This was no small matter; without the thunder god's best weapon, Asgard was left vulnerable to the attacks of the giants. In a rage, he searched everywhere for his most prized possession, but it was nowhere to be found.

Loki volunteered to go off in search of the precious hammer. Freya lent him her set of falcon feathers that enabled their bearer to shift his or her shape into that of a falcon. Loki donned the feathers and flew off in search of the treasure. He quickly surmised that it had probably been stolen by the giants, so he rode the winds to Jotunheim.

Upon his arrival in that chilling, gray land, he changed back into his regular form and approached the chief of the giants, Thrym, "Noisy." He questioned Thrym regarding the hammer, and the giant answered that he had not only taken it, but had buried it eight miles below the ground. And, added the lonely, ugly giant, he had no intention of returning it until Freya was compelled to be his bride.

Loki flew back to Asgard and told this news to his fellow gods, who were alarmed and furious - especially Freya. As they sat in counsel, Heimdall put forth the following solution: that Thor should go to Jotunheim disguised as Freya, and thereby win back his hammer and take vengeance on its thieves. Thor protested, saying that this was a dishonorable and unmanly thing to do, and that all of the inhabitants of Asgard would mock him for it for the rest of his days. Loki pointed out, however, that if he didn't consent to Heimdall's plan, Asgard would be ruled by the giants. Seeing no other way, Thor sorrowfully agreed to the plan.

No detail was spared in the assemblage of Thor's bridal dress. After the humiliated god had put on the costume, Loki - who had far fewer scruples when it came to sexual honor - offered to go with him as his maid-servant.

The pair climbed into Thor's goat-drawn chariot and rode across the sky to Jotunheim. When they arrived, they received a hearty welcome by Thrym, who boasted that the gods had at last brought him the prize he deserved.

At dinner, Thor and Loki found themselves in trouble. Thor singlehandedly ate an entire ox, eight salmon, and all of the dainties that had been prepared for the women - not to mention the many barrels of mead he drank. This made Thrym suspicious, and he declared that he had never in his whole life seen a woman with such an appetite.

Loki quickly devised an excuse: "The fair goddess has been so lovesick for you," he claimed, "that she hasn't been able to eat for a week." Thrym accepted this answer, and was overcome by a desire to kiss his bride. When he peeled back the veil, Thor's eyes glared at him so intently that they seemed to burn holes right through him. He exclaimed, "Never have I seen a maiden with such frightfully piercing eyes!" Loki, the master of deceit, explained to the giant that while Freya had been unable to eat, she had also been unable to sleep, so fierce was her longing for him.

The wedding ceremony soon followed. As was customary, Thrym called for the hammer to be brought out to hallow their union. When Mjollnir was laid in Thor's lap, he grabbed its handle and slew first his groom, then all of the assembled guests.

With Loki at his side, Thor returned triumphantly to Asgard, and was relieved to be able to change back into his preferred clothes.

# Chapter 37:
# Thor's Contest with
# Alviss

This story comes from the Eddic poem *The Song of Alviss* (*Alvíssmál*). Alviss ("All-Wise") is a dwarf who has evidently been promised the hand of an unnamed daughter of Thor in marriage. The poem was composed in the twelfth century by a poet who wanted to try his hand at imitating earlier didactic Old Norse poems such as *The Song of Vafthrudnir* and *The Song of the Hooded One*.[1]

Given that its chief concern is with aping a genre form that was by then dead – essentially a nostalgic aesthetic exercise – it should come as no surprise that the "lore" it relates along the way, as well as its pseudo-mythological framing story, have no basis whatsoever in authentic Viking Age mythology and religion.[2] As with *The Poem of Thrym*, its very premise is absurd: Thor occupies Odin's role as master of wisdom and "wanderer," and challenges another being renowned for his wisdom to a contest. The poet was evidently ignorant of even the basics of the mythology and religion from which he drew. The whole thing reads like a homework assignment by some medieval schoolboy. But Snorri quotes it in his *Prose Edda*, which shows that, for all its flaws, *The Song of Alviss* eventually became a somewhat important text for the medieval scholars who crafted their own version of Norse mythology.

## THOR'S CONTEST WITH ALVISS

Alviss the dwarf had been promised the hand of the daughter of none other than Thor himself. As he trekked to Asgard from his dark, dank home under a mountain, his heart was giddy and filled with joy. He thought about how, when he returned to his home, he would have the gorgeous daughter of one of the greatest gods with him. He traveled by night, for dwarves turned to stone when daylight touched them.

When Alviss arrived in Asgard, Thor squinted his eyes and surveyed his figure and features in the firelight for a long minute. Then the thunder god shook his head and said, "Your complexion is pale beyond belief. Have you been sleeping in a pile of corpses, or what? In any case, you don't look fit for my daughter."

The mildly offended Alviss replied, "Well, I do live beneath the soil and the rocks, you know. But that's not important. The important thing is that the gods and I made an agreement, and I would very much like to see that agreement kept."

Thor snorted. "That deal concerns my daughter, and as her father, if anyone has the right to break that deal, it's me. I wasn't consulted when it was originally made, but I'm the one who would be granting you her hand in marriage. And so far, you've done nothing to demonstrate that you're worthy of my consent in the matter. As of now, you don't have my permission to marry my daughter."

Alviss pleaded, "Is there anything I could do that would prove me worthy in your eyes? I long for the hand of your dazzling daughter."

Thor kept scowling at the dwarf while pondering his quest. Eventually he said, "Despite your great ugliness, you are famous for your wisdom. Let's see if your skills match your reputation."

Thor then fired at him a volley of questions about what names the various kinds of beings had for many different things – the earth, the sky, the moon, the sun, the clouds, the wind, and seemingly countless others. Alviss answered each question in great detail.

At last, when Alviss was clearly exhausted, Thor raised his hands and smiled. "I must confess that I have never seen so much knowledge in one head before." A flutter of hope rose in the dwarf's chest. "But," continued Thor, "I must also confess that this entire test has been a ruse. One glance eastward will tell you why."

Alviss turned his head to the east just in time to see the first glimmer of the rising sun make its way over the mountains. In that same instant, it touched the dwarf's skin, and his shocked and terrified form was turned to stone.

# CHAPTER 38:

# BALDER'S DREAMS

*Balder's Dreams* (*Baldrs Draumar*), one of the poems in the *Poetic Edda*, apparently serves as a prelude to the story of Balder's death. It has come down to us only in a single, fourteenth-century manuscript of the *Poetic Edda*.[1] The poem has one stanza in common with *The Prophecy of the Seeress* and one with *The Poem of Thrym*, so it might have known those poems and incorporated those stanzas from them, but the three poems could also be drawing on other, older sources that are now lost.[2] After all, we've already noted at least one instance of *The Prophecy of the Seeress* incorporating older material word-for-word. These factors make it difficult to determine a date for the composition of *Balder's Dreams*, and to assess its reliability as a source of information about the Viking Age.

## BALDER'S DREAMS

Balder, a son of Odin and one of the most beloved of all the gods, began to have ominous dreams that tormented him night after night. When he told his fellow deities what he was going through, they assembled in council to determine what to do about these dreams. They realized that they couldn't decide on a particular course of action until they knew what the dreams meant, so they sent the wise and well-traveled Odin to find out.

Odin saddled Sleipnir and rode down Yggdrasil's branches to its trunk, and then down its trunk to its roots, where he came to the land of the dead. The hound at the door, whose face and neck were covered in blood, bayed furiously at him, but Odin had traveled this path plenty of times before, and knew how to appease the dog. Once inside the gate, Odin found the high hall of Hel, the death-goddess, decked out lavishly and the many long tables set, as if in preparation for a feast to welcome someone of very high stature to the dark, damp realm.

By the eastern door of the hall lay the grave of a powerful sorceress. Odin made his way there and, using the spells he knew so well, got her into such a condition that she was able to sit upright and talk to him in a trance. "I have been dead for long – rain has rained upon me, snow has snowed upon me, and dew has settled upon me many times. Now a stranger has awakened me. Who are you?"

As usual, Odin gave one of his lesser-known names: Vegtam, "Traveler." Then he implored the reanimated woman to tell him in whose honor the hall had been so grandly prepared.

"For Balder," she answered, "has the mead been brewed and the tables set." You could almost hear Odin's heart sink in agony. This is what Balder's dreams had been warning him of. "While we are celebrating his arrival, the gods will be weeping over him at his funeral." Then she began to slump over, and said, "I have already said more than I would have liked to, and now I will go back to sleep."

"No, please," Odin pleaded. "Stay awake for just a little longer. Who will snatch away Balder's life from him?"

The sorceress replied, "It shall be Hod, who bears in his hand a slender branch that will soon become world-famous." Slurring her words from exhaustion, she added, "and now, at last, I will return to my slumber."

"Sorceress, please, just a moment longer. Who will seek vengeance for Balder's death?"

"It shall be Vali, whom Odin shall beget upon the giantess Rind. From the day of his birth, he will never wash his hands nor comb his hair until he has slain his brother's killer. Now," she said in a barely audible murmur, "I am too tired to go on. Let me lie down..."

Odin leaned down to prop her up with his hands. "Wise woman, before you do, just one more question, please."

The sorceress glared at him through her fatigue. "Now I see that you are no 'Vegtam,'" she said scornfully, "but rather Odin, that old necromancer. Go home. I will answer no more of your questions, and no one will get another word out of me until Loki breaks free from his bonds, and the giants meet the gods at Ragnarok."

# CHAPTER 39:

# BALDER'S DEATH

# (VERSION I)

The tale of the tragic event that Balder's dreams foretold is recounted in two startlingly different versions in the sources. The two are more or less irreconcilable, so we'll look at each of them separately. We'll start with the better-known one: Snorri's version from the *Prose Edda*.

Three of Snorri's sources are known to us: *The Prophecy of the Seeress*, *Balder's Dreams*, and Ulf Uggason's *House Poem* (*Húsdrápa*). However, Snorri seems to have also relied on other sources, perhaps several of them, which have been lost.[1] Thus, while some of the details of Snorri's account are corroborated by other sources (many of which have their own problems when it comes to reliability), there's much in Snorri's retelling that is unique to it. Some of those elements probably come from those lost sources, but others seem to have come from Snorri's own mind.

Snorri's aim of presenting the Norse religion as a groping toward Christianity surely colored his retelling of this myth, as it did his retelling of others – and, for that matter, the way he framed the whole *Prose Edda*.[2] This is perhaps most evident in his treatment of Balder as an innocent, passive sufferer that cannot help but remind a reader of Christ himself. Numerous other Old Norse sources – one of which we'll examine in the following chapter – portray Balder as a capable and fierce warrior, the very opposite of Snorri's characterization of him. While this version of the myth of Balder's death certainly wasn't invented out of thin air, it can't be taken at face value as representing an authentic product of the Viking Age. It's a mixed bag in that regard.

# THE DEATH OF BALDER

Although the gods knew what fate was to befall their cherished Balder, they couldn't bring themselves to admit that they were helpless against it. Instead, they did everything within their power to forestall the inevitable. Frigg, Balder's mother, went around to everything in the cosmos – all animals, all plants, fire, water, iron, rocks, disease, and anything else that can be found in all the worlds – and obtained solemn oaths from them that they would never harm her son in any way.

After this had been completed, the gods amused themselves by throwing anything they could get their hands on at Balder, and watching in amazement and laughter as their arrows, axes, swords, and stones bounced off of him without wounding him in the slightest. Balder was as amazed and heartened by this as anyone else, and everyone thought it was a fitting way to honor his invincibility.

But this invincibility was soon to be exposed as a sham, for Frigg had made a mistake that would cost the gods dearly.

The devious Loki went to Frigg disguised as an ordinary woman and asked her if there was anything from which she had failed to secure an oath to not injure her son. "Well," Frigg said casually, "I didn't bother to ask the mistletoe. After all, it's such a small, slight, and weak thing; what damage could it possibly do to Balder?" This was exactly the kind of information Loki had been hoping to hear. He went away at once, found some mistletoe growing to the west of Valhalla, and set about crafting a spear out of it.

Loki took the mistletoe spear to where the deities were merrily throwing things at the impervious Balder. He found Hod, Balder's brother, standing in the back of the assembled gods. Hod was blind, and couldn't take aim at Balder on his own, so he contended himself with listening to what was going on rather than participating.

Loki approached the blind god and said to him, "Hod, my dear friend, it's simply improper that you alone of all the gods are not honoring Balder by demonstrating his invincibility to all present. Here," and he put the mistletoe spear into his hands. "I will direct your aim, and when I tell you, let it loose." Loki positioned Hod's arms until the mistletoe was pointing straight at his brother's chest. "Fire!" shrieked Loki with delight.

Hod threw the missile into the empty darkness ahead of him. Then he heard a loud thwack, a nightmarish scream of pain, and a thud that almost seemed to echo through the utter silence that followed.

The stunned gods remained speechless for a long moment. Balder lay lifeless in a pool of red on the ground in front of them, felled by a mere piece of mistletoe.

The first sounds to rupture the silence were muffled sobs, which gradually gave way to open weeping by everyone present. But none felt their sorrow more deeply than Odin, who understood better than any of them the full ramifications of the death of his son: it was a presage of Ragnarok, of the death of all the gods, and of his own death along with them.

Everyone knew who was responsible for this murder, but Asgard was such a holy sanctuary that none dared to shed blood within its walls, even in punishment for such a cruel and destructive act.

The first one to speak was Frigg. "My son is now surely in Hel with the other shades of the dead. If any of you will volunteer to travel to that gloomy, grimy realm and negotiate Balder's release with the goddess for whom that place is named, you will thereby earn my eternal esteem and love." One god stepped forward: Hermod, another son of Odin. With a look of noble resolve on his tear-stained face, he volunteered for the mission. Odin let him borrow Sleipnir, the most capable horse to bear him on such a perilous task, and off he sped for Hel.

The gods then turned their attention to holding a funeral for their fallen companion. He was to be given a stately send-off, with his own magnificent ship serving as his pyre. But when it came time to launch the boat from the land, the puzzled gods found that it wouldn't budge from the bank. Exasperated, the gods called on Hyrrokkin, "Withered by Fire," an exceedingly mighty giantess. Hyrrokkin rode all the way from Jotunheim on a wolf and using vipers for reins. When she arrived, it took four berserkers to subdue and tie up her vicious steed. Hyrrokkin was able to get Balder's ship into the water with one heave so tremendous that it set the rollers on fire and caused the whole land to quake. Thor, that great hater of Hyrrokkin's kind, suspected that she was trying to kill everyone present. He brandished his hammer and would have smote her then and there had the other gods not held him back.

Balder's body was carried with the utmost ceremony onto the ship. His wife, Nanna, stood amongst the mourners, and when she saw her husband's body being carried up to be burned, she collapsed in anguish and died on the spot. The gods thought it fitting to place her body beside that of her husband on the pile of wood on the ship, and commemorate both of them together. A fire was lit underneath them, and Thor hallowed it with his hammer as it began to slowly consume the wood upon which they lay. A dwarf named Lit, "Colorful," ran in front of Thor as he held his hammer over the ship, and the thunder god kicked the dwarf into the flames. Odin solemnly placed his legendary ring Draupnir, from which eight other rings fall every ninth night, onto the fire. Balder's horse, fitted with all his trappings, was led alive into the blaze.

As all who were in attendance – all the gods, the elves, the dwarves, and even some giants – looked on, the fire slowly devoured the entire boat, sending a thick plume of black smoke and the rancid stench of burning flesh into the air. The fire was quenched only when the charred debris of the ship sank beneath the waves. Then, on the spot where this violent sensorial and emotional ordeal had just taken place, the water and air became perfectly still and calm – almost eerily so.

Meanwhile, Hermod was riding Sleipnir to Hel in hopes of freeing him from the clutches of the death goddess. He rode for nine nights through ever deeper and darker valleys. Eventually, the lack of daylight in those sunken lands and thick, twisted forests became such that he couldn't see at all, and had to rely on Sleipnir's subtler senses.

Then, in the murky blackness in front of him, he saw glittering gold – first faint, then brilliant. This was the golden bridge over the furiously churning river Gjoll, "Loud Noise," which encircled the underworld.

When he came to the bridge, a fearsome giantess named Modgud, "Fierce Battle," stopped him. "Who are you, and what kind of being?" she demanded. "Yesterday, five whole armies of dead men passed over this bridge. But it shakes just the same when you cross it alone, and for that matter" – and she eyed him suspiciously – "you have more color in your face than a dead man does."

Hermod answered her, "I have been sent to seek Balder in Hel. Have you seen him?" She answered that he had passed that way some time ago, and that she would let him proceed on his journey.

On the far side of the bridge, the weary but persistent traveler reached the gate of Hel. It was closed, and he had no means of prying open the heavy doors. But no wall was too high for Sleipnir, who jumped over the fence with the god on his back. The two made their way to Hel's hall. Hermod dismounted, left Sleipnir outside the door, and went into the hall. Inside, he found Balder, pale, stone-faced, and unmoving, sitting in the seat of honor next to Hel herself.

After spending the night there as a polite guest, Hermod got down to business. He implored Hel to let his brother go free, telling her how everything in the universe was weeping over his absence.

Hel listened to his entreaties with a grim expression. When he had finished, she said, "You say that all the gods and their creation weep for Balder. That claim can be put to the test, and that is what I propose to do. If you can make every last creature in the cosmos cry and mourn over the loss of Balder, then I will allow him to return with you to the world of the living. But if even one stone, one flea, or one blade of grass withholds its tears, then Balder shall remain with me." Hermod enthusiastically agreed to these terms, and thanked Hel profusely for her willingness to compromise. As Hermod was preparing to leave, Balder handed him Draupnir so that Odin would have something to remember him by, and Nanna gave him fine clothes and jewelry for Frigg.

When Hermod returned to Asgard and told the gods what Hel had said, they wasted no time in going around to everything in the universe and ensuring that they were all weeping – every elf, every dwarf, every human, every plant, every animal, every mountain, every river, every star. By the time they were nearing the end of their quest, everything they had come across so far had sobbed bitterly over Balder, and the gods were becoming hopeful that they would pass Hel's test.

But then they found a lone giantess named Thokk, "Thanks," in a cave. Her eyes were dry. When they asked her to find enough compassionate sadness in her heart to cry over Balder and allow him to return to life, she scoffed and told them, "I never loved that churl of yours. Let Hel hold what she has." Some say that Thokk was none other than Loki in disguise, and they are probably right. In any case, the gods failed that day, and Balder was doomed to remain with Hel until Ragnarok.

# Chapter 40:

# Balder's Death

# (Version 2)

The second "full" version of the myth of Balder's death that has come down to us is that of the medieval Danish historian Saxo Grammaticus in his *History of the Danes* (*Gesta Danorum*).

Saxo's version is radically different from Snorri's. Balder and Hod aren't brothers. Hod isn't blind. Nanna is in love with Hod, and Balder tries to steal her from him against her wishes. Balder is killed by a sword (albeit still a weapon with something "special" or "magical" about it) rather than a mistletoe spear. Loki doesn't feature in the tale at all. Perhaps most significantly, Balder's entire personality is almost the exact opposite of the way it's portrayed in the *Prose Edda*. Here, rather than an irreproachable, almost martyr-like figure, Balder is a belligerently ambitious warlord – a character and career far more fitting for a Norse god than what Snorri makes him out to be. As we've seen, this view of Balder is corroborated by numerous references from Old Norse literature, as well as the most likely meaning of his name, "Bold."[1] The same goes for Hod, too; Snorri's characterization of him as an unwitting pawn of Loki stands in remarkable tension with his name – Old Norse *Höðr*, "Warrior."[2]

Many of the other elements of Saxo's tale also find support elsewhere in the Norse sources, so it's clear that Saxo's account is based on a traditional version of the myth, and didn't come solely from his own imagination. (Nevertheless, Saxo weaves into his version threads of pseudo-historical stories of Danish kings, which are irrelevant and have been filtered out of my retelling below as much as possible.) Famed Old Norse scholar E.O.G. Turville-Petre has made a convincing case that Snorri's version is based predominantly on Icelandic sources, whereas Saxo's is mostly indebted to Danish ones.[3] In that case, some of the differences between them could be explained as regional variations.

Either way, the gaping differences between Snorri's and Saxo's accounts of what is clearly the same underlying story provide an excellent example of the startling diversity of the pre-Christian Norse myths. They reinforce a point that has been made repeatedly throughout this book: that the Vikings were quite content with what to modern sensibilities is a downright shocking lack of rational order and systematization in their mythology, and, more broadly, the religion of which it was a part. There was never one single "standard" version of any of their myths, and modern attempts to create an appearance to the contrary are illusions. Whether or not this is a good thing or a bad thing will naturally depend on your own aesthetic preferences, but it's something that every honest student of Norse mythology must grapple with one way or another.

Finally, Turville-Petre has made another intriguing suggestion regarding this myth. In his well-reasoned estimation, there very well may have been another version – or a common interpretation of the other versions – in which Balder was killed by none other than Odin, his father. In this view, Hod is nothing more than yet another one of Odin's countless disguises. It's not difficult to see what Odin's motivations for committing such an otherwise grisly and tragic murder would have been; after all, did he not often arrange the deaths of other heroes in order to have them join his army in Valhalla and fight at his side during Ragnarok?[4]

# THE DEATH OF BALDER

Hod was an extremely precocious boy who grew into an extremely talented man. He spent his childhood as the foster-son of the rich and powerful god Gevar, the father of the beautiful goddess Nanna. Gevar sought out the best experts in all fields to educate the god he had adopted as his son, and by the time he had grown up, Hod was a master of swimming, archery, wrestling, all fields of scholarly learning, and music. In fact, he was one of the finest players of virtually every instrument there was. When he opened his mouth to sing, or placed his hands on a harp, the emotions of anyone within earshot became his playthings. Because of his many accomplishments, Nanna became quite attracted to him.

But Nanna soon found that she had another suitor. One day, Balder, a brash warrior and one of Odin's favorite sons, happened to catch sight of her while she was bathing in a river. He hid behind a tree and watched for as long as he could as she ran her washcloth along the perfect curves of her naked body. He became so smitten with lust for her that he resolved to kill Hod to remove his competition for her embraces.

Meanwhile, Hod was hunting in another part of the forest. A thick fog rolled in, and he lost his way. While wandering over the hills and trying to get his bearings, he stumbled upon a troop of Valkyries who addressed him by name.

"Who are you, and how do you know my name?" he asked, mystified.

"We are the women who decide the outcomes of battles, who bless and guide certain heroes, and ensure the doom of others," they replied. Then they told him about what was happening in Balder's heart and thoughts and gave him an impenetrable coat of mail to wear in his coming struggle with Balder. However, they warned him not to immediately challenge Balder to a fight, but to wait until the time was right. Then, as Hod was already overwhelmed and bewildered by this news, the women vanished, and he found himself alone in the forest.

When Hod returned to Gevar's house, he told his patron what had happened and what he had been told. Then he promptly asked for Nanna's hand in marriage. Gevar sighed resignedly and said, "Although I would greatly prefer Nanna to be married to you than to Balder, I fear what Balder might do to me when he finds out."

After a moment of melancholy silence, Gevar's expression became lighter, and his body moved with a sudden pulse of inspiration. "However," he added, "I may be able to help you get rid of your competitor. Even though he is so strong that his body might as well be made of steel, there is one weapon that might be able to fell him. Acquiring it, however, will subject you to great peril. Deep in the mountains in the north, where the cold is so relentless that nothing but wretched lichens can grow on the rocks, there lives a giant named Miming. Miming owns a sword that never fails to slay anyone whom it is turned against, and a golden bracelet that can make its wearer almost as rich as Njord. There is no road that leads to where Miming lives. Only an expert navigator can successfully traverse those frozen wastelands, and only if he has a team of reindeer to drive his chariot. When you reach Miming's cave, set up your tent in a space near the entrance exposed to the daylight. When you see the giant's shadow approach your tent, stab him with your spear before he has a chance to kill you or to flee into the endless blackness of his cave. Then you can take his sword and his bracelet."

Hod did as Gevar instructed, made it to the mouth of the giant's cave, set up his tent, and waited. For many days, he went without sleep in case Miming arrived during the night. And one night, as Hod sat in anxious contemplation in the bitter cold, fighting hard not to doze off, a shadow fell upon his moonlit tent. At just the right moment, Hod lunged at the dark form with his spear. A piercing shriek of pain echoed across the mountains as Hod ran from his tent, captured Miming, and bound him. He threatened him with all kinds of grisly torture if he didn't give up his sword and ring. With little choice,

Miming did just that. The giant then disappeared into his cave to nurse his wound, and the triumphant warrior broke camp and headed home.

Back at Gevar's house, Balder was courting Nanna. She refused him as politely and cleverly as she could, saying that his strength and power made her undeserving of him, and that she feared what he might one day do to her because of their different statures.

When Hod returned and learned what Balder had been doing, he became furious. Figuring that enough time had elapsed since the Valkyries' warning in the woods, he decided, after much deliberation, to fight Balder openly.

The two sides met in a fierce sea battle. Odin and Thor led a great army of gods who fought on behalf of their beloved Balder, while Hod commanded another formidable host. Hod, clad in the coat of mail he had been given by the Valkyries, ran wildly through the ranks of Balder's soldiers, cutting down anyone who stood in his way. But Thor took up his hammer and rampaged through Hod's fighters. No shield, no helmet, and no armor could withstand the force of Mjollnir when swung by the thunder god. Hod's warriors were about to give up and flee when Hod charged at Thor, struck Mjollnir, and lopped off its handle, rendering it useless. Deprived of their best weapon, Thor, Odin, Balder, and all who remained of their force had no choice but to retreat. The victors, to celebrate their triumph, hacked to pieces the ships that had been left behind. But they went out of their way to honor the strength and bravery of their foes by giving them a splendid and dignified funeral.

Hod returned to Gevar's house a war hero. When he asked Gevar once more for his daughter's hand in marriage, Gevar delightfully consented. Hod and Nanna were at last joined in that union for which both had yearned so passionately and for so long. At their wedding, joke after mocking joke was told at the expense of the vanquished Balder.

Though defeated in both war and in love, Balder refused to relinquish to his foe what his heart desired. Hod and Balder met in battle again, and this time Balder won. However, he failed to gain

Nanna from Hod, and this loss tormented him so thoroughly that by day he could think of nothing else, and by night he could dream of nothing else. His obsession chipped away at his health until he grew so weak that he lost the ability to walk, and had to be carried on a litter or driven in a chariot to get anywhere.

But this only strengthened his desperate resolve. He engaged his hated rival in battle yet again. Just as before, he won the battle, but without gaining the prize for which he had fought.

Yet these repeated losses weighed heavily on Hod's heart. His honor had been tarnished. He could no longer bear to look anyone else in the eye, and he grew to loathe the company of others. One day, he pulled himself together just enough to announce to his most trusted friends that he was going away to live alone in a remote wilderness, and didn't know when, or if, he'd return. Then he departed, and no one heard anything from him for a long time.

In his vast, wild refuge of solitude, Hod spent his days hunting, fishing, gathering berries and herbs, and trying to forget about his earlier life. One day, while wandering in the woods, he found himself face to face with the same Valkyries who had given him his matchless armor those many years before.

"Why are you here?" they asked him.

"Because I have lost too many battles to be able to hold my head high when I am among other men," he replied despondently. "You promised me victory," he charged with a flash of anger in his voice, "but that's not the way things have worked out, is it?" Then he sat down on the dirt and began to sob helplessly.

One of the women walked over to him and began to stroke his hair. "But you've defeated Balder at least as often and as severely as he has defeated you, have you not?" she reminded him. "Though you may have lost more battles than he, you still have the one thing that he desires above all else, and which he has been unable to wrest from you: the love of your wife Nanna." She sat down next to Hod. "Balder is renowned for being so strong as to be almost invincible, but he has a weakness that few know about. Were it not for a rare food that another band of Valkyries feed him, he would be no stronger than any other spoiled king's son. If you can obtain some of this vivifying fare for yourself, Balder will be no match for you, and you will have no trouble dealing him a resounding, final defeat."

These words gave Hod the courage and confidence he needed. He wasted no time in leaving his squalid hovel in the wilderness and walking the many miles back to his grand home. His wife, his companions, and his servants were all overjoyed by his return. He immediately set about devising plans to renew his feud with his adversary.

Soon thereafter, Hod and Balder met in battle once again. By the end of the first day of fighting, the wide plain was littered with countless corpses. Hod went to sleep that night with his heart troubled about the prospects for the coming day, and his anxieties awoke him long before dawn. Unable to fall back asleep, he got up and crept toward his enemy's camp to spy on them and plan his moves for the coming day. His heart leapt when he saw three mysterious-looking women emerge from Balder's tent with a tray of food. Could this be the magically empowering nourishment the Valkyries had told him about during his time in the wilderness?

He surreptitiously followed the maidens through the forest until he came to their encampment. When he stepped into their firelight, they demanded to know who he was. He replied that he was a simple minstrel who had approached them in search of hospitality for the night. To back up his claim, he picked up a lyre they had with them amongst their possessions, tuned it, and began to serenade them with the most moving music they had ever heard. Their hearts were alternately roused, broken, and mended.

As Hod played, an enormous, sinister viper dribbled venom into a bowl, whose contents the women periodically poured out and mixed with food. This, Hod understood, was how Balder's special nourishment was made. When the minstrel had finished his set, the Valkyries debated whether or not it was proper to reward him with a sample of this potent food. In the end, they decided to give him a taste

– after all, he was only a minstrel and couldn't use this gift against Balder, could he? Having obtained what he wanted, Hod left them and, brimming with happiness, began to make his way back to his camp just as the first rumors of dawn began to lighten the sky.

Along the way, he had to pass near the camp of his enemy's forces. As it turned out, Balder had just emerged from his tent to prepare himself for the day's fight. Hod snuck up on him and plunged Miming's sword into his side, dealing him his mortal wound.

But Balder didn't die immediately. Instead, he spent the next days wasting away while being carried around on his litter so that his troops could pretend that he was still relatively well. One night, Hel came to him in a dream and told him that, in three nights' time, he would join her in her subterranean kingdom. And, on the third night after that dream, its message came true. Balder succumbed to his wounds, and was buried in a tall mound.

All of the gods who had remained on Balder's side throughout this conflict mourned him long and intensely. None felt this loss more deeply than Odin, who not only understood its magnitude more than the others, but had lost one of his foremost sons. As the seeress in Hel had predicted, he vowed revenge.

Odin mounted Sleipnir and rode to Jotunheim, where he located the giantess Rind, whom the prophecies had said would be the mother of the child who would avenge Balder's death. But Rind would have nothing to do with the sorcerer god, and he succeeded in impregnating her only by disguising himself as a female doctor who had come to help her when she was ill, and then raping her. She gave birth to a son named Bous, who went on to fight Hod in battle. Each dealt the other his death blow.

# CHAPTER 41:
# LOKI'S TAUNTS

This story, in which the gods' dirty laundry is aired spectacularly, comes from the poem *Loki's Taunts* (*Lokasenna*) in the *Poetic Edda*. The date of the poem's composition is disputed, with arguments ranging from the tenth to twelfth centuries, but virtually all scholars agree that it dates from the period of transition to Christianity (tenth century) at the earliest.[1]

The poem's dialogue alludes to numerous other myths, some of which are known from other sources, and some of which are unattested outside of this poem. For the ones that fall into that latter category, it's unclear to what degree the poet had access to sources we don't and based the cryptic passages in the dialogue on these, and to what degree he was making stuff up to give Loki and the other gods something to say as they hurled insults back and forth at each other.[2]

The poem says that Loki had prevented Balder from coming to the feast, but it's unclear whether he had first killed Balder, or whether Balder was still alive and Loki had just prevented him from going to that one particular event because he couldn't find anything insulting to say to him.[3]

Nor do we know whether or not the framing story is a traditional Viking Age myth. It could have been, but it could have also been the invention of a poet sympathetic to Christianity, who wanted to cast the deities of his forebears in an unflattering light by drawing attention to their shortcomings.

## LOKI'S TAUNTS

The giant Aegir, "Sea Giant," was usually on friendly terms with the gods. Once, he invited them to a feast in his splendid hall, which was covered in so much shining, reflective gold that there was hardly need for fire to see by. All gladly accepted the offer, but when the night of the feast came, Thor was elsewhere slaying other, more hostile giants, and was unable to make it. But scores of other gods and elves arrived at Aegir's hall and were shown in by two servants, Fimafeng, "Busy," and Eldir, "Fire-Lighter."

The ale was served, and everyone was jovial and at peace. Much praise was heaped on Aegir's servants. This made Loki jealous, and when Fimafeng came over to fill his horn, he drew his sword and slew him. The other gods screamed at Loki, banged on their shields, and chased him out of the bright hall and into the forest. There he stewed in his anger for a while before deciding to force his way back in and make known his feelings about the gods.

At the door of the hall, Loki met Eldir. He grabbed the servant roughly by the arm and said, "Tell me, Eldir, what are the guests talking about now? Answer me, or I'll make sure that you never take another step."

Eldir replied nervously, "They're talking about their accomplishments in war, and how marvelous their weapons are. If I were you, Loki, I wouldn't go back in there, for you will find no one who will be well-disposed toward you."

Loki frowned. "I'm going in anyway. The gods deserve to have their boasts ruined, like poison in their drinks."

Eldir tried one more time. "If you go in there and try to smear the gods with slander, be prepared for them to fling it back at you."

A wormlike, hateful smile wriggled its way into Loki's lips. "Foolish Eldir, the more you try to dissuade me, the more practice you're going to give me." He released his grip on Aegir's servant as he violently shoved him aside. Then he opened the door and entered the hall.

When the guests saw him, all their merriment ceased, and they sat in silence and scowled at him. He barked, "I'm thirsty after my long journey. Someone pour me a drink!" When no one budged and no one said anything, he continued, "Come on, you arrogant cowards! Either make room for me at your table or make me leave."

Finally, Bragi, the bard of Valhalla, spoke up. "The gods know very well who they want at their feasts and who they don't. They've made the mistake of finding you a seat with them in the past, but they will surely do so no more."

Loki turned to Odin and spoke to him in a sarcastically pleading tone of voice. "Don't you remember, Odin, that we once mixed our blood together? On that occasion, you promised you'd never taste alcohol unless both of us drank together."

Odin, knowing that his honor was at stake, grudgingly gestured for Loki to be given a seat and a drink. "Go ahead and give the wolf's father what he wants, lest he should speak ill of us here."

Before Loki took a sip of his drink, he made a toast. "Hail to you, gods! Hail to you, goddesses! Hail to all of you -- well, except for Bragi over there."

Bragi tried to bargain with the intruder to prevent the situation from escalating. "I'll give you a horse, a sword, and a ring if you can hold yourself together and not incite any more anger in the hearts of the gods."

Loki quipped, "You've never been rich enough in horses, swords, or rings to make such an offer. But perhaps you would be if you had ever shown the slightest bit of bravery in battle."

Bragi snarled, "If it weren't for the fact that we're guests in another's hall, I'd pay you the price you deserve for your lies by chopping off your head here and now!"

Loki laughed. "Oh, Bragi, you ornament of benches, you're so much bolder while sitting than while standing!"

Before Bragi could respond, his wife Idun grabbed his arm and said to him in a calming tone of voice, "Consider, husband, how close in kinship he is to the others here. Stop this rash chatter between the two of you."

But this only made Loki turn his ire toward her instead. "Shut up, Idun! Of all of the slutty goddesses here, you may be the worst of all! Remember that time you wrapped your arms around the man who killed your own brother?"

Idun remained resolutely calm. Looking straight ahead and not at Loki, she said, "I'm not going to speak to Loki here in Aegir's hall."

Then Gefjun spoke up, addressing everyone present. "Why are we bothering to match hate with hate? We already know that Loki is an idle mocker who hates us all."

"Ah, Gefjun," said Loki with a tone of amusement, "What has turned your heart so black? Was it the time you wrapped your legs around a handsome boy who gave you a necklace?"

Odin intervened. "It doesn't strike me as wise, Loki, to incur the wrath of Gefjun. She has the power of insight and prophecy just like I do, you know."

"Shut up, Odin!" Loki shouted. "You meddle in the outcomes of countless battles, yet not once have you awarded victory justly. To the lesser party you grant a resounding triumph, and to the greater a crushing defeat."

"Well," Odin retorted, "at least it wasn't me who lived underground for eight winters, milking the cows like a woman, and even bearing children. That was rather *argr* of you, now wasn't it?"

"But it wasn't me who donned the dress of a woman and traveled among men as a witch, chanting, beating the drum, and casting spells. Now *that*, it seems to me, is wholly *argr*."

Frigg had a look of shame on her face and interjected, "Neither of you should speak of the deeds you did in olden times."

Her attempt at peacemaking fell flat. The next words spoken were Loki's. "Shut up, Frigg! Speaking of olden times, do you recall that you slept with Vili and Ve while your husband was away?"

Frigg scolded, "If Balder, my hawkish son, were here by my side, you wouldn't emerge from this hall alive."

Loki snorted. "Would you like to know why Balder isn't here, Frigg? I myself prevented him from coming. So much for your son's fabled strength."

Freya chimed in. "Loki, only an idiot would go out of his way to let others know what shameful crimes he has committed. And to tell them to Frigg, who knows the fate of all beings, even you, is that much more ill-advised."

"Shut up, Freya!" sneered Loki. "You're not exactly blameless yourself. In fact, of all of the gods and elves who are gathered here now, there isn't a single one of them who hasn't been inside you."

Freya had a look of mixed terror and hate on her face, and said to him, "If you don't stop taunting the gods with your false tongue, it will be the weapon that finally kills you."

"Shut up, Freya, you witch! Don't you remember that time the gods walked in on you and your brother, as you moaned with delight in his arms?"

Njord entered the fray on his daughter's behalf. "It seems to me that it's no big deal if a woman has an affair here and there. But it's a marvel that such a taunt would come from a man so *argr* that he's borne children of his own!"

"Shut up, Njord! You once let giantesses use your mouth as an outhouse!" jabbed Loki.

"But my son Frey is the foremost of all the gods, and is hated by no one," replied Njord. "I'd say I've done quite well for myself."

Loki scoffed, "You mean the son you had with your own sister?"

Tyr spoke up. "We all know that Frey is the bravest of all the heroes who sit in this hall. And unlike you, Loki, he harms no one who doesn't deserve it, but instead liberates them from those would do them wrong."

"Shut up, Tyr! You've never been able to bring men to peace, but only to war. And need I tell the story of how you lost your hand to my son, the wolf?"

"It's true that I lost my hand to Fenrir," Tyr conceded, "but you thereby lost your son, who lies in chains for aeons."

"Shut up, Tyr! Your wife deemed it a great honor when I let her have a son by me. And what vengeance have you gotten for that grave dishonor? Hah!"

Then Frey reciprocated Tyr's remarks on his behalf. "Fenrir howls and rattles his chains impotently for millennia on end, and so shall you, Loki, if you don't master your tongue."

"The only way you could get a wife was by buying her from her father with gold," jeered Loki at Frey. "When the fire-giants ride from Muspelheim to torch your pretty little world, you will find yourself helpless against them."

Byggvir, Frey's servant, came to his master's defense. "If I were as high-born as Frey, and had won so much admiration for my deeds, I would beat this scoundrel until he's nothing but a slushy puddle on the floor."

Loki snapped, "What a pathetic little creature you are, always crawling around at your master's heels. Never have you been seen anywhere else – except toiling hard in his stead."

Byggvir made a point to sit up especially straight in his chair. "I have earned the respect of all of the gods for my dutiful service."

"But when it came time for battle, you hid in the straw on the floor!" cackled Loki.

Heimdall tried to be the voice of reason. "Loki, listen to yourself. You're drunk. Why don't you leave before you embarrass yourself further? Intemperance will lead anyone to say ill-considered things."

Loki, of course, would have none of that. "Heimdall, you're just upset because the gods long ago appointed you to guard their fortress, and that's all you do, day in and day out – stand there and stand there while your back grows stiff."

Then Skadi said to Loki, "Enjoy your freedom while it lasts. Soon the gods will bind you in chains made from the bowels of your own son, whose body will be as cold as ice."

"Perhaps it is so," replied Loki, "but the last sight your father Thjazi ever saw was me as I slew him."

Skadi's face grew pale, and her eyes narrowed. "If that is true, then I have nothing for you but words and deeds as cold as the glaciers where I live."

Loki burst into contemptuous laughter. "You certainly had something else for me that time you beckoned me to your bed!"

Sif, Thor's gracious wife, walked over to where Loki was sitting. She filled with mead a hearty cup made of fine crystal. "Take this gift from me," she said to him, "because you know that, of all those gathered here, I alone am blameless."

Loki saw through the brazen attempt to bribe him. After downing the entire glass unceremoniously, he smacked his lips and said to her, "Well, Sif, what you say would be true if you had remained faithful to your husband. But I'm sure that everyone here would be interested to know to whom you went while Thor was away." He looked at her with a knowing smile while he waited for her response. For, of course, it had been none other than Loki.

A faint rumbling was heard in the distance. Beyla, the wife of Byggvir, addressed the guests: "Surely that is Thor returning from his journey. When he gets here, he won't put up with this slimy disparager for long."

As if to get in one last lick before the mighty thunder god's arrival, Loki growled, "Shut up, Beyla! As if it weren't shameful enough to be married to someone as lowly as Byggvir, you've done plenty of other misdeeds that we all know about."

Thor entered the hall and heard what was going on. He walked to Loki's chair and loomed over him, holding his hammer up menacingly. "*Argr* wretch! Keep your mouth closed or I'll close it for you with my hammer. Then I'll rip your neck from your shoulders, and that will be the end of you."

Loki pretended he wasn't afraid. "Son of Jord, why treat me so coarsely? Save your energy for when you have to fight the great serpent at Ragnarok."

Thor tightened his grip on Mjollnir. "End your insults now or I'll throw your helpless body to the giants and let them do with you what they will."

Loki smiled up at Thor mockingly. "It's not as though you've exactly fared well among the giants, either. Remember that time you cowered in one of their gloves?"

Thor bellowed, "The hammer that slew Hrungnir can certainly slay you, *argr* lowlife, and if you don't cease your taunts, it will crush every bone in your body to dust."

Loki chuckled. "I think I'll live a long time yet. After all, you were quite confident in your ability to open the straps of Skrymir's bag, but you went hungry that night, didn't you?"

Thor hissed through his teeth, "One more taunt from you and I'll knock you all the way down to the gates of Hel!"

Loki sighed and looked around the hall with an expression of contemplation. After a few moments, he said, "Everything I have spoken here tonight has been true, and all of you know it. But all of us also know that I am no match for the great Thor, so here I will cease to speak my mind and go forth from this splendid hall." Looking around the room once more, he added, "Aegir, your feasts and your ale have lived up to their reputation. It is perfectly plain why you are so famous a host. But enjoy your banquets while you can, because in less time than you may think, the flames of Ragnarok will leap and dance through your hall and all over your body."

With that, the trickster fled, with the other gods in hot pursuit.

# CHAPTER 42:
# LOKI'S PUNISHMENT

The tale of the punishment the gods meted out to Loki for his countless misdeeds comes from the prose ending of the Eddic poem *Loki's Taunts*, as well as a longer version from Snorri's *Prose Edda*. Other Old Norse sources contain passing references to details from the narrative.

In *Loki's Taunts*, the fact that the binding of Loki directly follows his almost bottomless slandering of the deities seems to clearly indicate that this was the crime for which he was caught and bound. Snorri, by contrast, explicitly connects Loki's punishment to his culpability for the death of Balder. But we can assume that, whatever the proximate causes for Loki's imprisonment were – and surely these differed from telling to telling during the Viking Age – the ultimate cause was simply who Loki was: one of the foremost enemies of the gods. Despite his highly ambivalent character, which led him to sometimes aid or even rescue the gods (usually after putting some or all of them in grave danger in the first place), on balance Loki proved to be a bringer of misfortune and ruin. Therefore, the gods did what they could to get him out of the way – at least for as long as he was fated to remain there, which was not forever. But Loki's liberation will have to be left for another story.

## LOKI'S PUNISHMENT

The gods pursued Loki until they lost him in a deep, trackless wilderness. He fled to the top of a mountain, where he built a house with four doors so that he could see the land below from all directions.

Not too far from his house, a cold stream tumbled through the ice and rocks. Salmon swam in that stream, and some days, when the fear of the gods finding him struck him especially hard, he turned himself into a salmon and hid under a waterfall in the stream.

One day, the crisis Loki had feared arrived. As he sat in his house weaving a net for fishing, he saw a troop of figures approaching from below. He ran to one of his doors and peered out from behind it. As the people below drew close enough for him to make out their forms, he saw that they were indeed the gods. In a panic, he flung the net into the fire so as not to leave any clues about his activities, then vanished from his house.

When the gods entered Loki's empty house, the wise Kvasir noticed the remnants of the net in the fire. The gods examined it, and determined that it must have been a net for fishing. They set about crafting another net in the likeness of the one Loki had abandoned. Upon finishing it, they took it down to the stream and cast it into the waterfall. Loki, who had taken up the form a salmon, darted out of its way just in time and hid between two rocks in the streambed. The gods pulled the net out and cast it in a second time, having added weights to it so that it would scoop up anything and everything at the bottom of the stream. Loki evaded the snare once more. Seeing that the open ocean was just a short distance away, Loki leapt out of the stream and over the net in hopes of outsmarting the gods and swimming to safety. But Thor caught him with his hand in mid-flight. Loki tried to squirm out of the mighty hand, but Thor held him fast by the tail – and the firmness of Thor's grip left the salmon with a tapered back, which it still has to this day.

The gods carried the terrified Loki to a cave. There they brought his two beloved sons, Vali and Nari. The gods turned Vali into a wolf and made Loki watch as one of his sons tore apart the helplessly screaming and flailing body of the other. The gods then drew Nari's entrails out of his corpse, drilled holes in three large rock formations in the cave, and tied Loki to the rocks with his son's bowels. As soon as

Loki was bound with the intestines, they turned to solid, thick iron, imprisoning him.

Skadi approached the furious, despairing trickster with a huge viper in her hands. With a malicious smile, she said to him, "This is your payment for killing my father, Thjazi." Then she placed the serpent on a ledge just above him. Venom dripped from its jaws and onto Loki's forehead, stinging intolerably every time. Loki yelped and writhed in pain, shaking the earth.

But Loki was shown mercy by his faithful, dutiful wife, Sigyn. To mitigate his suffering as best she could, she ran to his side and held a bowl over his head to catch the drops of poison from the snake. There by his side she has sat ever since. But every now and then, the bowl becomes full, and she has to leave the cave to empty it. During her absences, a few drops of venom reach Loki's head, causing him to thrash about in uncontrollable agony. When that happens, we who live on the surface of the earth experience earthquakes.

# CHAPTER 43:
# ANDVARI'S CURSE

The story of how Odin, Loki, and Hoenir got themselves into trouble over the killing of an otter survives in three versions: one from *The Song of Regin* (*Reginsmál*) in the *Poetic Edda*, a second from Snorri's *Prose Edda*, and a third from *The Saga of the Volsungs*. In addition to being a standalone story in its own right, this tale also sets the stage for the life of Sigurd – the exemplary Norse hero of whom we'll read in the next chapter. Due to the number of versions of the story that have come down to us, we can confidently say that this myth originated in the Viking Age, or quite possibly even earlier.

## ANDVARI'S CURSE

Odin, Loki, and Hoenir were traveling in Midgard, the world of humankind, following a river to mark their course. They came to a waterfall in the river, and on a rock by the waterfall sat an otter munching on a salmon he had just caught. Loki picked up a rock and threw it skillfully at the otter, striking his head and knocking him dead on the spot. The mischievous god giggled with delight, and boasted that he had caught both an otter and a salmon in just one throw.

The shadows were growing longer and the air beginning to chill, so the three sought lodging for the night in a nearby farmer's house. They offered the farmer, Hreidmar, the otter and the salmon for dinner, in hopes of repaying him for his hospitality.

But when Hreidmar saw the otter, his eyes grew wide with anger, and he nearly lost his balance. He called to his sons Fafnir, "Embracer," and Regin, "Mighty," who were within the house. When they came to his side, he showed them the dead otter and said to them, "These men who seek lodging with us tonight have killed your brother. What should we do with them?" The question was practically rhetorical. The three men glared up at the three disguised gods, seized them, and bound them. The otter had been Hreidmar's third son, Ot, "Otter," who had been a very successful fisherman on account of his ability to turn himself into an otter to do the fishing.

As Hreidmar and his sons were sharpening their axes in preparation for their vengeance, Odin proposed a settlement: in exchange for sparing their lives, the farmer and his family would receive as much wealth as they desired from the gods. This seemed like a good bargain to Hreidmar. He skinned the otter's body and demanded that his prisoners give him enough gold to cover the skin, inside and out.

Loki was sent to the underground homeland of the dwarves to acquire the gold. There he found the dwarf Andvari, "Careful," swimming through a stream in the shape of a fish. He caught Andvari and demanded all of his gold as the condition for his release. The terrified dwarf agreed, and took Loki to the rock in which all of his wealth was stored – and it was a great deal of wealth indeed. Andvari dutifully scooped almost all of his gold into Loki's bag, but tried to pocket one small ring without his kidnapper noticing. Loki saw the trick. "We agreed that I would receive *all* of your gold," he said, pointing to the dwarf's pocket. The exasperated Andvari handed Loki the ring, but placed a curse on it, saying that, from that day forward, the trinket would be the death of whoever owned it. Loki laughed and kept the ring despite the curse, gloating over the misfortune that he would be secretly bringing to Hreidmar through it.

Andvari's gold hoard proved to be just the right amount to cover the otter's skin, inside and out. Just before the gods presented it to the farmer, however, Odin noticed the ring. It seemed to him to be an especially beautiful ring, and he put it in his pocket to keep for himself.

Then Odin, Loki, and Hoenir handed the gold-covered hide to Hreidmar, and said to him, "Here is the restitution you are owed, according to our agreement. Now will you let us go on our way?"

The farmer inspected the hide in great detail and for a long time. At last, he said disapprovingly, "There is still one whisker that remains exposed. Cover it, too, with gold, or else you will not have fulfilled the terms of our deal."

With a look of sadness, Odin took the ring out of his pocket, and the whisker disappeared beneath it. "There," he said. "We have kept our end of the bargain. Now you keep yours. Let us go."

Hreidmar nodded and untied the gods. When they had gathered their belongings and weapons and were on their way out the door, Loki gleefully informed Hreidmar of the curse that had been placed on the ring. Then they went on their way.

As soon as the gods had left, Regin and Fafnir approached their father and told him sternly that they were owed a portion of the gold, since Ot had been not only Hreidmar's son, but their brother as well. Hreidmar scoffed at their demand, and said he had no intention of giving either of them so much as a penny of the treasure. The angry brothers slew him.

Fafnir picked up the gold and began to make off with it, but Regin grabbed him and told him that the fair thing to do would be to split the hoard in half between them. Fafnir refused, saying, "This treasure is worth so much to me that I murdered my own father for it. There's no chance that I will share it with you. Now leave me alone, or else you'll end up like our father."

In order to keep the gold from Regin, Fafnir fled with it to a desolate, uninhabited moor. He hid the hoard in a cave, turned himself into a gigantic, snakelike dragon that crawled along the ground on its belly, and lay on his treasure day and night.

263

# Chapter 44:
# The Saga of Sigurd

Sigurd (Old Norse *Sigurðr*, probably "Guardian of Victory" or "Fated to Victory"), a descendent of Odin, a member of the illustrious Volsung family, a slayer of dragons, a liberator of bewitched and imprisoned maidens, a possessor of shamanic abilities, and a warrior whose valor and accomplishments on the battlefield were without parallel, was by far the greatest human hero for the Norse – and, indeed, for virtually every other branch of the ancient Germanic peoples, too. The story of his life survives in too many different versions from too many parts of the Germanic lands to list them all here. The retelling in this chapter is primarily based on the version from *The Saga of the Volsungs*, the best-known, best-loved, and most detailed Old Norse version.

Parts of this myth *may* have had some kind of historical basis,[1] but whether or not that's the case is really beside the point. If elements that we today would consider "historical" are present in the tale, they're buried to the point of being indecipherable. The significance of the tale for the Vikings lay in its status as a myth – a timeless, sacred narrative – and not in any potential "historicity." The ancient Germanic peoples didn't share our modern concept of "history," so in order to understand and appreciate the story as they would have, we have to momentarily disregard our own concept of "history" and immerse ourselves in the much less precise but much more colorful world of myth.

# THE SAGA OF SIGURD

King Sigmund, the son of Volsung, the son of Rerir, the son of Sigi, the son of Odin, had obtained the hand of the stunningly beautiful princess Hjordis in marriage. Sigmund had won countless battles and overcome countless obstacles in his life, and now, in his old age, he had won yet another prize for which he had passionately yearned.

But Sigmund hadn't been the only suitor of Hjordis. The princess had also been courted by King Lyngvi, a younger but less accomplished man. In the end, Hjordis had chosen Sigmund due to his proven virtues. Lyngvi turned out to be a sore loser, and led his forces against Sigmund in hopes of wresting his bride by force.

In the thick of battle, King Sigmund found himself face to face with a tall man whose one-eyed face loomed darkly from beneath a broad-brimmed hat. The stranger came at Sigmund with a great spear, which Sigmund met with his sword. Sigmund's sword was no ordinary weapon; it had been given to him in his youth by Odin, and it sliced through iron like cloth. But on that day, it proved no match for the spear of the god who had given it to Sigmund those many decades ago. Odin's spear struck Sigmund's sword and broke the blade in two, then dealt the defenseless king his death blow. Then the shadowy form vanished, and returned to Valhalla to prepare for Sigmund's arrival.

Hjordis found her dying husband on the battlefield, and did everything within her power to staunch his wound. But it was no use. Sigmund turned to her, gently traced the outline of her face with his hand, and said to her, "You are with child. He shall grow up to become a truly magnificent man, and he shall avenge my death. Keep the pieces of my broken sword, for it will one day be forged anew. Then it will be stronger than ever, and it will be called Gram. Our boy shall wield it, and with it he will achieve many things that men think are impossible. As long as there are mouths to sing songs, the name of our son will be on their lips. But now, dear wife, I must go and be with my kinsmen who have come before me." With that, King Sigmund died.

Some months later, Hjordis, who had been granted protection by another king named Hjalprek, gave birth to a son. The king marveled at the boy's piercing eyes, and predicted that he would become such a man that none would be his equal. Hjordis named him Sigurd.

Regin, the son of Hreidmar, was appointed to be Sigurd's foster-father. Regin instructed the boy in all kinds of athletic and martial activities, foreign languages, and writing in runes – all fitting skills for a king's son.

When it came time for Sigurd to choose a horse for himself, he happened to meet a one-eyed man with a long beard in the forest. The man advised him to put the horses he was considering to a test: drive them into a mighty river and see if any had the strength and courage to swim to the other side rather than turn back in fear. Sigurd did as the old man had suggested, and all the horses fled except one: a young, handsome, gray stallion. Sigurd chose this one. The old man told him that he had chosen wisely, and that this horse – whose name was Grani – was a descendent of Sleipnir, the steed of Odin. Then the man disappeared.

When Sigurd brought Grani back to Regin's house, his foster-father admired the horse. Then he said to Sigurd, "Now, at last, you've found a fine, fitting horse for yourself. But you still have far too little wealth for someone of your parentage and stature. I know where and how you could obtain an enormous hoard of treasure, and win fame among all men in the process." Then Regin told him the story of his father, Hreidmar, and his brother, Fafnir – how Fafnir had killed Hreidmar, taken his gold, and stored it in a lair in the moors while changing himself into a dragon to guard it.

When Regin had finished, Sigurd said solemnly, "I am truly sorry for your loss. Your kinsmen have behaved cruelly and unjustly toward you." He agreed to fight Fafnir the dragon for the gold, and, in so doing, avenge Regin. But first, he said that Regin, who was a great smith, must fulfill Sigmund's prophecy and forge the sword Gram from the pieces of Sigmund's broken sword.

Sigurd obtained the pieces of Sigmund's sword from Hjordis and gave them to Regin. When Regin had finished and pulled the sword out of the fire, Sigurd tested it by striking it against an anvil. The anvil was split from the top to the bottom, but Gram didn't even have a scratch. Then he went down to a river, threw a tuft of wool into the current, and held the sword downstream from the wool. Instead of getting caught on the blade, the wool was split perfectly into two smaller tufts, which then floated on downstream. Sigurd praised Regin's work highly. "Now I have fulfilled my end of the bargain," said Regin, "and it is your turn to fulfill yours." Sigurd put his hand on his foster-father's shoulder and said, "I will fulfill my vow to you. But first, I must avenge my own father."

King Hjalprek gave Sigurd everything he needed for his quest of vengeance, and the sturdy young man set off with a large fleet of ships toward the lands of King Lyngvi. Along the way, a storm arose that threatened to rip the sails. They were passing by a craggy headland, and a man called out to them from the rocks, asking who was in charge of the fleet. When they told him it was Sigurd, he asked to join their expedition. They asked him what his name was, and he replied with a list of many of Odin's names. The men brought him on board with them, and immediately the wind and rain abated and the sun came out. They soon landed in Lyngvi's kingdom, and the stranger disappeared.

As soon as they had stepped on dry land, Sigurd and his men wasted no time, and immediately set about burning and plundering everything in their path. Those few peasants who escaped with their lives fled to warn King Lyngvi about the invasion of his realm. When the king heard that their leader was Sigurd, the son of Sigmund – heir of the Volsung line, which Lyngvi had thought he had ended – his face grew gray. But he refused to flee or surrender. He summoned every able-bodied man under his rulership to fight, and set out to face Sigurd.

A brutal fight ensued. Arrows fell like hail, axes split shields asunder, armor gave way, swords stopped hearts, clubs smashed skulls, and countless men fell in what all who survived agreed was one of the most savage battles ever waged. Sigurd advanced through the enemy ranks, hewing down men and horses with Gram until his arms were drenched in blood all the way to his shoulders. Iron helmets and armor crumpled and broke like pieces of parchment under his sword.

At last, the great warrior met King Lyngvi face to face. Their combat was short, and ended with Sigurd slicing through the king's helmet, skull, armor, and torso with one furious stroke of his sword. Then Lyngvi's brother came at Sigurd, and was cut in half. Sigurd rounded up all of Lyngvi's sons and slaughtered them, then turned to hew down the remnants of the king's forces. He confiscated all of Lyngvi's gold and other portable wealth, drank his ale, and then returned to the ships and headed home with his men and his spoils.

When Sigurd arrived at King Hjalprek's court, a lavish feast was held in his honor. At its end, Regin reminded Sigurd of his promise to slay Fafnir. "I have not forgotten it," said Sigurd, "and now that I have avenged my own father, I will avenge yours – and you."

Some days later, Regin and Sigurd rode to the heath where Fafnir lay on his gold. It wasn't hard to find evidence of the monster's presence: a barren track wider than several men ran from the dragon's cave to the pond to which he slunk daily to have a drink of water. Sigurd turned to Regin and said, "You had told me that Fafnir was no bigger than an ordinary serpent, but this trail seems to suggest otherwise."

Regin looked nervous, and evaded the question. He instead began giving Sigurd instructions: "The best way to kill the dragon will be to dig a ditch across his pathway, crouch down in it, and then stab him in the heart when he crawls to his watering hole. If you do that, you will win great fame for yourself."

Sigurd asked sensibly, "But what should I do if the ditch fills with the dragon's blood? Might I not drown?"

Regin replied, with obvious agitation in his voice, "Do I have to spell everything out for you? It sounds like you're afraid, and that you lack the courage of your famous kinsmen."

Sigurd set to work digging a ditch. But as for Regin, the fear of Fafnir overcame him, and he rode away. After a short while, a one-eyed old man approached Sigurd and asked him what he was doing. When Sigurd answered, the stranger gave a disapproving look, and said, "It will go much better for you if you dig a network of ditches so that the running blood has somewhere to go. *Then* you can safely sit in one of them and strike at the beast's heart." Sigurd thought that this was a marvelous idea, but when he turned to thank the old man for his advice, he was gone. Sigurd dug the ditches, sat down in one of them, and waited.

The ground began to rumble and shake. The dragon spewed poison all over the moor as he slithered down to the pond. When the heart of the dreadful beast was directly above him, Sigurd thrust his sword into it through the soft flesh of his underbelly, right up to the hilt. As blood began to flow in torrents from the wound, Sigurd pulled out his sword and leapt from the ditch. The ground was now quaking even more violently as Fafnir thrashed from side to side and in all kinds of contortions, filling the air with bloodcurdling howls as thickly as the ditches were being filled with his blood. Anything in his way – trees, rocks, hillocks – was utterly destroyed.

When Fafnir saw Sigurd, he regained his composure enough to ask him: "Who are you, and of what family do you come?"

The warrior replied, "I am Sigurd, the son of Sigmund, of the Volsung family."

"Ah," the dragon gargled through his throat full of blood. "Your pedigree will be no match for my treasure, which, you might like to know, is cursed to become the death of anyone who owns it."

Sigurd replied, "That is true of all wealth. Everyone wants it for himself, until the day when others kill him to take it for themselves. As for you, your hoard already belongs to another, and you already belong to Hel." Then the dragon breathed his last and slumped to the ground with a booming thud.

When Regin saw that the beast was dead, he finally emerged from the stand of bushes where he had been hiding, and congratulated Sigurd on his victory – "even though," he said darkly, "you *have* killed my brother." Regin then asked Sigurd to do him a favor – "nothing more than a trifle for you, really," he said – and roast the dragon's heart for him to eat.

Sigurd complied with Regin's request. When he thought the organ might be done cooking, he touched it with his finger to get a taste and see. As soon as he had put his finger to his mouth, he found, to his amazement, that he could understand what the birds around him were saying.

In a nearby tree, three nuthatches were chirping and chattering with each other. One of them said, "If only Sigurd knew that by eating this heart he would become wiser than any man alive, he would surely do so." The second added, "Yes, and if he knew that Regin was about to kill him, I have little doubt that he'd kill Regin, too. After all, does he really think that Regin is going to just let him go after he killed his brother?" The third chimed in: "Yes, and if Sigurd is wise, he will then take all the gold for himself and ride to Hindarfell, the mountain where the Valkyrie Brynhild, 'Armor of Battle,' is imprisoned. She can teach him even more wisdom."

Sigurd contemplated their words for a few moments before declaring, "Hreidmar's second son should go the way of the first." Then he drew Gram and sliced off Regin's head. He ate part of Fafnir's heart, stored the rest away for later, and rode up to Fafnir's lair. He found the two huge, ornate iron doors at its entrance open. Inside, there was enough gold and other precious things to fill two large chests. Sigurd mounted them on Grani's back, and the horse didn't seem to be troubled by the load in the slightest, even when Sigurd got on his back, too. So as to follow the rest of the birds' advice, man and horse set off for Hindarfell.

After many days of riding through dense forests, over windy plains, and across frothing rivers, Sigurd caught his first glimpse of Hindarfell in the distance. The mountain seemed to be glowing with a light that reached all the way up to the sky.

At the mountain's cold, rocky peak, Sigurd found a rampart made of shields with a banner flying over it. Inside of the wall of shields lay a sleeping warrior in full armor. When Sigurd removed the man's helmet, he found that the man was actually a woman – and a breathtakingly beautiful woman at that. The lady's armor clung to her body so tightly that it almost seemed to have grown into it. Sigurd unsheathed Gram and cut her body free of the tight metal clothing. Then he said over her, "Awaken, for you have slept too long."

The woman began to twitch and yawn, then rubbed her eyes and opened them. She stared up at Sigurd for a long moment, then asked him sleepily, "Who are you, who have cut me free and roused me from my sleep? Could you be Sigurd, the son of Sigmund, as has been foretold?"

"I am," replied Sigurd.

Then she told him how she had gotten into the predicament from which the hero had rescued her. "I was one of the choosers of the slain, the deciders of battle, in Odin's service. Two kings were fighting, and Odin had determined that one of them was due the victory. But I granted the triumph to the other one. In revenge, Odin dragged me here and cast a spell over me so that I fell into a long, deep sleep."

"Now that I have awoken you," said Sigurd, "I would very much like it if you would tell me some of the wisdom for which you are renowned." Brynhild got up and poured him a goblet of beer. Then the two sat in conversation for a long time, sharing their tremendous lore with each other.

When they had finished their conversation, Sigurd gazed deep into Brynhild's eyes and announced, "I have never met anyone wiser than you, nor anyone more beautiful. I swear to you here and now that I will marry you." A smile like a sunrise came over Bynhild's face, and she replied, "Even if I could choose any man in the world for my husband, I would choose you." As they savored each other's company, neither of them had any idea what terrible misfortunes fate had in store for them.

Sigurd took Brynhild to the hall of her sister Bekkhild and Bekkhild's husband, the chieftain Heimir. Word of Sigurd's victory over Fafnir had spread throughout all lands. For this and for freeing Brynhild, he was given a hero's welcome, complete with a splendid feast. Everyone marveled that Brynhild had found a man she was willing to marry and pour drink for, because she had always spurned men in the past.

One day, Gudrun, the daughter of the powerful King Gjuki, arrived at Heimir's hall. She was despondent, and no one could cheer her up, no matter how hard they tried. When Brynhild asked her what was troubling her, Gudrun told the Valkyrie that she had had strange, upsetting dreams. She knew that Brynhild was very skilled at interpreting dreams, so she had come to get her advice. Brynhild sat down with her and asked her what she had dreamt.

"I dreamt," said Gudrun, "that you and I went into the forest one day and came upon a mighty stag. He was far bigger than any other stag I had ever seen, walked with a regal posture, and had hair made of gold that glistened in the sunlight that filtered down through the leaves. Both of us desired this stag more than anything else, and we chased after it, but only I was able to catch it. Then you shot an arrow through his chest, and he fell down dead. I was distraught beyond measure."

Brynhild sat in silence for a long time, her face stony and grim. "Here is what your dream means," she said at last. "You will obtain Sigurd, the man to whom I have pledged myself in marriage, as your own husband. But you won't have him for long before I bring about his death."

Gudrun gasped and said, "Because I know this, I am overwhelmed by grief." Then she left and went back to her father's court.

Sigurd's adventures soon found him approaching the hall of the same King Gjuki. One of the king's sentinels saw Sigurd approaching and ran to his master, telling him, "My lord, a man who might be a god is approaching. He is dressed from head to toe in gold, his weapons are the finest I have ever seen, his horse is far larger than other horses, and he himself is far larger than other men."

King Gjuki rode out with his attendants to meet the stranger. When they met, the king stopped Sigurd and asked him, "Who are you? No one may enter my fortress without the permission of my sons, who are all heroes of many battles."

Sigurd hailed the king and replied, "I am Sigurd, the son of Sigmund."

A look of great surprise and joy came over Gjuki's face. "Then by all means," he said, "come in and feel welcome to anything you desire."

Sigurd was treated very well by everyone, and stayed with Gjuki and his family for some time. He would often ride horses and engage in other sports with the king's sons, Gunnar and Hogni, and though all competed with great skill and strength, Sigurd handily won every competition.

Grimhild, King Gjuki's wife, noted how much Sigurd loved Brynhild, whom he spoke of often and fondly. But the devious Grimhild also noted how much of an asset Sigurd would be to her family if he could be enticed to marry her daughter Gudrun. He was the most capable, most handsome, and most accomplished man alive. He was a king's son, and he was the owner of immense wealth. So she concocted a plot to manipulate the hero's affections.

Grimhild was not only devious – she was also a powerful sorceress. One evening, at dinner, she handed Sigurd a horn of ale that she had bewitched to cause him to forget his love for Brynhild and the vows he had made to her. Sigurd drank it, and when the potion had taken effect, Grimhild said to him, "Your presence here has brought us incalculable joy, and you certainly seem to have been enjoying yourself, too. Why not let King Gjuki become your father, and Gunnar and Hogni your brothers, and Gudrun your wife?" Gudrun went over to where Sigurd was sitting, and honored him by pouring him another drink. He couldn't help but notice her beauty, her grace, and the impeccable courtliness of her manner. He accepted the queen's offer.

Sigurd and the sons of Gjuki made a solemn pact that they would henceforth treat each other as brothers. A magnificent feast of celebration lasting several days was held. The food, drink, and entertainment got better and better each day. At the height of the feast, Sigurd and Gudrun were married.

For a long time thereafter, Sigurd, Gunnar, and Hogni traveled to countless lands, slew countless sons of kings, and obtained more fame and riches than anyone before or since.

One day, Grimhild approached Gunnar and said to him, "My beloved son, you have done superbly well for yourself in all realms of life but one: you are still unmarried. Why don't you ask for the hand of Brynhild? It seems to me that there is no more fitting match for you in all the world. Sigurd could go with you and endorse the proposal."

Gunnar thought that this was a phenomenal idea. When he told his brother-in-law of it, Sigurd readily agreed to accompany him and speak on his behalf.

Gunnar, Hogni, and Sigurd set out for the hall of King Budli, Brynhild's father. They were all dressed in extraordinarily fine clothes and weapons, and were quite a sight to behold. When they arrived at Budli's hall and requested the hand of his daughter in marriage, Brynhild was devastated. How could the only man she had ever loved, who had sworn solemn oaths to marry her, now be in her house advocating that she marry another? She adamantly refused the men's request. Gunnar did not take her rejection well, and declared that he would burn the hall to the ground and slay everyone under Budli's command if his wish were not granted.

Budli tried to persuade Brynhild to take Gunnar's hand, pointing out how high-born, wealthy, and successful he was. But Brynhild remained obstinate, and instead offered to lead the king's forces in battle against the sons of King Gjuki. Budli scorned this suggestion, and told her that if she were to take up arms against her suitor, she would forfeit her inheritance and his goodwill from that moment on. And, he warned her, his friendship would serve her far better than his wrath.

Brynhild thought the matter over, and her ruminations became ever darker and more despairing. How could she hope to fight not only the forces of King Gjuki, but her father as well? But then an idea came to her. She would arrange a test, and whoever passed it would receive her hand in marriage – but she would make sure that the challenge was one at which only Sigurd could succeed. She rode to her own golden-roofed hall and kindled all around it a circle of fire, whose insatiable flames leapt as high as the walls of the fortress itself. She announced that whoever would cross the wall of fire would obtain her hand in marriage.

Gunnar, Hogni, and Sigurd arrived at Brynhild's fortress, eager to prove that Gunnar was worthy of Brynhild. But try as he might, Gunnar found himself unable to summon the courage to ride through the thick, roaring blaze. He recalled that Grimhild had taught him and Sigurd how to exchange shapes, so that each would take on the appearance of the other, and he asked Sigurd if he would be willing to take on his form and ride into the flames on his behalf. Sigurd agreed, and the swap was made.

With his body perfectly disguised as that of Gunnar, Sigurd mounted Grani, let out a great yell, and charged into the wall of fire. The earth trembled, and the flames shot up toward the heavens, as if a god had blown his breath into them. Then, just as quickly as they had swelled, they subsided, and Gunnar and Hogni saw Sigurd and Grani safe on the other side of the embers. Neither had suffered the slightest singe. Sigurd, still in Gunnar's form, dismounted and walked proudly into Brynhild's hall.

The Valkyrie was shocked when she saw that, by all indications, Gunnar, and not Sigurd, had made it through the trial. Sigurd walked up to her gilded seat and said to her, "Your father has given me his permission to marry you. Now I have passed the test that you set before any man who desired your hand, and I have come to gain your permission, too, so that I may finally have what my heart has yearned for so ardently and for so long."

It took Brynhild some time to regain her composure. She held up her sword, and its reflection gleamed on her helmet and coat of mail. "I am a woman of war," she said gravely, "and I do not wish to be torn away from battle to take up a domestic life."

"Nevertheless," replied Sigurd, "did you not give your word that you would wed the man who would dare to cross your wall of fire?"

Though these words filled Brynhild with more sorrow than she could express, she could not deny their truth, nor their justice. She rose from her seat and accepted the marriage proposal.

For three nights, Sigurd stayed with Brynhild and slept in her bed beside her. But each night, he unsheathed Gram and placed it between them. When Brynhild asked him why he did this, he said that a sorceress had prophesied that if he did not thus postpone the consummation of his marriage, he would die. Brynhild didn't question this, because it suited her just fine. But Sigurd did give her a ring. When the two had exchanged vows to marry on the mountain Hindarfell, he had given her the ring that Andvari the dwarf had tried to withhold from Loki. Now, he took this ring from her and gave her another fine ring from the hoard of Fafnir the dragon.

King Gjuki and Queen Grimhild prepared a sumptuous feast at their hall to celebrate the marriage. Sigurd and Gunnar rode there separately from Brynhild, and along the way they changed back into their proper shapes. The feast lasted many days, and every guest was full of joy - except for Brynhild, who sat quietly and snuck glances at Sigurd with hopeless longing, and Sigurd, who had begun to come out of Grimhild's spell and to realize what had been done to him.

One day not long thereafter, Brynhild and Gudrun went to bathe in the river. In the course of their conversation, they got into a heated argument about whose husband was greater. Brynhild taunted Gudrun, "Only Gunnar had the courage to ride through the wall of fire to claim me as his bride. Your Sigurd evidently just didn't have a stout enough heart."

Gudrun shot back, "Do you really think that a man as pathetic as Gunnar did what you say he did? It was Sigurd who rode through the flames in Gunnar's shape, lay with you, and gave you a ring. If you don't believe me, here, look at this!" She tossed Brynhild Andvari's ring. Brynhild's face became as pale as a corpse.

After this, Brynhild took to her room and refused to leave. When Gunnar entered with the hope of consoling her, she tried to kill him. Gunnar restrained her, and Hogni tied her up. Then Gunnar looked at her pleadingly and said, "I don't want you to remain in chains forever."

Brynhild glared back at him and snarled, "It doesn't matter. Either way, you will never again see me happy in your house." For a long time after that, she filled the wide hall with hideous screams of sorrow and rage day and night.

At Gudrun's insistence, Sigurd went in to talk to her. He tried to justify his actions, and to convince her to be content with Gunnar. "If you think that anything I have done has been done out of malice," he said, "you are mistaken. My forgetfulness of my pledge to you was not my doing, but it is the greatest sorrow of my life nonetheless. I love you now as much as I ever have."

She hissed at him through clenched teeth, "Of all of the scoundrels who have tricked me and betrayed me, none are more loathsome than you, Sigurd. And now I wish to live no longer." Sigurd's heart heaved so hard in his chest that his coat of mail burst asunder.

The next time Gunnar came in to see her, she said to him, "You have two choices: either I will leave you, return to my father's hall, and live there in misery for the rest of my days, or you will kill Sigurd."

This distressed Gunnar deeply. Either way, he would bring grave dishonor upon himself. It was a shameful thing for his wife to leave him, but it was also shameful for him to break the oath of brotherhood he had sworn to Sigurd. He consulted with Hogni, and the two decided that the best course of action would be to have their younger brother, Guttorm, who had never sworn an oath to Sigurd, carry out the murder. They cooked the meat of a snake and a wolf and fed this to Guttorm. Then they proposed their plan. The boy was then so full of strength and wrath that he agreed.

That night, Guttorm snuck into Sigurd's room with his sword. He saw his brother-in-law sleeping soundly, with Gudrun in his arms. Even while asleep, Sigurd was a fearsome sight to behold. Guttorm turned back and tiptoed out of the room without performing the deed. Outside, he gathered his courage, and then crept back in. But once again, he couldn't bring himself to strike at such a colossal opponent.

On the third try, however, he mustered all of his strength and stabbed Sigurd straight through the chest, so that the blade went into the bed underneath him. He tried to run out of the room, but Sigurd hurled Gram after him. It struck him in the back and severed his body at the waist. His legs and abdomen fell forward, and his head and arms fell backward. Then Sigurd died. Gudrun awoke drenched in her husband's blood, and let out a piercing scream. Brynhild laughed from her room.

Soon, however, Brynhild's cackles turned to sobs and wails. Gunnar put his arms around her and begged her to agree to live and accept any compensation she desired for the loss of Sigurd's life. But Brynhild refused. Instead, she had her servants bring all of her many heaps of gold and other treasures in front of her. She screamed to everyone in Gjuki's hall, "If any of you want any of this, take it! I care about it less than a bird cares about his excrement." Then she picked up a dagger that lay beside her and stabbed herself under the arm.

As everyone ran to her side – whether to see if they could save her or to take some of her gold – she told them, in such a calm, lucid tone of voice that everyone was astonished, what would happen to them in the future. Each one was to suffer greatly, and their family line would die with them. At the end, she added, "I have one final request. When you burn Sigurd's body on a magnificent funeral pyre, as I know you will, burn my body beside his. Then, at last, we will be together, if not in the way that I had hoped." With that, she died.

All that Brynhild prophesied, as well as her last request, came to pass.

# CHAPTER 45:

# RAGNAROK

Ragnarok (Old Norse *Ragnarök*, "Final Fate of the Gods"[1]) is a word the Vikings used to refer to the cataclysmic event that will bring about the destruction of the cosmos. Ragnarok is the final chapter in Norse mythology.

The story is told in the most detail in *The Prophecy of the Seeress*, *The Song of Vafthrudnir*, and the *Prose Edda*. While these sources, as we've seen, are all rather late and suspect, the basic theme of the final battle between the gods and the giants that ushers in the end of the world is referenced repeatedly in older and more reliable sources.[2] Thus, while some of the details in the following tale may belong to a Christianized, medieval version of Norse mythology, the underlying idea and plot is undoubtedly ancient and pre-Christian.

As we saw in Chapter Four, we can be reasonably certain that the idea of a rebirth after Ragnarok only came about in the conversion period, when the Viking religion was being replaced by Christianity. The following retelling takes that into account.

## RAGNAROK

One day, perhaps tomorrow, or perhaps thousands of years in the future, that dreaded time of which the prophecies have long spoken in hushed, furtive whispers will finally come to pass. The army of countless elite warriors that Odin has been amassing in Valhalla will pour out of their lord's golden hall to fulfill their long-awaited purpose. The simmering strife between the gods and the giants will at last come to a head, and the whole world will hang in the balance.

The first sign of the coming of Ragnarok will be the Fimbulwinter, "Great Winter," three winters that follow each other in a row with no summer in between. Darkness, ice, and wind will grip the earth and refuse to let go, and the sun will be pitifully distant and weak. All virtue shall leave humankind; even the bonds of family will fail to restrain brothers, fathers, and sons from killing each other. It will be an age of swords and of axes, and no shield will remain in all the world that is not broken into pieces.

The wolves who have pursued the sun and the moon throughout the millennia will at last catch their prey. Under the dark sky, the land will heave and quake. Trees will be torn up from their roots, mountains will crumble, and valleys will be filled in. Yggdrasil itself will tremble and totter. Heimdall will blow the Gjallarhorn to warn the gods of the impending disaster. Odin will desperately consult with Mimir's head, which was severed from his body so long ago in the war between the gods, to see if there is anything he can do to avert the inevitable. He will not like the answer he receives.

Then those monsters the gods have taken such pains to get rid of will find themselves free. Jormungand, the great serpent who has lain in the ocean encircling the world, will rise up from the waves and slither onto land, displacing so much water that no one will be able to tell any longer where the land ends and the sea begins. Fenrir, the dreadful wolf, will break the chain with which he was bound. He will run furiously over all the earth, with his lower jaw on the ground and his upper jaw against the roof of the sky, devouring everything unfortunate enough to be caught in between. Fire will roar from his eyes and nostrils. Naglfar, "Nail Ship," a longship made from the fingernails of all dead men and women, will become unmoored from its former resting place at the bottom of the ocean. When it floats up to the surface, the gods will recoil in terror at the sight of its countless oars all manned by giants, and its helm captained by none other than Loki.

Then the fire-giants will arrive from Muspelheim, the land of elemental fire. Surt, "Black," will lead them, all the while swinging his flaming sword that shines brighter than the sun. They will march across Bifrost, the rainbow bridge that leads to the door of Asgard, and the bridge will snap and collapse under their weight. They will ransack the gods' sanctuary, forcing its inhabitants to flee.

All will converge at Vigrid, the "Place of Surging Battle," a plain no less than a hundred leagues wide and long. There will stand on one side all the giants, along with Fenrir, Jormungand, and Loki. On the other side will stand all the gods, backed by Odin's army of dead champions. Odin will ride into battle first, and will come up against Fenrir. The wolf will swallow Odin in his gaping maw. But then Vidar, Odin's son and avenger, will stride forth and rip the wolf's jaws from his face, and that will be the end of Fenrir.

Thor will long to come to the aid of his father, but he will be powerless to do so, for he will have his hands full with his own arch-enemy: Jormungand. Vigrid will become a morass of lightning, thunder, and venom as the two ancient foes finally face each other. Thor will slay the snake with his hammer, but by that time his body will be so full of the monster's poison that he will only be able to take nine steps before falling down dead.

The gods' ablest defender, Heimdall, will finally get the chance to take on the gods' betrayer, Loki. Both will slay each other, as will Tyr and the wolf Garm, and Frey and Surt. All the other gods and giants will perish in the same manner.

By that time, Surt's fire will have covered all the world. With no gods left to uphold it, its charred mass will sink into the sea from which it arose. Then the unbroken silence, stillness and emptiness of Ginnungagap, the "Yawning Abyss," will reign forever, unchallenged and uninterrupted.

There are those who say that the downfall of the cosmos will not be final, and that after the land sinks into the sea, it will somehow arise again, fresh and green. It will yield vast crops without any work having to be done to sow, tend, or harvest them. The gods Vidar and Vali will survive to see that day, as will Thor's sons Magni and Modi. Balder and

Hod will return, too, to join these other gods. Two humans, Lif and Lifthrasir, "Life" and "The One Who Strives after Life," will have waited out the destruction of the world by hiding in a tree-trunk, and they will then emerge to repopulate the earth. The daughter of the sun will rise into the sky and follow her mother's course, bringing a light even fairer than that of the old sun to the lands below.

The gods will find in the grass golden game pieces that their forebears had once enjoyed. All will spend their days in merry pleasure, with no giants to disturb their contentment. A new, all-powerful god will appear in the heavens, and he will rule over all with perfect justice and virtue.

But those who say these things lack understanding, and have not attentively considered the lore that has come down to them.

# EPILOGUE

# Chapter 46: Conclusion

## "MYTH IS ETERNAL, BUT IT NEVER STOPS CHANGING."

The picture of the Vikings' mythology and religion that has come down to us is quite a vibrant and nuanced one indeed. The sources for that picture are many and varied, and they've supplied us with reams of information concerning what the Vikings believed about their world and the otherworld, and dozens of sacred stories that they told to one another.

Nevertheless, there are significant pieces missing from the available data. As vivid as the picture we have is, it's far from complete. This is inevitable given the historical distance that stretches between us and the Viking Age, as well as the problematic and incomplete nature of the sources that enable us to partially bridge that gap.

Understandably, many people - especially those for whom Norse mythology and religion are important for creative or spiritual reasons - want to fill in those missing pieces. There are two ways to attempt to do that. The first way is with more scholarly research and analysis. There's always more work to be done in this field, but scholarly work, which tries to stick quite closely to the sources, is necessarily limited by the limitations of the sources themselves.

The second way involves using your imagination to overcome those limitations, to fill in the gaps and to reinterpret what's already there. Unless you're a scholar writing for an audience that expects a certain level of scholarly rigor, or in some other kind of situation where historical and factual claims matter, there's nothing methodologically wrong with that. After all, that's what the Vikings themselves did. Why do you think that so many different versions of the Norse myths have come down to us from the Viking Age, for example? It's because the people who told those stories to one another were constantly adding new material to them, subtracting old material from them, and recasting them in ways that spoke to the needs and challenges of their particular time and place. That's how living traditions work; they're not static fossils that can only be mindlessly turned over again and again, but are constantly changing as the people who enact them change. No tradition can truly *live* without innovation.

The forms in which the Norse myths, and the religion of which they were a part, have come down to us are products of that very process. Consider just four examples of this that we've already noted: 1) the rebirth narrative that was added to the end of the tale of Ragnarok during the period of transition to Christianity, 2) the demotion of Tyr from the status of highest god to a much more minor role over the course of the centuries that preceded the Viking Age, 3) the splitting of Freya-Frigg into two goddesses over the course of the Viking Age, and 4) the splitting of the gods into two tribes, the Aesir and the Vanir, over the course of the Viking Age.

This process of development continued even after Christianity supplanted the Vikings' religion throughout northern Europe. The changes wrought by Snorri, Saxo, and the like shouldn't be seen as perversions of the "original" myths – and an "original" version of a myth exists only as a hypothetical abstraction rather than a fact, anyway – but instead as further developments in an ongoing line of transformation. In the words of Old Norse scholar Christopher Abram,

> [R]ather than seeing the Norse myths as diminishing over time as elements from genuine traditions were lost, we might look on the creation of this mythology as an additive process. The Norse myths get fuller, more sophisticated and more interesting over time, as elements from these different traditions are combined in new and innovative ways. Even as the myths moved further away from their

putative origins in pagan culture, they continued to grow and develop and capture the imaginations of new poets, scholars and presumably their audiences.[1]

This process of ceaseless development is not unique to Norse mythology and religion, but is intrinsic to myth and religion as such. Consider the ways in which the stories people tell about Jesus or Oedipus, to cite but two examples, have evolved over time. Freud's version of the Oedipus myth would have been hardly recognizable to the ancient Greeks, but it's clearly still the same story in many ways. To quote Abram once again, "Myth is eternal, but it never stops changing."[2]

Paradoxically, then, the best way to be "true" to the Norse myths and religion is to continue to reinvent them for one's own time and place.

## THE VIKING SPIRIT

Now that we've reached the end of this book, we've peered into the Vikings' world and worldview long and deeply enough to be able to tell what "the Viking spirit" was and is.

It was highly fatalistic, but its fatalism was not one of resignation or complacency. It saw life as being ultimately doomed to tragedy, but with the opportunity for grand and noble heroism along the way. The Vikings sought to seize that opportunity, to accomplish as much as they could – and be remembered for it – despite the certainty of the grave and "the wolf." How one met one's fate, whatever that fate happened to be, was what separated honorable and worthy people from the dishonorable and the unworthy.

Norse religion and mythology were thoroughly infused with this view. The gods, the "pillars" who held the cosmos together, fought for themselves and their world tirelessly and unflinchingly, even though they knew that in the end the struggle was hopeless, and that the forces of chaos and entropy would prevail. They went out not with a whimper, but with a bang. This attitude is what made the Vikings the Vikings.

# Notes

### Chapter One

1. Winroth 2014.
2. Davidson 1988: 5-8.
3. Otto 1923: 6.
4. Otto 1923: 25-30.
5. Otto 1923: 9.
6. Otto 1923: 12-40.
7. Price and Mortimer 2014; Turville-Petre 1964: 190-195.
8. Abram 2011: 2-11.
9. Abram 2011: 11-16.
10. Abram 2011: 16-20, 222-223; Turville-Petre 1964: 8.
11. Turville-Petre 1964: 22-25.
12. Abram 2011: 208-213.
13. Turville-Petre 1964: 18-21.
14. Abram 2011: 28-30.
15. Abram 2011: 2-11.

### Chapter Two

1. Orel 2003: 20-21.
2. Price 2002: 55.
3. Simek 2010.
4. Simek 2004; Simek 2010.
5. Price 2002: 91.
6. Adam of Bremen 2002: 207.
7. Turville-Petre 1964: 54.
8. Price 2002; Kershaw 2000.
9. Nietzsche 1954: 159.

10. Hárbarðsljóð, stanza 24; translation after Price 2002: 96.

11. Turville-Petre 1964: 51.

12. Eiríksmál, stanza 6, my translation.

13. Hávamál.

14. Hákonarmál.

15. Turville-Petre 1964: 56, 70.

16. Price and Mortimer 2014.

17. Price 2002: 56.

18. Ynglinga Saga, chapter 6.

19. Tacitus 2010.

20. Ynglinga Saga, chapter 7.

21. McKinnell 2008: 5.

22. Orel 2003: 429.

23. Turville-Petre 1964: 81.

24. Turville-Petre 1964: 75.

25. Simek 1993: 37.

26. Price 2002: 56.

27. Hárbarðsljóð, stanza 24. My translation.

28. Turville-Petre 1964: 75-86.

29. Davidson 1990: 83-84.

30. Adam of Bremen 2002: 207.

31. Turville-Petre 1964: 177-178.

32. Lokasenna, stanzas 30, 32.

33. Turville-Petre 1964: 159.

34. Lokasenna, stanza 36.

35. Völuspá, stanza 22.

36. Ynglinga Saga, chapter 4.

37. Price 2002: 56.

38. Turville-Petre 1964: 175-176.

39. Simek 1993: 280; Gylfaginning, chapter 23.

40. Grímnismál, stanza 14.

41. Egils Saga, chapter 78.

42. Orel 2003: 114.

43. Turville-Petre 1964: 189.

44. Lokasenna, stanza 26.
45. Saxo Grammaticus 1996: 26.
46. Saxo Grammaticus 1996: 26.
47. Lokasenna, stanza 29.
48. Lokasenna, stanza 36.
49. Ynglinga Saga, chapters 4-13.
50. Turville-Petre 1964: 170.
51. Turville-Petre 1964: 175.
52. Price 2002: 221.
53. Adam of Bremen 2002: 207-208.
54. Simek 1993: 298.
55. Price 2002: 56.
56. Turville-Petre 1964: 175.
57. Flateyjarbók; Gylfaginning, chapter 48; Turville-Petre 1964: 173.
58. Simek 1993: 289.
59. Turville-Petre 1964: 173.
60. Grímnismál, stanza 5.
61. Turville-Petre 1964: 133.
62. Turville-Petre 1964: 127.
63. Heide 2009: 363.
64. Simek 1993: 284.
65. Simek 1993: 228.
66. Turville-Petre 1964: 129.
67. Turville-Petre 1964: 129.
68. Heide 2012: 82.
69. Turville-Petre 1964: 126.
70. Heide 2009: 363; Heide 2012: 90-91.
71. Gylfaginning, chapter 22.
72. Turville-Petre 1964: 106.
73. Grímnismál, stanza 12.
74. Turville-Petre 1964: 106.
75. Simek 1993: 155.
76. Simek 1993: 28.
77. Turville-Petre 1964: 115.

78. Turville-Petre 1964: 115; Simek 1993: 28.

79. Simek 1993: 227.

80. Turville-Petre 1964: 116-117.

81. Turville-Petre 1964: 153.

82. Gylfaginning, chapter 27.

83. Völuspá, stanza 27.

84. Gylfaginning, chapter 27.

85. Price 2002: 56.

86. Simek 1993: 135-136.

87. Turville-Petre 1964: 162-163.

88. Mallory and Adams 2006: 408-409.

89. Turville-Petre 1964: 181.

90. Lindow 2004: 21; Turville-Petre 1964: 185-186.

91. Simek 1993: 171.

92. Turville-Petre 1964: 186.

93. Lokasenna, stanza 17.

94. Turville-Petre 1964: 186.

95. Turville-Petre 1964: 186.

96. Turville-Petre 1964: 165.

97. McKinnell 2005: 63.

98. Turville-Petre 1964: 310.

99. Ellis 1968: 75; Völsaþáttr; Gylfaginning, chapter 35.

100. Lokasenna, stanza 20.

## Chapter Three

1. Simek 1993: 335.

2. Steinsland 1987.

3. Orel 2003: 86.

4. Orel 2003: 429-430.

5. ("Giant" in the Online Etymology Dictionary.
    http://www.etymonline.com/index.php?term=giant&allowed_in_frame=0)

6. Davidson 1988: 92.

7. Davidson 1988: 93.

8. Völsunga Saga, chapter 9.

9. Njáls Saga, chapter 156.

10. Davidson 1988: 96-97; Price 2002: 338-340.

11. Hall 2007: 36.

12. Gylfaginning, chapter 17.

13. Turville-Petre 1964: 230.

14. Þiðreks Saga; Hrólfs Saga Kraka.

15. Óláfs Saga Helga.

16. Turville-Petre 1964: 231.

17. Turville-Petre 1964: 233-234.

18. Price 2002: 57.

19. Gylfaginning, chapter 8.

20. Price 2002: 57.

21. Davidson 1988: 104-105.

22. Turville-Petre 1964: 234.

23. Davidson 1993: 120.

24. Ellis 1968: 117-118.

25. Davidson 1993: 113.

26. Davidson 1988: 104.

27. Turville-Petre 1964: 232.

## Chapter Four

1. Heide 2014: 119-120.

2. Heide 2014: 126.

3. Heide 2014: 120-121.

4. Davidson 1988: 23.

5. Davidson 1988: 170.

6. Heide 2014: 121-122.

7. Hastrup 1985: 143.

8. Hastrup 1985: 136-139.

9. Price 2002: 109.

10. Simek 1993: 261.

11. Grímnismál, stanzas 32-35.

12. Simek 1993: 167; Bauschatz 1982.

13. Simek 1993: 36.

14. Simek 1993: 232-233.

15. Völuspá, stanza 2.

16. Vafþrúðnismál, stanza 43.

17. Davidson 1993: 69.

18. Davidson 1988: 169-170.

19. Simek 1993: 222-224.

20. Simek 1993: 345; Abram 2011: 222-226.

21. Völuspá, stanza 8.

22. Völuspá, stanzas 38-39.

23. Völuspá, stanza 65. My translation.

24. Turville-Petre 1964: 282.

25. Abram 2011: 157-168.

26. Davidson 1988: 188-191.

27. Abram 2011: 157.

## Chapter Five

1. Eiríksmál, stanzas 1-7.

2. Bek-Pedersen 2011: 165-171.

3. Fáfnismál, stanza 11.

4. Simek 1993: 342.

5. Price 2002: 56.

6. Price 2002: 56.

7. Davidson 1988: 164.

8. Fáfnismál, for example.

9. Völuspá; Gylfaginning.

10. Davidson 1988: 164.

11. Davidson 1988: 166.

12. Price 2002: 53.

13. Sonatorrek 23-25, Egils Saga, chapter 78. My translation.

## Chapter Six

1. Nietzsche 2000.
2. Price 2002: 382-383.
3. Bauman 1986: 140.
4. Raudvere 2004: 295.
5. Bauman 1986: 142.
6. Gísla Saga Súrssonar, chapter 2.
7. Bauman 1986: 140.
8. Zoëga 2004: 94.
9. Heide 2004: 168.
10. Price 2002: 211.
11. Price 2002: 212.
12. Price 2002: 211-212.
13. Turville-Petre 1964: 131.
14. Price 2002: 213.
15. Byock 2000: 196-206.

## Chapter Seven

1. Price 2002: 59.
2. Heide 2006a.
3. Raudvere 2002: 102.
4. Price 2002: 59.
5. Raudvere 2002: 102.
6. Price 2002: 59.
7. Price 2002: 60.
8. Price 2002: 60.
9. Raudvere 2002: 102.
10. Raudvere 2002: 102.
11. Heide 2006a.
12. Zoëga 2004: 153.
13. Turville-Petre 1964: 28.
14. Ellis 1968: 128.

15. Turville-Petre 1964: 228-229.
16. Davidson 1993: 119.
17. Ellis 1968: 128.
18. Price 2002: 229.
19. Ellis 1968: 128-129.
20. Sommer 2007: 275.
21. Ellis 1968: 132.
22. Víga-Glums Saga, chapter 9.
23. Ellis 1968: 134.
24. Ellis 1968: 132-133.
25. Ellis 1968: 131-132.

## Chapter Eight

1. Ibn Fadlan 2012.
2. Price 2010: 131-137.
3. Price 2010.
4. Davidson 1993: 70.
5. Ellis 1968: 97.
6. Heide 2014: 128.
7. Simek 1993: 138.
8. Abram 2011: 165.
9. Ellis 1968: 84.
10. Ellis 1968: 85-86.
11. Eyrbyggja Saga, chapter 11.
12. Simek 1993: 137.
13. Grímnismál, stanza 14.
14. DuBois 1999: 80.
15. Hárbarðsljóð, stanza 24.
16. Grímnismál, stanzas 8-10.
17. Simek 1993: 71.
18. Vafþrúðnismál, stanza 41.
19. Simek 1993: 347.
20. Ellis 1968: 74.

21. Ellis 1968: 84.

22. Grímnismál, stanza 14.

23. Eiríksmál, stanza 6.

24. Turville-Petre 1964: 53.

25. Ellis 1968: 80-81.

26. Turville-Petre 1964: 55.

27. Ellis 1968: 100.

28. Ellis 1968: 105-111.

29. Völuspá, Baldrs Draumar, and Hávamál 157, for example.

30. Ellis 1968: 138-147.

31. Óláfs Saga Helga.

32. Laxdæla Saga.

33. Grettis Saga.

34. Hávamál 76. My translation.


## Chapter Nine

1. Davidson 1988: 13.

2. Turville-Petre 1964: 239.

3. DuBois 1999: 50.

4. Price 2002: 61-62.

5. Davidson 1988: 19.

6. Davidson 1988: 25-26.

7. DuBois 1999: 51.

8. Davidson 1988: 13-14.

9. Davidson 1988: 16.

10. Davidson 1988: 21.

11. Davidson 1988: 14-16.

12. Turville-Petre 1964: 238.

13. Davidson 1988: 14.

14. Turville-Petre 1964: 238.

15. DuBois 1999: 43.

16. Turville-Petre 1964: 246-248.

17. Davidson 1988: 18.

18. Price 2002: 61.

19. Davidson 1988: 31.

20. Davidson 1988: 32.

21. Davidson 1993: 88; Davidson 1988: 39.

22. Davidson 1993: 92-93.

23. Davidson 1993: 90-91.

24. Davidson 1988: 45-56.

25. Davidson 1988: 58.

26. Davidson 1993: 89-90.

27. Turville-Petre 1964: 251.

28. Turville-Petre 1964: 251.

29. Turville-Petre 1964: 259-260.

30. Davidson 1993: 92-93.

31. Price 2002: 62.

32. Turville-Petre 1964: 260.

33. Davidson 1988: 58-68.

34. Davidson 1988: 59.

35. Davidson 1988: 59.

36. Davidson 1988: 67.

37. Ynglinga Saga, chapter 19.

38. Turville-Petre 1964: 254-255.

39. Turville-Petre 1964: 46.

40. DuBois 1999: 186.

41. Davidson 1988: 135-136.

42. DuBois 1999: 197.

43. DuBois 1999: 186.

44. DuBois 1999: 188.

45. Davidson 1988: 104.

46. Jómsvíkinga Saga, chapters 73-74.

## Chapter Ten

1. Eiríks Saga Rauða, chapter 4.

2. Price 2002: 65-66.

3. Raudvere 2002: 88.

4. Price 2002: 66.

5. Heide 2004.

6. Price 2002: 175.

7. Heide 2004.

8. Davidson 1988: 70.

9. Price 2002: 162.

10. Price 2002: 207.

11. Price 2002: 205-206.

12. Raudvere 2002: 91.

13. Davidson 1993: 99.

14. Raudvere 2002: 91; Price 2002: 65.

15. Price 2002: 66.

16. Price 2002: 64.

17. Raudvere 2002: 96.

18. Price 2002: 354.

19. Price 2002: 64.

20. Lokasenna, stanza 24.

21. Ynglinga Saga, chapter 7.

22. Heide 2004: 167.

23. Heide 2004: 167-168.

24. Heide 2004: 167.

25. Price 2002: 178.

26. Price 2002: 209.

27. Heide 2006a: 355.

28. Heide 2006a: 355-356; Heide 2004: 168.

29. Price 2002: 123.

30. Price 2002: 112-114.

31. Price 2002: 112-114.

32. Raudvere 2002: 97.

33. Price 2002: 359-360.

34. Price 2002: 330.

35. Price 2002: 359-360.

36. Price 2002: 119-122.

37. Price 2002: 286.
38. Price 2002: 288.
39. Ynglinga Saga, chapter 6.
40. Price 2002: 369.
41. Price 2002: 336.

## Chapter Eleven

1. Pagels 2003: 28.
2. Davidson 1993: 71.

## Chapter Twelve

1. Simek 1993: 52-53.

## Chapter Thirteen

1. Simek 1993: 21.

## Chapter Fourteen

1. Turville-Petre 1964: 150-151.

## Chapter Sixteen

1. Turville-Petre 1964: 35-39.
2. Simek 1993: 208.

## Chapter Nineteen

1. Turville-Petre 1964: 48.
2. Turville-Petre 1964: 42-43.
3. Turville-Petre 1964: 50.

### Chapter Twenty

1. Price and Mortimer 2014.

### Chapter Twenty-One

1. Lokasenna, stanza 38.

### Chapter Twenty-Two

1. Turville-Petre 1964: 75.
2. Simek 1993: 324.

### Chapter Twenty-Three

1. Simek 1993: 315.
2. Turville-Petre 1964: 186.

### Chapter Twenty-Five

1. Turville-Petre 1964: 78-80.

### Chapter Twenty-Six

1. Simek 1993: 45.
2. Simek 1993: 45.

### Chapter Twenty-Eight

1. Simek 1993: 290-291.
2. Turville-Petre 1964: 175.

### Chapter Twenty-Nine

1. Simek 1993: 119.

## Chapter Thirty

1. Turville-Petre 1964: 187.

## Chapter Thirty-Two

1. Simek 1993: 130.

## Chapter Thirty-Three

1. Simek 1993: 37.

## Chapter Thirty-Four

1. Turville-Petre 1964: 138.
2. Simek 1993: 343.

## Chapter Thirty-Five

1. Simek 1993: 345.

## Chapter Thirty-Six

1. Simek 1993: 331.
2. Turville-Petre 1964: 81.

## Chapter Thirty-Seven

1. Simek 1993: 12-13.
2. Simek 1993: 12-13.

## Chapter Thirty-Eight

1. Turville-Petre 1964: 109.
2. Simek 1993: 30-31.

## Chapter Thirty-Nine

1. Turville-Petre 1964: 108-111.
2. Abram 2011: 214-221.

## Chapter Forty

1. Turville-Petre 1964: 115.
2. Simek 1993: 155.
3. Turville-Petre 1964: 114-115.
4. Turville-Petre 1964: 115.

## Chapter Forty-One

1. Simek 1993: 192-193.
2. Simek 1993: 192-193.
3. Simek 1993: 192-193.

## Chapter Forty-Four

1. Turville-Petre 1964: 196-205.

## Chapter Forty-Five

1. Simek 1993: 259.
2. Abram 2011: 157; Davidson 1988: 188-191.

## Chapter Forty-Six

1. Abram 2011: 229.

2. Abram 2011: viii.

# BIBLIOGRAPHY

(Not including primary sources in Old Norse.)

Abram, Christopher. 2011. *Myths of the Pagan North: The Gods of the Norsemen.* Continuum: New York, New York, USA.

Adam of Bremen. 2002. *History of the Archbishops of Hamburg-Bremen.* Translated by Francis J. Tschan. Columbia University Press: New York, New York, USA.

Anthony, David W. 2007. *The Horse, the Wheel, and Language: How Bronze-Age Riders from the Eurasian Steppes Shaped the Modern World.* Princeton University Press: Princeton, New Jersey, USA.

Bauman, Richard. 1986. "Performance and Honor in 13th-Century Iceland." In *The Journal of American Folklore* Vol. 99, No. 392. University of Illinois Press: Champaign, Illinois, USA.

Bauschatz, Paul C. 1982. *The Well and the Tree: World and Time in Early Germanic Culture.* University of Massachusetts Press: Amherst, Massachusetts, USA.

Bek-Pedersen, Karen. 2011. *The Norns in Old Norse Mythology.* Dunedin Academic Press: Edinburgh, UK.

Blain, Jenny. 2002. *Nine Worlds of Seid-Magic: Ecstasy and Neo-Shamanism in North European Paganism.* Routledge: London, UK.

Branston, Brian. 1974. *The Lost Gods of England.* Oxford University Press: New York, New York, USA.

Byock, Jesse. 1995. "Choices of Honor: Telling Saga Feud, *Tháttr*, and the Fundamental Oral Progression." In *Oral Tradition* Vol. 10, No. 1. Slavica Publishers: Bloomington, Indiana, USA.

Byock, Jesse. 2000. *Viking Age Iceland*. Penguin Books: London, UK.

Chadwick, H. M. 2013. *The Cult of Othin: An Essay in the Ancient Religion of the North*. Cambridge University Press: Cambridge, UK.

Clunies Ross, Margaret. 1994. *Prolonged Echoes, Vol. I: Old Norse Myths in Medieval Northern Society*. University Press of Southern Denmark: Odense, Denmark.

Clunies Ross, Margaret. 2004. "The Measures of Old Norse Religion in Long-Term Perspective." In *Old Norse Religion in Long-Term Perspectives: Origins, Changes, and Interactions*. Edited by Anders Andrén, Kristina Jennbert, and Catharina Raudvere. Nordic Academic Press: Lund, Sweden.

Clunies Ross, Margaret. 2005. *A History of Old Norse Poetry and Poetics*. D.S. Brewer: Cambridge, UK.

Clunies Ross, Margaret. 2011. "Images of Norse Cosmology." In *Myths, Legends, and Heroes: Essays on Old Norse and Old English Literature*. Edited by Daniel Anlezark. University of Toronto Press: Toronto, Ontario, Canada.

Davidson, Hilda Roderick Ellis. 1967. *Pagan Scandinavia*. F.A. Praeger: New York, New York, USA.

Davidson, Hilda Roderick Ellis. 1988. *Myths and Symbols in Pagan Europe: Early Scandinavian and Celtic Religions*. Syracuse University Press: Syracuse, New York, USA.

Davidson, Hilda Roderick Ellis. 1990. *Gods and Myths of Northern Europe*. Penguin: New York, New York, USA.

Davidson, Hilda Roderick Ellis. 1993. *The Lost Beliefs of Northern Europe*. Routledge: London, UK.

Davidson, Hilda Roderick Ellis. 1998. *Roles of the Northern Goddess*. Routledge: London, UK.

Detienne, Marcel. 1996. *The Masters of Truth in Archaic Greece.* Translated by Janet Lloyd. Zone Books: New York, New York, USA.

Dobat, Andres Siegfried. 2004. "Bridging Mythology and Belief: Viking Age Functional Culture as a Reflection of the Belief in Divine Intervention." In *Old Norse Religion in Long-Term Perspectives: Origins, Changes, and Interactions.* Edited by Anders Andrén, Kristina Jennbert, and Catharina Raudvere. Nordic Academic Press: Lund, Sweden.

DuBois, Thomas A. 1999. *Nordic Religions in the Viking Age.* University of Pennsylvania Press: Philadelphia, Pennsylvania, USA.

DuBois, Thomas A. 2004. "Rituals, Witnesses, and Sagas." In *Old Norse Religion in Long-Term Perspectives: Origins, Changes, and Interactions.* Edited by Anders Andrén, Kristina Jennbert, and Catharina Raudvere. Nordic Academic Press: Lund, Sweden.

Dumézil, Georges. 1973. *Gods of the Ancient Northmen.* University of California Press: Berkeley, California, USA.

Dumézil, Georges. 1988. *Mitra-Varuna: An Essay on Two Indo-European Representations of Sovereignty.* Translated by Derek Coltman. Zone Books: New York, New York, USA.

Eliade, Mircea. 1959a. *Cosmos and History: The Myth of the Eternal Return.* Translated by Willard R. Trask. Harper & Row: New York, New York, USA.

Eliade, Mircea. 1959b. *The Sacred and the Profane: The Nature of Religion.* Translated by Willard R. Trask. Harcourt: Orlando, Florida, USA.

Eliade, Mircea. 1962. *Shamanism: Archaic Techniques of Ecstasy.* Translated by Willard R. Trask. Princeton University Press: Princeton, New Jersey, USA.

Ellis, Hilda Roderick. 1968. *The Road to Hel: A Study of the Conception of the Dead in Old Norse Literature.* Greenwood Press: New York, New York, USA.

Enright, Michael J. 1996. *Lady with a Mead Cup: Ritual, Prophecy and Lordship in the European Warband from La Tène to the Viking Age.* Four Courts Press: Portland, Oregon, USA.

Erickson, Carolly. 1976. *The Medieval Vision: Essays in History and Perception.* Oxford University Press: New York, New York, USA.

Flowers, Stephen. 1984. *Runes and Magic: Magical Formulaic Elements in the Elder Tradition.* University Microfilms International: Ann Arbor, Michigan, USA.

Flowers, Stephen. 1989. *The Galdrabók: An Icelandic Grimoire.* Samuel Weiser: York Beach, Maine, USA.

Gunnell, Terry. 2004. "Til Holts Ek Gekk...: The Performance Demands of *Skírnismál, Fáfnismál,* and *Sigrdrífumál* in Liminal Time and Sacred Space." In *Old Norse Religion in Long-Term Perspectives: Origins, Changes, and Interactions.* Edited by Anders Andrén, Kristina Jennbert, and Catharina Raudvere. Nordic Academic Press: Lund, Sweden.

Hall, Alaric. 2007. *Elves in Anglo-Saxon England: Matters of Belief, Health, Gender, and Identity.* Boydell Press: Woodbridge, UK.

Hastrup, Kirsten. 1985. *Culture and History in Medieval Iceland: An Anthropological Analysis of Structure and Change.* Clarendon Press: Oxford, UK.

Heide, Eldar. 2004. "Spinning *Seiðr.*" In *Old Norse Religion in Long-Term Perspectives: Origins, Changes, and Interactions.* Edited by Anders Andrén, Kristina Jennbert, and Catharina Raudvere. Nordic Academic Press: Lund, Sweden.

Heide, Eldar. 2006a. "Spirits through Respiratory Passages." In *The Fantastic in Old Norse / Icelandic Literature. Sagas and the British Isles.*

*Preprint Papers of the 13th International Saga Conference, Durham and York, 6th-12th August, 2006.* Edited by John McKinnell et al. University of Durham: Durham, United Kingdom.

Heide, Eldar. 2006b. "Approaches to the Study of Linguistic Identity in the Viking Age." Unpublished; presented at *Migration and Transcultural Identities in the Viking Age,* University of Nottingham, March 3 - April 1, 2006.

Heide, Eldar. 2009. "More Inroads to Pre-Christian Notions, After All? The Potential of Late Evidence. In *Á austrvega. Saga and East Scandinavia. Preprint Papers of the 14th International Saga Conference. Uppsala, 9th–15th August 2009.* Edited by Agneta Ney et al. Gävle University Press: Gävle, Sweden.

Heide, Eldar. 2011. "Holy Islands and the Otherworld: Places Beyond Water." In *Isolated Islands in Medieval Nature, Culture, and Mind.* Edited by Gerhard Jaritz and Torstein Jørgensen. University of Bergen: Bergen, Norway.

Heide, Eldar. 2012. "Loki, the Vätte, and the Ash Lad: A Study Combining Old Scandinavian and Medieval Material." In *Viking and Medieval Scandinavia* 7 (2011). University of Cambridge: Cambridge, United Kingdom.

Heide, Eldar. 2014. "Contradictory Cosmology in Old Norse Myth and Religion - But Still a System?" In *Maal og Minne* 1 (2014). Edited by Jon Gunnar Jørgensen and Torodd Kinn. Bymålslaget: Oslo, Norway.

Heide, Eldar. 2015. "*Hǫrgr* in Norwegian Names of Mountains and Other Natural Features." In *Namn og Nemne* 31 (2015).

Hultgård, Anders. 2004. "The Askr and Embla Myth in a Comparative Perspective." In *Old Norse Religion in Long-Term Perspectives: Origins, Changes, and Interactions.* Edited by Anders Andrén, Kristina Jennbert, and Catharina Raudvere. Nordic Academic Press: Lund, Sweden.

Hutton, Ronald. 1991. *The Pagan Religions of the Ancient British Isles: Their Nature and Legacy.* Blackwell Publishers: Oxford, UK.

Ibn Fadlan, Ahmad. 2012. *Ibn Fadlan and the Land of Darkness: Arab Travelers in the Far North.* Edited and translated by Paul Lunde and Caroline Stone. Penguin Books: New York, New York, USA.

Jón Hnefill Aðalsteinsson. 1998. *A Piece of Horse Liver: Myth, Ritual and Folklore in Old Icelandic Sources.* Translated by Terry Gunnell and Joan Turville-Petre. Háskólaútgáfan: Reykjavík, Iceland.

Kershaw, Kris. 2000. *The One-eyed God: Odin and the (Indo-) Germanic Männerbünde.* Institute for the Study of Man: Washington, D.C., USA.

Kure, Henning. 2003. "In the Beginning Was the Scream: Conceptual Thought in the Old Norse Myth of Creation." In *Scandinavia and Christian Europe in the Middle Ages: Papers of the 12th International Saga Conference.* Edited by Rudolf Simek and Judith Meurer. Universität Bonn: Bonn, Germany.

Kure, Henning. 2004. "Hanging on the World Tree: Man and Cosmos in Old Norse Mythic Poetry." In *Old Norse Religion in Long-Term Perspectives: Origins, Changes, and Interactions.* Edited by Anders Andrén, Kristina Jennbert, and Catharina Raudvere. Nordic Academic Press: Lund, Sweden.

Lindow, John. 1994. "Bloodfeud and Scandinavian Mythology." *Alvíssmál* 4. Freie Universität Berlin: Berlin, Germany.

Lindow, John. 1996. "Thor's Duel with Hrungnir." *Alvíssmál* 6. Freie Universität Berlin: Berlin, Germany.

Lindow, John. 2001. *Norse Mythology: A Guide to the Gods, Heroes, Rituals, and Beliefs.* Oxford University Press: Oxford, UK.

Lindow, John. 2004. "Narrative Worlds, Human Environments, and Poets: The Case of Bragi." In *Old Norse Religion in Long-Term Perspectives: Origins, Changes, and Interactions.* Edited by Anders Andrén, Kristina

Jennbert, and Catharina Raudvere. Nordic Academic Press: Lund, Sweden.

Looijenga, Tineke. 2003. *Texts and Contexts of the Oldest Runic Inscriptions*. Brill: Boston, Massachusetts, USA.

MacLeod, Mindy, and Bernard Mees. 2006. *Runic Amulets and Magic Objects*. Boydell Press: Woodbridge, UK.

Mallory, J.P., and D.Q. Adams. 2006. *The Oxford Introduction to Proto-Indo-European and the Proto-Indo-European World*. Oxford University Press: New York, New York, USA.

McKinnell, John. 2005. *Meeting the Other in Norse Myth and Legend*. D.S. Brewer: Cambridge, UK.

McKinnell, John. 2008. "*Vǫluspá* and the Feast of Easter." Alvíssmál 12. Freie Universität Berlin: Berlin, Germany.

Nietzsche, Friedrich. 1954. *Thus Spoke Zarathustra: A Book for All and None*. In *The Portable Nietzsche*. Edited and translated by Walter Kaufmann. Penguin Books: New York, New York, USA.

Nietzsche, Friedrich. 2000. *On the Genealogy of Morals*. In *Basic Writings of Nietzsche*. Translated and edited by Walter Kaufmann. Modern Library: New York, New York, USA.

Orel, Vladimir. 2003. *A Handbook of Germanic Etymology*. Brill: Leiden, The Netherlands.

Otto, Rudolf. 1923. *The Idea of the Holy: An Inquiry into the Non-rational Factor in the Idea of the Divine and its Relation to the Rational*. Translated by John W. Harvey. Oxford University Press: London, UK.

Pagels, Elaine. 2003. *Beyond Belief: The Secret Gospel of Thomas*. Vintage Books: New York, New York, USA.

Price, Neil. 2002. *The Viking Way: Religion and War in Late Iron Age Scandinavia*. Uppsala University: Uppsala, Sweden.

Price, Neil. 2004a. "The Archaeology of Seiðr: Circumpolar Traditions in Viking Pre-Christian Religion." Brathair 4.

Price, Neil. 2004b. "What's in a Name?: An Archaeological Identity Crisis for the Norse Gods (and Some of Their Friends)." In *Old Norse Religion in Long-Term Perspectives: Origins, Changes, and Interactions*. Edited by Anders Andrén, Kristina Jennbert, and Catharina Raudvere. Nordic Academic Press: Lund, Sweden.

Price, Neil. 2010. "Passing into Poetry: Viking-Age Mortuary Drama and the Origins of Norse Mythology." Medieval Archaeology 10. University of Aberdeen: Aberdeen, UK.

Price, Neil, and Paul Mortimer. 2014. "An Eye for Odin? Divine Role-Playing in the Age of Sutton Hoo." In *European Journal of Archaeology* 17 (3). Maney Publishing: Leeds, UK.

Raudvere, Catharina. 2002. "*Trolldómr* in Early Medieval Scandinavia." In *Witchcraft and Magic in Europe, Vol. 3: The Middle Ages*. Edited by Bengt Ankarloo and Stuart Clark. University of Pennsylvania Press: Philadelphia, Pennsylvania, USA.

Raudvere, Catharina. 2004. "Poetry and Practice: Egil's Art of Poetry and the Odinic Legacy." In *Old Norse Religion in Long-Term Perspectives: Origins, Changes, and Interactions*. Edited by Anders Andrén, Kristina Jennbert, and Catharina Raudvere. Nordic Academic Press: Lund, Sweden.

Saxo Grammaticus. 1996. *The History of the Danes, Books I-IX*. Edited by Hilda Ellis Davidson. Translated by Peter Fisher. D.S. Brewer: Cambridge, UK.

Simek, Rudolf. 1993. *Dictionary of Northern Mythology*. Translated by Angela Hall. D.S. Brewer: Cambridge, UK.

Simek, Rudolf. 2004. "The Use and Abuse of Old Norse Religion: Its Beginnings in High Medieval Iceland." In *Old Norse Religion in Long-Term Perspectives: Origins, Changes, and Interactions*. Edited by Anders Andrén, Kristina Jennbert, and Catharina Raudvere. Nordic Academic Press: Lund, Sweden.

Simek, Rudolf. 2010. "The Vanir: an Obituary." In *The Retrospective Methods Newsletter*, December 2010. Edited by Helen F. Leslie and Mathais Nordvig.

Sommer, Bettina Sejbjerg. 2007. "The Norse Concept of Luck." In *Scandinavian Studies*, Volume 79, No. 3.

Steinsland, Gro. 1987. "Giants as Recipients of Cult in the Viking Age?" In *Words and Objects: Towards a Dialogue Between Archaeology and History of Religion*. Edited by Gro Steinsland. Oxford University Press: New York, New York, USA.

Ström, Folke. 1974. Nið, Ergi, *and Old Norse Moral Attitudes*. T. & A. Constable Ltd.: Edinburgh, UK.

Sturtevant, Albert Morey. 1916. "A Study of the Old Norse Word 'Regin.'" In *The Journal of English and Germanic Philology*, Vol. 15, No. 2. University of Illinois Press: Champaign, Illinois, USA.

Tacitus. 2010. *The Agricola and the Germania*. Translated by Harold Mattingly. Penguin Classics: London, UK.

Turville-Petre, E.O.G. 1964. *Myth and Religion of the North: The Religion of Ancient Scandinavia*. Holt, Rinehart and Winston: New York, New York, USA.

Turville-Petre, E.O.G. 1972. *Nine Norse Studies*. Western Printing Services: Bristol, UK.

Vernant, Jean-Pierre. 1996. *Myth and Society in Ancient Greece*. Translated by Janet Lloyd. Zone Books: New York, New York, USA.

Vernant, Jean-Pierre. 2006. *Myth and Thought among the Greeks.* Translated by Janet Lloyd and Jeff Fort. Zone Books: New York, New York, USA.

Veyne, Paul. 1988. *Did the Greeks Believe in Their Myths?: An Essay on the Constitutive Imagination.* Translated by Paula Wissing. University of Chicago Press: Chicago, Illinois, USA.

Vries, Jan de. 2000. *Altnordisches Etymologisches Wörterbuch.* Brill: Leiden, The Netherlands.

Winn, Shan. 1995. *Heaven, Heroes, and Happiness: The Indo-European Roots of Western Ideology.* University Press of America: Lanham, Maryland, USA.

Winroth, Anders. 2014. *The Age of the Vikings.* Princeton University Press: Princeton, New Jersey, USA.

West, M.L. 2009. *Indo-European Poetry and Myth.* Oxford University Press: New York, New York, USA.

Zoëga, Geir T. 2004. *A Concise Dictionary of Old Icelandic.* University of Toronto Press: Toronto, Canada.

Made in the USA
San Bernardino, CA
07 July 2017